De Officiis/On Duties

THE LIBRARY OF LIBERAL ARTS

THE LIBRARY OF LIBERAL ARTS

published by
THE BOBBS-MERRILL COMPANY, INC.
Indianapolis   New York

Marcus Tullius

CICERO

De Officiis/On Duties

Translated, with an introduction and notes, by Harry G. Edinger

PA
6308
D5
E3

FOR MY MOTHER AND FATHER

CONTENTS

INTRODUCTION

Cicero's subject in this book is *officium*. Matthias Gelzer, the Swiss historian, once suggested[1] that the proper meaning of this word is "reciprocal personal relationship." While this phrase conveys the meaning of *officium* quite precisely, it is obviously too cumbersome for purposes of translation. Unfortunately, neither "duty" nor "responsibility" nor "obligation," which are the ordinary English translations, reproduces fully the essential notion of reciprocity. A "duty" in everyday English is an action that one must perform without consulting the possibility of reward, and without stopping to consider whether one's action will put another person under an obligation in return. Cicero never quite abandons the implications of reciprocity in the word *officium;* wholly disinterested "duty," in the ordinary English sense, he probably would have regarded as an unattainable philosophical refinement. This difficulty in conveying the nuances of *officium* in translation suggests that we should attempt at the outset to understand its range of meaning more completely.

The importance of *officium*, and the reason why Cicero felt that it was a worthy subject for an entire book, are rooted in the structure of Republican Rome's government and society. A Roman in public life acquired power and prestige by putting

[1] Matthias Gelzer, *The Roman Nobility* (Trans. by Robin Seager) Oxford: Basil Blackwell, 1969, p. 66.

other men under an obligation to himself. An ambitious politician would attempt to surround himself with a following of dependents, which the Romans called his *clientela* or clientship. This could be formed of individuals, groups, districts, or even of whole provinces on whose behalf he had performed or could perform services or favors. In return he could expect the support of his clientship at all decisive moments of his career, especially at elections. The Roman in the political arena or in public life (and they were much the same thing) did not represent a party or a platform in the modern sense of these terms. His constituency and his supporters should rather be thought of as a personal following, at greater or lesser remove.

The performance of services or the rendering of favors by such a man might be called a *beneficium*. In return for such *beneficia* the client was expected to acknowledge that he owed his patron certain *officia*. The relationship naturally supposes that the more powerful man will abide by his obligation (*officium*) to protect or favor those who have entered his *clientela*. The sense of obligation works both ways and that sense on either side would be called *officium*. Cicero's point of view in *On Duties* is consistently that of the more powerful half of the relationship, of course. This basic relationship, infinitely complicated by many social and financial considerations, underlay all Roman Republican society. Terms like *officium, beneficium* and many related ones could be used to describe the relationship between people and groups on all social levels: owner and slave, father and son, lawyer and client, seller and buyer, the government and the individual, the Roman Senate and foreign powers. This being true, the subject of *officium* opens the way for Cicero to discuss all the most important relationships in human life.[2]

[2] The matters briefly summarized in these two paragraphs should be grasped as thoroughly as possible by the reader approaching *On Duties*. The following chapters are helpful and might be read: "Morality and Politics," Chap. I of *The Moral and Political Tradition of Rome* by Donald Earl (Ithaca:

Officium, then, may be understood on many levels. The utterly practical relationships of everyday life are the basic manifestations of the concept. But Cicero takes a wide philosophical view and wants to demonstrate that *officium* has a nearly universal importance. All philosophers, he points out (I.5), have felt the obligation to transmit some teaching about the duties of man. *On Duties* therefore examines the moral and philosophical dimensions of what was basically a practical and largely unwritten Roman way of doing things. It might be said that in part Cicero is codifying a Roman state of mind, a frame of daily thinking that ordinarily would never be the subject of analysis. To offer such a codification was not Cicero's announced intention, of course. The "reciprocal personal relationship" of the everyday world is a meeting of interests, the exchange of favors between a man who wields or who seeks power and those who can support him. Cicero does not start with such a low evaluation of the concept and build upwards to the philosophical sphere; rather he works downward from the lofty and venerable Stoic virtues of wisdom, justice, courage, and moderation, tracing the obligations that are implied by the desire to attain these virtues.

Yet Cicero never loses sight of the practical advantages of observing *officia.* Various words expressed to the Romans the prestige attached to the man who commanded a large clientship. The chief word was *dignitas,* a single term that summed up the position of a leader in the state. More interesting, perhaps, are the terms *fides* and *gloria. Fides,* one might say, is the power of inducing men to entrust themselves to you as a person. It is the power that stems from a wide and solid reputation for being a man of your word, a man whom people can trust

---

Cornell University Press, 1967); "Introduction—*Clientela,*" in *Foreign Clientelae (264–70 B.C.)* by E. Badian (Oxford: Clarendon Press, 1958); *"Virtus* and *Imperium,"* Chap. I of *Roman Imperialism in the Late Republic* by E. Badian (Oxford: Basil Blackwell, 1968); fundamental to all these discussions is the book of Gelzer cited in fn. 1.

completely. *Gloria* is fame and glamor and, in the best sense, notoriety. Once achieved, *gloria* is self-generating; it is the power that derives from being looked up to because of great achievements and that creates the possibilities of even greater achievements. These two qualities are both the cause and the product of an impressive *clientela*. Made visible in dealing with a group of clients or in public life in general, these qualities attract men who will enlarge your *clientela*. Cicero was anxious to have his son, to whom *On Duties* is addressed, understand clearly how the qualities of *fides* and *gloria* could be attained, as well as the connection between them and the observance of *officia*.[3]

To a certain extent Cicero possessed an outsider's sensitive knowledge of the social and political factors that he touches upon in *On Duties*. The nobility of Rome was an oligarchy of a restricted number of families, whose members had for generations filled the highest military, religious, judicial, and governmental offices. Nobility was achieved when a member of the family attained the highest political office, the consulship. Although Cicero's family had distant connections with some leading figures of the Republican nobility, his father was of the equestrian order, an official rating of citizens by property and birth that fell below the nobles. None of his ancestors had attained the consulship and the young Cicero, therefore, could not count on the advantages like *clientelae, dignitas* and *gloria* that were inherited by the younger sons of the ruling oligarchy. He had to become acceptable to this oligarchy by force of talents and proved that he had done so when he became consul in 63 B.C. But even then he was marked as a *novus homo,* a "new man," the first member of a family to attain the rank of consul.

The force of Cicero's talent was extraordinary. He is known as the greatest of Roman orators, but to call his abilities merely

---

[3] *Fides* is discussed in II.33–35; *gloria* in II.42–51.

a talent for oratory is gravely misleading, especially since "oratory" is largely a pejorative word in contemporary terms. Roman oratory in fact was a combination of legal training, public speaking, diplomacy and statesmanship and literature in an unbroken spectrum. The interdependence of these varied fields can be illustrated from the career of any of the prominent Romans of the first century B.C. and was such that by winning a case in court a man could at the same time advance his political prospects and increase his prestige with the electorate. In 80 B.C., for example, when he was 26 years old, Cicero undertook the defense in court of a certain Sextus Roscius, who had been falsely accused by agents of the all-powerful dictator of Rome, Sulla. This was not merely a defense of a man falsely accused of murder, but the trial forced Cicero to oppose the man, Sulla, who had first seized power through the Roman army and who held an extraordinary dictatorship. Cicero's success in defending Roscius and in winning the case without offending the dictator was the start of his reputation as an orator. Continued work in the courts widened his political influence so that in 76 B.C. he stood for election to the quaestorship and won this office, which gained one admittance to the Senate. Another trial in 70 B.C. again helped to extend his reputation. This was the prosecution of Verres on a charge of rapaciously extorting a fortune in cash and moveable property from the province of Sicily when he was governor there. The case against Verres was an outstanding moment in Cicero's career, not only because it demonstrated his legal industry and talent but also because it strengthened his influence and showed that he was willing to take greater political risks and to profit from them. He was aedile-elect[4] when he won this success, and following the normal roster of offices, he served as praetor in 67 B.C.

Cicero was eligible to stand for election to the consulship of 63 B.C. His holding of this office was the crowning moment in

[4] Cicero refers to his own aedileship in II.57 and II.59.

his career, at least in his own estimation, and he frequently referred afterwards to what he had achieved, the first man in thirty years to become consul whose family had not previously held the office. Furthermore, during his consulship Cicero earned the title *pater patriae*, "Father of his Country," for suppressing a conspiracy against the government led by Catiline, a man whom Cicero pictured as a violent revolutionary.[5] Cicero took and undoubtedly deserved credit for discovering Catiline's intentions and for forcing him out into the open and crushing him and his supporters. Henceforward Cicero regarded himself as the savior of the Roman state in its hour of extreme peril. He shared, however, in the responsibility for putting to death Catiline's fellow conspirators, some of whom were of noble rank. They were hastily executed without proper trial, and this action, which was of doubtful legality, clouded the rest of Cicero's career.

This most glorious moment of Cicero's fulfilled ambitions, when the "daggers," released by the force of his eloquence, "slipped from the hands" of the conspirators, was a source of pride and satisfaction to him for the rest of his life. He was convinced that the crushing of Catiline's conspiracy had resulted in a harmonizing of conflicting segments of the state and that this new harmony would provide future stability for Rome. But in 62 B.C. Pompey the Great returned from a series of military victories in the East and celebrated a splendid triumph. Cicero proudly recalls how Pompey told him that the triumph was only possible because Cicero had preserved the state by vigorous action during his consulship. But within a year Pompey had made a political agreement with Caesar and Crassus that clearly showed that the traditional Republican institutions were rapidly losing their effectiveness and that the course of history would

---

[5] Cicero mentions the conspiracy in II.84, where he objects to schemes for the general cancellation of debts, the kind of radical proposals that were made by Catiline but that Cicero could assume would be abhorred by all good elements among the knights and nobles.

henceforth be in the hands of a few powerful men like Pompey, Caesar, and Crassus, contending among themselves for supremacy. Cicero was never comfortable with power politics, never sufficiently resolute or single-minded to take a place for himself and fight to keep it. He could not bring himself to cooperate with the first Triumvirate and refused to be part of it. Lacking its protection, he was forced to go into exile in 58 B.C. as a delayed penalty for having caused the execution of the Catilinarian conspirators. Later he reluctantly left Rome again for another extended period to serve as proconsular governor in a province of Asia Minor in 51 B.C.

Events at Rome moved steadily toward the inevitable war between Pompey and Caesar. Cicero chose the side of Pompey. Caesar's victory and dictatorship were of course not welcome to Cicero. In *On Duties* he laments the decline of public life that began at this time, especially the restricted opportunities to practice oratory and the stifling of Rome's legal system.[6] The assassination of Caesar and the ascendancy of Marc Antony were, for Cicero, no solution. He felt excluded from public life, moved about restlessly, and was agonized with characteristic lack of decision about what course he should take. At last he decided to attack Marc Antony and did so in a brilliant series of speeches known as the *Philippics*. But by the beginning of 43 B.C. Antony, Octavian (Caesar's adoptive son and the future emperor Augustus), and Lepidus had arrived at the political accommodation known as the second Triumvirate. They divided the Roman world among themselves, and Cicero's enmity with Marc Antony now endangered his life. He was executed in a purge of the Triumvirate's enemies on December 7, 43 B.C.

Throughout his mature life, then, Cicero was at or near the center of events. His philosophical writings, a long series of which *On Duties* is only one, were produced during intervals of enforced retirement, especially in the last years of his life. The

---

[6] Cf. II. 2–4 and 65–67.

nature of the book and explicit statements by Cicero in the book make abundantly clear his motivations in writing it. Primarily, as we have seen, the book is a discussion of *officium*, "duty, responsibility, obligation." The underlying purpose is to bridge the gap between philosophical ideals and public life. The great past schools of Greek philosophy, in their discussions of ethics, had produced descriptions of the perfectly wise man or the perfectly good man. They had also produced descriptions of the ideal goals of human conduct, such as justice, or happiness or virtue. Cicero, and the Romans in general, recognized that, while it was possible to study and absorb these ideals on an abstract level, it was far more desirable to translate these ideals into a guide for daily conduct. Cicero conceives that the student of philosophy has two choices. Either he can withdraw from the society of men and pass his life in study and contemplation, or he can spend his life in society, where he will regulate his conduct according to the ideals he has studied. The first possibility was not really taken seriously by Cicero or by most Romans. Consequently the second possibility must be provided for, and hence the discussion of the duties that a man in public life who has once studied philosophy will best know how to perform.

In addition to this task of showing the links between philosophy and daily conduct, *On Duties* also appears to us to be a manual of practical wisdom. Ancient ethics were far more prescriptive than modern writings on the subject usually are; philosophers were not timid about expounding actual regulations of conduct or descriptions of how men should act in particular circumstances to achieve happiness or justice. These regulations embraced the whole of life to a degree that is now astonishing. Cicero finds space to discuss even such topics as dress, posture, and facial expressions. He apologizes slightly for taking up such items as physical condition and one's bank balance, but he recognizes that they are not topics utterly remote from morality. *On Duties,* then, is to some extent a handbook of daily conduct, or pointers on how a young man should behave in order to be a success.

The book is also a criticism of Roman life and politics. The values and forms of conduct that Cicero presents and praises are rooted in philosophical ideals, to be sure. But he was near the end of a long, ambitious life. He had witnessed the political failure of two men, Pompey and Cato, who he had hoped would revive the dying Republic. He had also witnessed the triumph of Caesar, who had finally destroyed the Republic, and then the growing menace of Antony after the liberation of Rome from Caesar's tyranny. It follows from these events and from Cicero's attitude toward them that the prescriptions of conduct in On Duties involve, almost of necessity, much criticism of the directions that Roman political life had taken and of the abandonment of ideals that Cicero felt were necessary to justice.

There can also be little doubt that Cicero wished to leave a kind of last testament to his only son concerning social and political conduct. The younger Cicero (born 65 B.C. and also named Marcus Tullius Cicero) was twenty-one at the time his father wrote On Duties. The family, as we have seen, ranked high in Roman life and politics. Cicero had raised himself to consular rank and thereby had laid an obligation on his son not to diminish the family's standing. He displays pride at the opening of On Duties that the younger Cicero is now in a great cultural center, Athens, and that he is studying with one of the leading teachers of the day, Cratippus. Cicero feels, nevertheless, that he himself has something to contribute to the boy's education, even beyond the instructions of Cratippus. The younger Cicero, he explains, will be absorbing the doctrines of one philosophical school, the Peripatetic, but the points of view of other schools, notably the Stoic and Academic, must also find their place. The young man will be studying philosophy, but this pursuit must not exclude oratory; he will be studying in Greek, but he should also cultivate Latin. The young man must never forget what people will expect of him because of his father.

The relationship is both banal and poignant, for, while Cicero appears in these sentiments to be the typical self-made father trying to steer his son's life, he was indeed talking about the qualities that had contributed to his own success. But the younger Cicero was not to live in a world where those qualities could be useful, even if he had been a good student of his father or had had his father's talents. His first love, however, seems to have been the military life; he had served in Pompey's armies, then had joined the forces of Brutus in Greece and later those of Sextus Pompy in Spain. He did, it is true, become consul in 30 B.C. with Octavian, but by then the office was without its previous significance. Men remembered the younger Cicero as a hard drinker.[7]

On Duties was written late in 44 B.C., the year in which Julius Caesar was assassinated. The assassination lies in the background of Cicero's book. He had expressed joy when he first learned of the deed; Caesar, he thought, had become a tyrant, and it was a proper action, indeed a very Roman act, to strike him down. But Cicero's relations with the "liberators" were very problematical. He withdrew from Rome late in March 44 B.C. when it became clear that he was not going to fit in easily with the plans of the conspirators. Shut out in this way from the direct course of events, Cicero, as the months passed, took to moving distractedly from place to place in Italy, absorbing himself deliberately in literary projects. As the year drew toward its end, the growing ascendancy of Marc Antony meant growing danger to Cicero. He was pulled out of his literary distractions by the composition and publication of his speeches against Antony.

Cicero's movements can be followed rather closely at this period, and consequently some limited information about the composition of *On Duties* is available. He was working on it

---

[7] A detailed consideration of the rather limited information about the younger Cicero may be found in Maurice Testard, "Le fils de Cicéron, destinataire du *De Officiis*," *Bulletin de l'Association Guillaume Budé*, Series 4, vol. 21 (1962), pp. 198–213.

on October 25, 44 B.C., when he wrote to his correspondent, Atticus, the following:

I am philosophizing and giving a splendid account of the main points about duty. I am addressing it to young Cicero, of course; what better topic is there for a father to talk about to his son? Other essays will follow. Don't be surprised! I want my vacation to produce some results.[8]

About ten days later Cicero wrote to Atticus again with the news that the first two books of his treatise were finished. But the third book still waited to be written because the scheme of Panaetius he was following was not completely written out by the Greek philosopher. In order to complete his third book Cicero had to turn to Posidonius, who did write about the required topics. Cicero tells Atticus that he has to send to a certain Athenodorus for outline summaries. These summaries are mentioned again in a subsequent letter that dates probably from the middle of November; there Cicero tells Atticus that they have arrived.

These are the only fixed dates that can be attached to the composition of *On Duties*. They do not reveal how long Cicero had already been working on or thinking about the book when he wrote to Atticus on October 25th, nor do they reveal precisely when it was finished. During this year, however, we know that Cicero finished a great deal of other writing and that, as we have seen, he was soon absorbed in turning out the long series of political speeches or pamphlets against Antony. The impression of haste and sketchiness that the work conveys in some parts is probably not false.[9]

Before proceeding to consider the outline of the work that Cicero put together with such industrious haste in the fall of 44

---

[8] Cicero, *Letters to Atticus*, XV. 13.

[9] A full discussion of the information in ancient sources about the composition of *On Duties* may be found in M. Fiévez, " 'Opera peregrinationis huius' ou les étapes de la composition du De Officiis," *Latomus* vol. 12 (1953), pp. 261–274.

B.C., some attempt must be made to place Cicero in relation to the philosophies of his day. Philosophy was then thought of in terms of schools, each philosophy derived from the fundamental teachings of a great master. Four principal schools dominated the scene in Graeco-Roman philosophy in the first century B.C. The Academy recognized Socrates and Plato as its founders; the Peripatetic school regarded itself as the intellectual descendent of Aristotle; the Epicurean school was founded by Epicurus of Samos; and Stoicism revered as its founder Zeno of Citium, a town on Cyprus. Now Cicero was a man of extraordinarily wide interests and education, and we can trace more or less close relationships to all four of these schools at some point in his life, whether it was his young manhood, when, as he says, he was immersed in philosophy (II.4), or during his travels and later life.

As a young man Cicero studied with Philon of Larissa, an Academic who had moved to Rome in 88 B.C. Later, in Athens, he also studied with another representative of the New Academy, Antiochus of Ascalon. The sceptical strain in the Academic teachings of these men appealed very strongly to Cicero. He usually formulates this scepticism as the pursuit of the probable (II.7–8), rather than of what is certain. It has been suggested that the lawyer's temperament in Cicero was attracted to this scepticism, for while its advocates taught that absolute certainty in knowledge was not possible to achieve, they also taught that it was necessary to present as plausibly as possible the arguments both for and against a particular assertion so that what is probably true might become more clear.

While in intellectual matters this sceptical Academicism is Cicero's watchword and while he consistently claimed to belong to the Academy, in most questions of ethics and politics it was the Stoics to whom he gave his allegiance. The names of Posidonius and Diodotos are associated with Cicero's education in Stoicism. Diodotos lived for some twenty-five years as a houseguest of Cicero. Posidonius was a prolific Stoic writer from Syria who died in 50 B.C.; he identified certain traits in the philosophy of Stoicism with actual features of the Roman organization of the real world; we have already seen that Cicero was guided by summaries of some of Posidonius' views when he was working on the last book of On Duties. As important, perhaps, as the direct influence of these men is the strongly Stoic coloring of the so-called Scipionic Circle. This was a group of men who centered about the great figure of Scipio Aemilianus in the middle of the Second Century B.C., among them Panaetius, the Stoic philosopher. To Cicero these men were historical figures of special glamor, and he paid them a form of tribute that occasionally appears to be almost sentimental. He made some of them serve as speaking characters in philosophical dialogues, for example, and suggests that the great days of the Republic, the nearly heroic character of those men, and their philosophical interests were all intertwined.[10] Yet for all these influences Cicero is careful not to present himself as a doctrinaire Stoic. He asserts his independence in such matters as the revision of the categories of Panaetius, which will be discussed below, and also in his assertion that the doctrines of the Stoics have served him only as a source for a judicious personal selection of ideas (I.6). On balance, however, much of what is distinctly Roman in On Duties, the stern morality, the emphasis on the society of men that embraces all humanity under the law of nature, are Stoic through and through.

Toward Epicureanism Cicero consistently reacts with an irritating simplicity in On Duties. This is perhaps surprising, because he cannot be assumed to be ignorant of the tenets of the philosophy. He knew and possibly studied with a certain Phaedrus, both in Rome and in Athens. He was not so contemptuous of the school as to refuse to read the poetry of Lucretius, which

---

[10] A recent critical account of the Scipionic Circle, with interesting suggestions about its influence on Cicero, may be found in A. E. Astin, Scipio Aemilianus (Oxford: The Clarendon Press, 1967), pp. 294–306.

is the most moving and systematic statement of the philosophy of Epicurus that survives. And Cicero's lifelong and intimate friend Atticus was an adherent of Epicureanism. The abrupt dismissal of the notion that this philosophy can be taken seriously seems almost to be a rhetorical attitude on Cicero's part. He mentions Epicurean ideas in *On Duties* only so that he can scoff at them. His chief reasons for rejecting the philosophy are undoubtedly that it advocated a withdrawal from participation in public life that must have sounded nearly subversive to many Romans. That alone would be sufficient to condemn the whole philosophy in the eyes of a man like Cicero.

The Peripatetic school is one that Cicero does not differentiate sharply from the Academic. Indeed, in Athens in 79 B.C., when he heard the leading representatives of the Athenian schools debating among themselves, he got the impression that Academics, Peripatetics, and Stoics were very close to each other on some major doctrines and that many of their disputes were merely verbal quibbles. But he admired Cratippus so much that he considered him to be the best philosopher of the day and it was with this teacher that the younger Marcus Tullius Cicero was studying in Athens at the time of the writing of *On Duties*. The doctrine of the Peripatetics that Cicero most admired was that of the "mean," the teaching that the best kind of behavior is the moderate way that lies between the extremes on either side.

Working, then, principally from Stoic writings, but with an eye to the teachings of other philosophical schools, Cicero set out to give a formal philosophical framework to the body of his discussion. Specifically he borrowed this framework from the writings of Panaetius.[11] There he found a previous discussion about the obligations of men that suited his purposes and that

---

[11] The fullest presentation of the life and fragments of Panaetius will be found in M. van Straaten, *Panetius, sa vie, ses écrits et sa doctrine*, (Amsterdam: H. J. Paris, 1946). This book shows clearly the difficulties that arise when scholars attempt to assess precisely the extent of Panaetius' contribution to Cicero's writings.

he apparently followed rather closely. None of the numerous writings of Panaetius survives, and it is therefore impossible to tell the precise extent of Cicero's borrowings from his Greek predecessor. Historians of philosophy regard Panaetius, who lived from ca. 185 to 109 B.C., about two generations before Cicero, as the founder of the so-called Middle Stoa. This school developed modifications in the doctrines of the original Stoa, the tendency of these changes being to soften the absolute rigidity of several ethical propositions. In particular, the Middle Stoa modified the absoluteness of the Stoa's view of virtue or goodness. The Stoa had asserted that only the perfectly wise man can be good and that only the good man can perform a good action. But Cicero works with the Middle Stoa's distinction, as it must have been presented by Panaetius, between absolute and "secondary" qualities. An absolute duty must be performed at all times and places. But as our view of an action changes with time and circumstances, so may duties change: these are secondary duties (I.7–8). Cicero illustrates these distinctions particularly well in the case of promises, where the promised action should not be performed if more harm than good would result from the action, even though to keep a promise is an absolute duty.

Panaetius presented a framework of three distinctions among actions. They may be summarized as (1.) good vs. bad actions; (2.) useful vs. harmful actions; (3.) good vs. useful actions. Cicero professes to be dissatisfied with this outline arrangement and expands it into five categories (I.9–10). These are (1.) good actions distinguished from bad; (2.) good actions ranked among themselves; (3.) useful actions distinguished from harmful; (4.) useful actions ranked among themselves; and (5.) conflicts between good actions and those that are useful or expedient. This slight criticism and expansion of Panaetius' distinctions gives an impression of independence on Cicero's part, but constructing such categories is not Cicero's strongest talent and there is nothing unusually subtle in his revision.

The last of his proposed categories, however, which he claims is new with him, is the one that interests Cicero by far the most. It deals in general with situations in which morality is obscured because the clearly right action conflicts with an action that is clearly profitable or useful. A large group of hypothetical and sometimes amusing situations is brought forward as examples of decisions that must be made, ending with a long discussion of the moral implications of the actions of Regulus, which will be discussed in more detail below. This material occurs in the third book of *On Duties*.

It may be useful to examine briefly the way in which Cicero has distributed his material. The first part of Book One is devoted to establishing the categories of the whole discussion, as sketched above. The rest of the book takes up the discussion of good vs. bad actions, and what one should do when two good courses of action are presented at the same time, but only one of them can be performed. This discussion employs as an outline the four cardinal virtues of the Stoics: wisdom, justice, courage, and moderation. These virtues are taken up in turn, are defined, and shown to be both the source and result of good or morally right actions.

The second book is the shortest of *On Duties*. The main subject is man's relation to his fellow human beings, and in particular the methods by which he can cultivate and win permanently the esteem of other men. There are three methods by which this may be done. First we may cause men to esteem and honor us out of simple personal affection. This method is most worthy, but affects relatively few people. Hence the second method, which is to attain *gloria*. If many people have placed their confidence in us as a leader, or if we are extremely well-known as a man of action, or if we have performed some actions in the military or political sphere that people admire intensely, then we have attained what Cicero calls *gloria*, and men will hold us in favor and respect. But Cicero recognizes that such public esteem is not available to all men, since it is partly a matter of personality. Hence the third method of winning esteem, which is to practice generosity. Cicero discusses various grades of generosity. The vulgar, direct distribution of money is condemned, while Cicero praises expenditures on public works or welfare or, best of all, personal favors and services in public that do not involve the spending of money at all. These points all come under the general heading of what is or is not useful or expedient conduct. The book closes with a brief discussion of the problem of choosing between two actions that both appear to be expedient.

After a rather long introduction, Book Three takes up the topic that Cicero himself devised. What is to be the decision when we have to choose between an action that is good and correct and one that is useful and profitable? The answer is that in all such cases the conflict is only apparent and an illusion. The only good is right action. Expedient but morally doubtful actions can never be good. If the profit from an action seems to be more compelling than our feeling that the action is wrong or evil, the action is still to be avoided; it can never be profitable to perform an action that is known to be wrong. This conflict between good actions and expediency is discussed again within the framework of the four cardinal virtues of the Stoics. Cicero shows how the pursuit of private advantage, if the situation is examined carefully, can never come into conflict with wisdom or justice or courage or moderation.

It may also be helpful to explain one unusual feature of Cicero's way of writing philosophy, for it will undoubtedly puzzle or irritate many modern readers. I refer to his frequent allusions to episodes or personalities from Greek and Roman history to illustrate moral abstractions. These illustrations may even be taken from the tales of Greek mythology or from the characters of the Roman theater. Cicero's procedure is by no means very profound. For some particular point that he wishes to make he may cite one or several examples that occur to him of the characteristic or action in question. He seldom treats these in an elaborate or searching manner. Let us take Alexander the Great, for example, who is mentioned four times in *On Duties*. The first time Cicero mentions him (I.90), Alexander's character is contrasted with that of his father, Philip of Macedonia. The contrast is unfavorable to Alexander, whose good character was put under a strain and made worse by his successful military career. Cicero claims, along with the Stoics, that no good man would allow either good or bad fortune to change his character. At another point Cicero wishes to drive home the assertion that human society is based on mutual cooperation and the exchange of mutual benefits between human beings. Alexander is listed along with four other Greek generals (II.16) to show that their careers would have been impossible without the cooperation of other men. On the third occasion Cicero wishes to show the extent to which friendly and sympathetic speech contributes to the acquisition of a good reputation. Three Greek commanders are cited, Alexander among them, and Cicero states that the letters sent to these men by their fathers all gave advice on the power of speech to win over the minds of men (II.48). On still a fourth occasion Cicero refers again to a letter that Alexander received from his father in which Alexander was scolded for attempting to influence other men by bribery (II.53). The nature of Cicero's historical consciousness emerges clearly from these examples. He treats Alexander not primarily as a figure in history, but considers the biography of Alexander an excellent source of moral *exempla*. Modern historians, to be sure, debate the question of Alexander's personality and the position one takes in that debate will color one's evaluation of Alexander's entire career and the meaning of a whole period of Greek history. Cicero, by contrast, has in mind a fixed image of Alexander's personal qualities whose failings serve as a warning to later and lesser men.

    On Duties, then, is pervaded by the citation of dozens of similar *exempla* of human conduct. Since most of them, as Cicero himself notes (I.61), were stock examples often brought into play by public speakers, they posed no problem for the

Roman reader. For contemporary readers the point that Cicero is trying to make in his argument is usually perfectly clear, but why such-and-such a name should be mentioned in each particular connection is usually not evident. However, it must be remembered that Cicero is not making a display of his learning but is attempting to recall and put in their place many traditional stories and bits of historical knowledge that helped to illustrate to the Romans their own character as a people.

The most elaborate of these *exempla* and demanding a separate comment is that of Regulus. Sections 99 through 113 of the last book present an extended analysis of the meaning of certain acts supposed to have been performed by this Roman commander during the first Punic War. Regulus, after a defeat in Africa, was taken captive by the Carthaginians. When they decided to attempt to exchange prisoners with the Romans, they sent Regulus to Rome along with the Carthaginian officials. The reason for sending Regulus was possibly that he was to serve as a sign of the good faith of the Carthaginians, or perhaps that he was to help them by urging the Romans to agree to the exchange. (Variants of the story exist in which the subject of the mission was a peace treaty, not merely an exchange of prisoners.) Two features of the tale caused it to be retold often by later Roman writers and public speakers. The first of these was the oath Regulus swore to the Carthaginians before he set out. Apparently he pledged, or was forced to pledge, that whatever the outcome of the mission, he would return to Carthage and remain a captive. Regulus stood by this oath. The second fact that made Regulus almost revered was his refusal to say in the Roman Senate what the Carthaginians wanted him to say. He advised the Romans to reject the enemy's offer and not to negotiate with them. Although this course of action would clearly anger the Carthaginians, Regulus chose to take it and yet also chose to return to Carthage. Tradition says that he was severely punished by the Carthaginians, left to starve to death, or even more barbarously tortured and killed.

Cicero imagines that objections might be raised against the conduct of Regulus. He might, for example, have disregarded his oath to return to Carthage because it was given to an enemy. Another objection is that, even though the oath that Regulus gave invoked Jupiter, still Jupiter does not really punish individuals and besides could not have inflicted worse punishments on Regulus than he in fact eventually suffered because of his own decisions. Another objection is that it was worse to return voluntarily to be punished than to break the oath. Or to abide by an oath that was extracted under duress was foolish. And to urge that the Roman Senate should reject the Carthaginians' offers was foolish when Regulus might simply have said nothing at all. Cicero discusses these possible objections to Regulus' conduct so elaborately because he views the case as a parade example of the conflict between right action and expediency. To remain in Rome might appear to be the sensible and advantageous action. But that conclusion, Cicero argues, is deceptive because only what is right is expedient. The advantageous course of action for Regulus was to abide by his oath. The details of Cicero's arguments may be read in their place, but it should be clear that to him the value of the story of Regulus is above all a moral one.

Though drawn from Roman history, the story is treated as a problem in ethics rather than a problem in history.[12]

The long popularity of Cicero's *On Duties* began with the generations immediately following his death and lasted well into the nineteenth century. It came to be regarded virtually as a handbook of secular conduct. In the eighteenth century espe-

---

[12] Brief discussions of the Regulus legend in Roman writings may be found in Tenney Frank, "Two Historical Themes in Roman Literature," *Classical Philology* vol. xxi (1926), pp. 311–316; Erving Mix, "Cicero and Regulus," *Classical World* vol. 58 (1965), pp. 156–159, and *Marcus Atilius Regulus: Exemplum Historicum* (Studies in Classical Literature, 10.) The Hague and Paris: Mouton, 1970.

cially it was valued as highly as any other work of ancient philosophy, appealing to such diverse figures as Voltaire, Frederick the Great, and Kant. It was a prime source for certain leading Stoic ideas that permeated the Enlightenment, notably the concepts of natural law and the brotherhood of man. In the ⌐ twentieth century the work has, until recently, suffered unjustly in the general eclipse of Cicero and his writings. But with renewed interest in the dynamics of the disintegration of the Roman Republic and the transition to the Roman Empire, *On Duties* may now be read as important testimony to Roman values and ideals at that critical historical turning point.

The University of British Columbia
February, 1972

SELECTED BIBLIOGRAPHY

Badian, E. *Roman Imperialism in the Late Republic.* Oxford: Basil Blackwell, 1967.

Dorey, T. A., ed. *Cicero.* London: Routledge & Kegan Paul, 1965. An excellent collection of essays on various aspects of Cicero's career.

Douglas, A. E. *Cicero.* Oxford: Clarendon press, 1968. [*Greece and Rome:* New Surveys in the Classics, No. 2.]

Earl, D. *The Moral and Political Tradition of Rome.* Ithaca: Cornell University Press, 1967.

Gelzer, M. *Caesar: Politician and Statesman.* Translated by P. Needham. Oxford: Basil Blackwell; Cambridge, Mass.: Harvard University Press, 1968.

————. *Cicero: Ein biographischer Versuch.* Wiesbaden: Franz Steiner Verlag, 1969.

————. *The Roman Nobility.* Translated by R. Seager. Oxford: Basil Blackwell, 1969.

Holden, H. A. *De Officiis.* Cambridge: Cambridge University Press, 1899. [Reprinted, Amsterdam: Adolf M. Hakkert, 1966.] The fullest commentary in English.

Hunt, H. A. K. *The Humanism of Cicero.* Melbourne: Melbourne University Press, 1954.

Long, A. A., ed. *Problems in Stoicism.* London: The Athlone Press, 1971.

Nelson, N. E. "Cicero's *De Officiis* in Christian Thought: 300–1300," *University of Michigan Publications. Language and Literature.* Vol. X (1933), pp. 59–160.

Petersson, T. *Cicero: A Biography*. Berkeley: The University of California Press, 1920. [Reprinted, New York: Biblo and Tannen, 1963.]

Rist, J. M. *Stoic Philosophy*. Cambridge: Cambridge University Press, 1969.

Sihler, E. G. *Cicero of Arpinum. A Political and Literary Biography*. New Haven: Yale University Press; London: Oxford University Press, 1914.

Smethurst, S. E. "Cicero's Rhetorical and Philosophical Works, 1957–1963," *Classical World*, vol. LVIII (1964–65), pp. 36–45. An annotated bibliography.

———. "Cicero's Rhetorical and Philosophical Works, 1964–1967," *Classical World*, vol. LXI (1967), pp. 125–133.

Stockton, D. *Cicero: A Political Biography*. Oxford: Oxford University Press, 1971.

Suess, W. *Cicero: eine Einfuehrung in seine philosophischen Schriften*. Akademie der Wissenschaften und der Literatur, Mainz. Wiesbaden: Franz Steiner Verlag, 1966.

Syme, R. *The Roman Revolution*. Oxford: Oxford University Press, 1939. [Reprinted: Oxford Paperbacks, 1960.]

Taylor, L. R. *Party Politics in the Age of Caesar*. Berkeley and Los Angeles: University of California Press, 1964. (Sather Classical Lectures, vol. 21.) Excellent introduction to the political background of *De Officiis*.

NOTE ON THE TEXT

The translation has been made from the text of Paolo Fedeli, *Ciceronis De officiis libri tres*. Milan: Mondadori, 1965, which has been used with the permission of the editor and publisher. The numbers of sections of text are those given in standard editions of the Latin text; references to the text are customarily given by book and section (e.g., II.22). These section numbers do not necessarily coincide with paragraphing in the present translation.

A few passages of the translation are enclosed in square brackets. These are passages that Fedeli considers to be interpolations in the Latin text. Scholars do not agree about the extent and origin of these passages; if they are by Cicero himself, they would seem to be rough drafts or marginal notes that became incorporated into the final version.[1]

All footnotes to the translation are by the translator.

[1] On the state of this question see P. Fedeli in *Gnomon* vol. 40 (July, 1968), p. 357 with fn. 1.

ACKNOWLEDGMENTS

I wish to thank Helen Mounce, Billie Young, Robert Heidbreder and Elizabeth Edinger for their help with preparation of the manuscript, and William J. Dusing for fruitful consultations on various historical and legal points. Fee Whitehall was especially generous in devoting her time, patience, and editorial skill to this translation. The final version, of course, is my own responsibility.

H. G. E.

De Officiis/On Duties

BOOK ONE

[1] By now you should have a good supply of philosophical rules and theories, Marcus my son, since you have spent a year in Athens itself as a student of Cratippus. The reputation of both the teacher and the city is extremely high. Cratippus can provide you with knowledge, Athens with inspiration. Yet in spite of such advantages, I think you might follow my practice. I have always found it profitable to combine Latin and Greek studies, and I have done this not only in philosophy, but also in the practice of speaking. You, too, will eventually have equal command over both languages if you combine their study. In this respect I believe I have been very useful to the Romans,[1] so that beginners in Greek as well as educated people believe themselves far more at ease both in speaking and in judging the languages.

[2] You will learn, of course, from the leader of today's philosophers, and you will go on learning as long as you wish. Besides, you should wish to go on learning as long as you are satisfied with your progress. As far as the philosophical content of my books is concerned, you can form your own opinion as you read them. My general position fairly well coincides with that of the Peripatetics, since both they and I claim that we

---

[1] Cicero felt that his great contribution had been to write in Latin about philosophy, which, like the study and teaching of rhetoric, had largely been confined to being discussed in Greek, even among Romans. Thus even Romans already educated in Greek philosophy had benefited from Cicero's writings.

follow Socrates and Plato.² I have no wish to force the content upon you; but I am certain that your Latin style will improve as you read my writings. I should not like you to think that this is an arrogant claim. While I yield to many others in the technique of philosophizing, I reserve for myself that which is essential to an orator: speaking to the point, with clarity and with style. It seems to me that in some ways I have a personal right to claim this, since I have spent my life studying how to speak.

[3] So I strongly urge you, my Cicero, to read and study not only my public speeches but also my books on philosophy, which by now are almost as numerous as the speeches. The speeches display greater oratorical power, but the philosophical style of speaking, sustained and calm, must also be cultivated.³

I notice that not a single Greek ever succeeded in working and trying to achieve something in both areas; that is to say in forensic oratory and in the category of private discussion. Possibly Demetrius of Phaleron could be placed on a list of such men: he was subtle in debate, but not a very forceful orator. Yet he spoke with such charm that you could not fail to recognize him as a student of Theophrastus. How much I myself have accomplished in these two areas is for others to judge: I have at least made an effort in both disciplines.

[4] I think, as a matter of fact, that if Plato had wished to practice in the field of public oratory, he could have been an extremely impressive and eloquent speaker. I believe that De-

---

² Plato, the founder of the Academy, was Socrates' pupil; Aristotle, the founder of the Peripatetic school, was Plato's pupil. The New Academy, of which Cicero always regards himself a follower, thus shares the same background with the Peripatetics.

³ Cicero here introduces a distinction between the separate styles of speaking and writing required by ancient taste in oratory and philosophical discussions. Below he discusses Demosthenes and Isocrates as representatives of one (oratory) and Plato and Aristotle as examples of the other (philosophy). The distinction is very foreign to modern criticism; Cicero discusses it further in section 132 below. His pride in having successfully cultivated both areas underlies the whole present passage.

mosthenes, if he had remained interested in all he learned from Plato and had wished to communicate it to others, could have done so with style and elegance. I have the same opinion of Aristotle and Isocrates: each of these was devoted to his own concerns and ignored those of the other.

Since I have decided to write down something to send you on this occasion (there will be more later),[4] I especially want to begin with what is most suitable to your age and my position. Although in philosophy many profound and useful ideas have been the subject of subtle and eloquent debates among philosophers, the most widely relevant one seems to be their lessons and teachings about responsibility. No part of your activities can be free of responsibility, whether your business is that of a public official or an ordinary citizen, in the law courts or at home, whether you are acting alone or are entering into an agreement with someone else: all good actions in life come from maintaining your responsibilities; when you neglect them the result is discredit.

[5] The inquiry into duty is common to all philosophers: is there anyone who would dare to call himself a philosopher without having handed on instructions about duty? There are, of course, some schools of philosophy that completely distort duty when they define the greatest good and the worst evil. Take, for example, the man who has established the kind of highest good that has nothing in common with virtue, that is measured by the individual's convenience, not by his morality.[5] If that man is consistent and is not in the meantime overcome

---

[4] This parenthesis apparently refers to Cicero's expectation of eventually joining his son in Athens; see III.121.

[5] This paragraph attacks Epicureanism. The *summum bonum* ("highest good") of Epicurus' philosophy lent itself to the kind of distortion that Cicero illustrates here. In general, Epicurus advised men to achieve happiness by avoiding pain and by seeking personal detachment. Cicero declares that these goals are incompatible with the Stoic virtues of courage and temperance or moderation. He deals summarily with Epicureanism again in III.102 and 116–117.

by natural goodness, he cannot cultivate friendship, or justice, or openness of character. In fact, a man of courage who considers pain the greatest evil, or a temperate man who declares indulgence to be the greatest good, is surely an impossible contradiction. [6] Although these objections are so obvious that the matter does not require any argument, still, I have discussed them in other books of mine.[6]

Therefore, if these schools want to be consistent, they will not be able to say anything about duty. Only two schools of philosophy can issue irrefutable and consistent teachings about duty that are in harmony with nature. The one school asserts that men should pursue moral excellence for its own sake to the exclusion of all other goals in life; the other asserts that moral excellence is not the only goal, but the most desirable one. Thus teachings about duty properly belong to these two schools, the Stoics and the Academics and Peripatetics, since the opinion of Ariston, Pyrrho, and of Herillus[7] has long since been rejected. These men, however, would have their own right to discourse about duty if they had left some differences between things so there would be an opening for the discovery of duty. As a consequence I am following principally the Stoics, at least for the time being and in this inquiry, and not as mere spokesman; but as I customarily do, I shall use them as sources according to my judgment and choice and to the extent that seems best.

[7] The whole argument that follows concerns responsibility, and so it seems right first to define what that is. I am astonished that Panaetius omitted a definition. Every exposition undertaken on a systematic plan, whatever the subject, ought to start with a definition so that people can understand the subject of

---

[6] Cicero previously discussed these topics in *De Finibus Bonorum et Malorum* and in the *Tusculan Disputations*.

[7] The common tendency of these three philosophers was a scepticism that denied the possibility of absolute knowledge; they advocated indifference to the ordinary concerns of life; they would have looked upon a discussion of duties as irrelevant.

the argument.[8] . . . Every inquiry into responsibility has two aspects. One series of questions concerns the highest possible moral good. The other series involves the rules that lead to an improved conduct of life in particular areas. The following are examples of the first group: are all duties absolute or not? Is one duty more important than another? There are other questions in the same series. Philosophers have taught us rules that govern the second group of duties, and they also deal with the supreme good, although the fact does not stand out very clearly, because they seem to point rather toward the conduct of daily life. In these books I am going to deal with these practical rules.[9]

[8] There is also another subdivision of duty:[10] there is said to be an absolute duty and a secondary one. I shall call an absolute duty "upright," I think, because the Greeks call it *katorthoma,* while the secondary or ordinary duty is called *kathekon.* Their definitions are such that they call what is "upright" an absolute duty, while they call the other a secondary duty because an acceptable reason can be given why it is done.

[9] Now, in Panaetius' view, to reach a decision demands three kinds of deliberation. First of all, people try to determine whether the matter they are trying to decide is a good or wicked deed; opposing opinions often tear the spirit apart when men

[8] The definition of duty has apparently dropped out and the editor of the Latin text indicates a lacuna.

[9] The distinction here is the fundamental one between a theoretical consideration of duty and a practical set of rules intended to be applied in particular human situations. While Cicero states that he will discuss the latter part, he is perhaps anxious not to seem excessively practical and so claims that the practical always implies the theoretical.

[10] In the preceding paragraph Cicero distinguished between theoretical and practical duty. In this paragraph he makes essentially the same distinction but introduces Stoic terminology and discusses the Latin translation of the Stoic terms. The Stoic distinction is between absolute duties, those that must be performed at all times and in all places, and ordinary duties, those actions that in themselves are neither bad nor good but that take their moral coloring from the intention of the man who performs them. Stoics assigned the former class to philosophers, the latter to ordinary people.

consider this problem. Second, men either meditate or discuss whether or not what they are pondering contributes to the pleasure and enjoyment of life, to the acquisition and abundance of possessions, to riches, to power, things with which they might benefit themselves and their dependents; this whole train of thought falls under reasoning about advantage. The third area of deliberation comes when what seems to be advantageous conflicts with what is good: when usefulness seems to be dragging you forward but goodness is calling you back, then the mind thinking over the situation is torn apart and applies anxious care to its deliberations.

[10] When we divide things into categories our greatest fault is to omit something; in this category two things have been left out. One does not usually ponder only whether something is good or wicked but also which one of two good alternatives is the better, and in the same way, which of two useful proposals is the more advantageous. Consequently one finds that the analysis that Panaetius believed to have three parts ought to be laid out in five parts. In summary, then, our first inquiry is the one concerning what is good, but in two senses; then in a similar double analysis it will investigate what is advantageous, and afterwards the inquiry will compare the two.

[11] To begin with, nature has bestowed on every species of living things the instinct to protect its own life and limb, to avoid what it believes will be harmful, and to hunt and provide everything necessary to maintain life, such as nourishment, shelter and other similar requirements. Other instincts common to all living things are the desire for intercourse for the sake of procreation and some degree of affection toward the offspring thus brought forth. The greatest difference between man and beast, however, is this: that the beast adapts itself to what is at hand and what is present only to the extent that a physical reaction impels it; it perceives the past and the future only slightly. But man is endowed with reason, by which he perceives inferences and sees the causes of facts, that is, he is fully aware of what we might call their antecedents or their origins; he com-

pares resemblances and connects with or weaves into present circumstances those in the future; he easily sees the entire course of life and prepares beforehand the things necessary to its conduct.

[12] By the power of reason nature also associates one man with another to form a society of common culture and life; to begin with, it implants in the parents a certain individual love toward those children born from them; then it drives a man to desire the existence of groups and gatherings of people and to participate in them. For these reasons he is then anxious to acquire the necessary accompaniments of civilization and comfort, not for himself alone, but for his wife, his children, and others he holds dear and ought to defend. This concern also stimulates men's characters and makes them superior in accomplishment.

[13] Inquiry into and searching for truth are primary characteristics of mankind. So when we are free from business obligations and other preoccupations, we become eager to see something new, to hear and learn something; we begin to think that knowledge about the mysteries and wonders of the world is necessary to a happy life. This eagerness leads to the recognition that what is true, simple, and straightforward is most congenial to human nature. A striving for independence accompanies this eagerness to contemplate the truth, so that a man whose character is well-formed by nature does not wish to obey anyone except an adviser or teacher, or someone who holds power lawfully and correctly for the common good. This striving creates breadth of character and indifference to external conditions.

[14] The power of natural understanding is not negligible, because by it man, alone among living things, experiences the essence of order, the essence of *decorum*[11] and develops a true

---

[11] This paragraph illustrates very well the range of meaning in *decorum*, a word that I have chosen to leave in Latin here and elsewhere. The word clearly refers to a harmony and measure in the whole personality that is comparable to the symmetry and attractiveness of beautiful objects.

knowledge of moderation in action and speech. This is also particularly true of whatever objects the eyes perceive: no other animal grasps their beauty, their attractiveness, or the symmetry of their parts. The natural understanding, transferring an image of this perception from the eyes to the mind, begins to think that it should respect beauty, symmetry, and order a great deal more in planning and action. This understanding begins to see to it that none of its actions are unseemly or unmanly; eventually in every thought and deed it is careful neither to do nor to think of anything dishonorable. The particular good that we are seeking is gathered and constructed from these attitudes, and even if men do not commonly admire it, it is still good. What we say about the good is correct: even if no one praises it, it is by nature praiseworthy.

[15] So you see the real shape of the good, Marcus my son, its face, so to speak, which, as Plato says, "would arouse a wonderful love [of wisdom]" if the eyes could see it.[12] Now everything good arises from any one of four categories: either it is involved in perceptions of, and concern for, the truth; or in maintaining the society of men, in rendering to each man his due and in respecting the sanctity of agreements; or in the scope and strength of an exalted and unyielding spirit; or in discipline and in moderation in everything a man does or says, the moderation that constitutes modesty and self-control.[13]

Although these four categories merge and combine with each other, nevertheless special types of responsibility arise from each one. For example, the category first described, in which we place wisdom and knowledge, includes the search for and discovery of truth, and that search is the specific function of that category. [16] Someone, for example, has the best insight into the essential truth in a situation and is able to grasp and explain its causes very clearly and rapidly. A man like that is

[12] Plato, *Phaedrus* 250 D.

[13] These are the four cardinal virtues of Stoicism: wisdom, justice, courage, and temperance.

correctly said to be extremely wise and filled with knowledge. For this reason truth underlies wisdom like the basic material that wisdom deals with and with which it is concerned.

[17] The necessity to acquire and maintain the circumstances in which men conduct the business of life is the sphere of the other three virtues. Their purpose is to preserve human society and relationships and to allow the distinction and scope of a man's character to reveal itself, as he increases resources and advantages for himself and his dependents, but even more as he begins to understand that such things are not of the highest value. This area also includes discipline and self-control and moderation and similar qualities, in which some action is brought to bear, not merely the activity of the mind. By maintaining a certain moderation and order in the practical affairs of life we shall preserve goodness and *decorum*.

[18] Of the four subdivisions into which I have separated the nature and essence of goodness, the first, which consists of the knowledge of the truth, touches man's nature most closely. We are all drawn and led to a desire for knowledge and skill. We think it is attractive to be distinguished in knowledge, while we consider it disgraceful and shameful to make a slip, to go astray, to be ignorant, and to be deceived. In this natural and honorable pursuit of knowledge there are two faults that must be avoided: we should not mistakenly believe that we know what is unknown and quickly lend our belief to it. Whoever wants to escape this fault, and everyone should have that desire, will take time and care to investigate the facts. [19] The second fault is that some people spend too much enthusiasm and too much energy on obscure and difficult questions, on questions that are irrelevant. If you avoid these faults, men will be justified in praising the care and effort you spend on subjects that are respectable and worth knowing about. For example, in astronomy I have heard about Gaius Sulpicius; in geometry I was a personal friend of Sextus Pompeius; I had many friends among logicians, even more among civil lawyers. All these dis-

ciplines involve research into useful knowledge. It is contrary to duty, however, to allow enthusiasm for such research to draw you away from public affairs. The only merit of any virtue lies in the activities to which it leads.[14] But interruptions often occur in one's activities, and many opportunities arise to return to one's intellectual interests. Also, the ferment of the mind, which never dies down completely, can keep us in the pursuit of knowledge even though we do not actually exert ourselves. Thus all perception and energies of the mind will be involved either in making plans about goals that are honorable and that pertain to living well and happily, or in the disciplines of knowledge and skill. This ends my discussion of the first source of duty.

[20] The principle that applies most broadly to the three remaining virtues is the one that holds together the society of humans among themselves or what might be called the "community of life." It has two parts: justice, in which virtue's splendor is unsurpassed and from which good men derive their reputation; and, related to justice, generosity, which may also be called kindliness or beneficence.

The first function of justice is to see that no man shall harm another unless he has been wounded by wrongdoing. The second is to see that each man uses public property for public benefit and his private property for himself. [21] In nature nothing is private property. Property becomes private by long-standing occupation, that is, people once settled on vacant land; or by conquest, that is, someone gained control in a war; or by a law, by a contract, a stipulation or by casting of lots.[15] It is on this principle that the Arpinates own the land of

---

[14] Cicero's attitude in this passage is not unique to him, but is a common Roman viewpoint. Public activity is the obligation of the ruling oligarchy. To withdraw from public life to pursue personal studies in private is an act that the Roman must explain as owing to perversity. As a kind of hobby, however, or to fill in periods of enforced absence from public life, it is acceptable, even potentially profitable. Cf. the last two sentences of section 70 below.

[15] Two or more heirs would presumably cast lots to divide a single inheritance in which they all shared.

Arpinum and Tusculum belongs to the Tusculans. The definition of individual private possessions is analogous.[16] It follows that each man should remain in possession of what he obtains for himself, since what had once naturally been shared becomes each man's own. It follows from this that whoever craves another's possessions violates a basic condition of human society.

[22] Plato wrote brilliantly on this point: "We have not been born for ourselves alone; our native land claims a portion of our origin, our friends claim a portion."[17] The Stoics like to repeat that everything that comes into being in the world is created for the benefit of man, that even men themselves are born for mankind's sake, that people can be helpful among themselves, one to another. The Stoics say that we should follow nature's lead in this and that we should contribute to the public benefit by the mutual interchange of obligations, by both giving and receiving. By our skills, by our efforts, by our capacities we should thus link men together into a human society.[18]

[23] Trust is basic to justice. By trust I mean stability and truth in promises and in agreements. I may risk repeating a discovery of the Stoics: they conduct industrious research into the derivations of words and they would have us believe that men devised the word "trust" (fides) because what an individual promises "is done" (fiat).[19] Of course, the derivation will probably seem rather forced to some people.

There are two classifications of injustice. One part includes those who act unjustly. The other part includes men who, even if they have the power to do so, fail to protect from abuse those

[16] Cicero often raises the question of property. See especially section 51 and following; also II.73. Nowhere is his essential conservatism and that of most Romans clearer than here. Proposals for agrarian reform, general cancellations of debt, and politically inspired confiscations of property presented themselves to Cicero and others as destructive attacks on private property.

[17] [Plato] Epistle IX to Archytas 358 A.

[18] This lofty Stoic overview of civilization is presented more elaborately in sections 51 and following.

[19] Cicero half-seriously brings forward one of the forced etymologies that certain Stoic writers cited in expounding principles of ethics.

people against whom other men commit violence. The man who unjustly does harm to someone else, either in anger or because some other passion arouses him, acts as if he were striking a companion. But the man who does not avert an act of violence, or offer resistance if he has the power, is just as much at fault as if he betrayed his parents, or friends, or his fatherland. [24] Those crimes that men commit deliberately to cause harm often arise from fear. I mean that a man who makes up his mind to harm someone else fears that he might suffer some injury himself unless he commits the crime. On the whole, however, men resort to criminal activity to get possession of what they crave. Greed is the clearest motive of crime.

[25] Now men pursue wealth both for the basic needs of life and for the easy enjoyment of pleasures as well. More ambitious men, however, desire wealth because it leads to power and the ability to obligate other people. Not long ago, for example, Marcus Crassus said that no one who wants to be the chief power in the state has sufficient property unless he can maintain an army on his income. Men also take pleasure in impressive furnishings and luxurious living along with elegance and abundance. Yet these are the objects that stimulate an unending desire for wealth. Of course, no one should criticize an increase in a family's estate that harms no one else, but it should never involve breaking the law. [26] Blindness to the claims of justice seizes men (and most people do not resist it) when they have conceived an ambition for military commands, or public offices, or glory. The quotation from Ennius:

No society is sacred

No trust is safe in questions of kingdom,[20]

has a rather wide application. Whatever is by definition a sphere in which not more than one person can be first, usually stirs up such competition that it is extremely hard to maintain a [sacred] society. The recklessness of Julius Caesar recently made this clear. He twisted every divine and human law to get the ruling

---

[20] The quotation (fr. CLXIX in H. D. Jocelyn, *The Tragedies of Ennius*, Cambridge, 1967) comes from a tragedy of Ennius, perhaps his *Thyestes*.

position that he imagined in some distorted fancy should belong to him. It is unfortunate in this matter that the craving for
office, for command, for power and glory usually occurs in
people of the finest energy and most brilliant ability.[21] This fact
provides an additional warning against any weakness in this
area.

[27] In all cases of injustice it makes a vast difference whether
the crime arises from some mental aberration, which is usually
brief and temporary, or whether it is deliberate and premedi-
tated. Crimes that occur because of some momentary disturbance are less blameworthy than those that men commit after
meditation and preparation. This is sufficient discussion of the
actual commission of injustices.

[28] As for protection of the weak, several causes may be
mentioned why men overlook and abandon this duty. Perhaps
they wish to avoid unpopularity, or hard work, or expense. Or
indifference, laziness, or weariness, or some private concerns
and preoccupations hamper them so much that they allow
people whom they ought to shelter to remain unprotected. For
this reason you have to examine whether what Plato says about
philosophers is adequate.[22] He says that because they are busy
searching for truth and because they condemn and despise what
most men pursue eagerly and usually fight over among themselves, for these reasons philosophers are men of justice. They
pursue one [type of justice] by inflicting a wrong so they do not
harm anyone, . . . they fall into another.[23] Their concern for
learning hobbles them, and so they abandon people whom
they should protect. He therefore thinks that they would not be
inclined to participate in government unless they were compelled to do so. Yet their participation would be more reason-

[21] A kind of epitaph of the recently assassinated Caesar. Note the praise
within the condemnation: Caesar was brilliant but criminal.

[22] The following passages in Plato's *Republic* are referred to: VI. 485 F;
VII. 520 D; I. 347 C, and VII. 519.

[23] The editor of the Latin text believes that some words have dropped
out of this sentence; the meaning is not certain.

able if it were voluntary, because a right action is only just on the condition that it is voluntary. [29] There are also men who, because they concentrate on protecting their private interests or because they have some dislike for mankind in general, say that they are minding their own business and to all appearances do not do anyone else any criminal harm. They escape one category of injustice but fall into another, because they abandon the society of life by devoting neither attention, nor any effort, nor any of their abilities to it.

Since I have set forth two categories of injustice and added the reasons for each group, and since I have previously established the features that define justice, we shall easily be able to decide what a man's obligation is for each occasion, unless we are excessively self-centred. [30] Concern for other people's interests is hard to arouse. I grant that Chremes in Terence "thinks nothing human alien to himself."[24] Nevertheless our decisions about others differ from those about ourselves, because we have more feeling for and experience of the things that will turn out successfully or adversely for ourselves than for the things that affect others. We see other men's affairs across a long intervening gulf, as it were. So philosophers who strictly forbid you to act when you have any reason to doubt whether your action is just or unjust, are good teachers. Justice stands out brightly by itself, while the mere fact of doubt indicates a suspicion of wrongdoing.

[31] On the other hand, occasions often arise when acts that seem preeminently worthy of a just man and of the man we call good reverse themselves and become their own opposites. Examples of this are to return something [even to a madman] that someone has left with you, or to fulfill a promise. Occasionally it turns out to be just to violate and disregard facts that contribute to truth and integrity. We ought to think back to the

---

[24] The famous quotation, *homo sum: humani nil a me alienum puto*, is from Terence's *Heautontimorumenos* ("The Self-Tormentor"), I.i.25.

bases of justice that I laid down in the beginning: first, that no harm comes to anyone and second, that the common good is served. [When circumstances change with occasions, responsibility changes also and is not always the same.] [32] It can happen that a man promises and agrees to do something that is not advantageous to carry out; there might be no advantage either to the man who gave the promise or to the man who received it. To give an example from mythology: if Neptune had not fulfilled his promise to Theseus, Theseus would not have lost his son, Hippolytus. The legend goes that this was the fulfillment of the third of three wishes: Theseus in a rage had said that he wished Hippolytus were dead. He got his wish and fell into great fits of mourning.[25] Therefore you should not keep those promises that might be of no benefit to those to whom you have made them. Again, suppose that what you promised to do might cause you more harm than the man who took your promise might stand to profit. In that case it is not a neglect of responsibility to prefer the greater good to the lesser. For example, if you have agreed with someone that you would go to court as a witness[26] and meanwhile your son began to suffer from a grave illness, it would be consistent with your responsibility not to carry out what you promised. On the contrary: the man who received your promise abandons his responsibility if he complains that you deserted him. Beyond this, who fails to understand that no one should honor promises that fear forced him to make, or that fraud deceived him into making? In fact praetorian law annuls many such promises and statute law quite a few more.[27]

[25] Cicero uses this same example in III.94.

[26] An *advocatus* ("witness") was not so much a witness in the modern sense of the term as anyone who would appear in court to support or help another man and do so not necessarily as a legal expert. He was not legally bound to appear before the court.

[27] Each praetor issued an edict when he began his year-long term of office. This edict, which in fact became stereotyped and did not reflect annual

[33] A perversion of justice, some extremely clever but harmful interpretation of a statute, also is a frequent cause of wrongdoing. Hence we have the saying *summum ius summa iniuria,* "Extreme legality is the worst law," a proverb become a cliché by daily use. Many crimes take place under this heading, even in public life. There is the case of the general who, during a thirty days' truce with the enemy, used to lay waste the fields by night, because the truce was for "days," not for "nights." Another story that I have only on hearsay involves the Roman, Quintus Fabius Labeo, or perhaps it was really someone else; in any case it was not an action that one would commend. The Senate appointed him to arbitrate a boundary dispute between the Nolans and the Neapolitans. When he arrived, he consulted each side separately, telling them not to behave greedily or selfishly. He urged them to choose to yield a little ground rather than to press forward. When both sides had in fact drawn back, they left an open patch of field between themselves. Labeo let the boundary stand just where they had said; what was left in the middle he appropriated for the Roman people. This is simply deception, of course, not the act of a judge. For this reason, such subtlety should be avoided in all cases.

Yet there are certain responsibilities that you should preserve even toward those who have done you an injury. There is a limit to vengeance and punishment; and I rather think that it is enough when the person who committed the wrong repents his crime, so that he does not do something similar later and so that others are less inclined toward crime.

[34] In a government's foreign policy the laws of warfare in particular should be observed. There are two ways of settling disputes: one by reasonable discussion, the other by force. Al-

---

changes, described the various circumstances in which the praetor would or would not undertake legal actions. The praetor's *edictum perpetuum* was thus a permanent set of regulations that supplemented the common or statute law. For praetor see *Glossary*.

though reason is characteristic of men and force of beasts, you must resort to force if there is no opportunity to employ reason. [35] Therefore wars should be undertaken only so that one may live in peace without wrongdoing. But if you win a victory, you should spare those enemies who were not cruel or barbarous in warfare. Remember that our ancestors even received the Tusculans, the Aequians, the Volscians, the Sabines, and the Hernicians into citizenship, while they completely obliterated Carthage and Numantia. I wish the Romans had not destroyed Corinth, but I believe they had some reason, most likely the excellence of its site: they did not wish the location itself[28] to tempt them to make war again. My firm opinion is that you should always work toward a peace that is not going to conceal any trap. If the Romans[29] had followed my advice in this we would have a government, not the best perhaps, but government of some kind, where none at all exists now. You must also have consideration for those you have conquered by strength, and in the same way you should welcome those who may put down their arms and flee to the protection of the generals, even though a battering ram has broken through their defense.[30] We have cultivated justice in this area to such an extent that men who have received the parole of cities or nations conquered in war are their *patroni*,[31] according to a long-established custom.

[36] Roman fetial law,[32] in fact, prescribes very minutely the equity of warfare. The existence of this law makes it clear that no war is just unless it is waged after the government has de-

---

[28] Corinth, situated on the Isthmus between the Gulf of Corinth and the Saronic Gulf, commanded a very strategic location both by land and by sea.

[29] Cicero presumably refers primarily to the disputes between Julius Caesar and Pompey that led to civil war.

[30] The Romans by tradition spared enemies in a besieged city who surrendered before the battering rams were brought forward.

[31] See *Glossary*.

[32] See *Glossary*.

manded restitution or unless the war is previously announced and declared. [The general Popillius governed a province, and a son of Cato was serving as a private in his army. However, when Popillius thought he should dismiss one legion, he also dismissed Cato's son, who was serving in that particular one. Because the son had remained in the army because of his love for fighting, Cato wrote to Popillius to put the young man under a second military oath if he was going to allow him to remain under arms. The reason was that, having invalidated his first oath, the son could not go into combat against enemies of the state. That was remarkably complete legality in waging war.]

[37] A letter exists, sent by Marcus Cato the Elder to Marcus his son, in which he writes that he has heard that the son had received a discharge from the consul when he was a soldier in Macedonia in the war against Perseus.[33] Accordingly, he warns his son to beware of going into battle; he says, you see, that it is not lawful for someone who is not a soldier to fight a state enemy. I call to mind also that the word *hostis* ("stranger") was applied to a person who would correctly have been called *perduellis* ("enemy"), the harshness of the fact being softened by the gentleness of the word. Among our ancestors the person we now call "stranger" was called a "guest" (*hostis*). The Twelve Tables[34] have this phrase: "or a day fixed with a foreigner *(hostis),*" and also, "in respect to a stranger *(hostis)* ownership is inalienable." What is more gentle than to call a person with whom you wage war by such a soft name? Of course, long use has by now made it a harsher word; *hostis* has lost the meaning "stranger" and now is applied accurately to one who bears arms offensively.

[38] When the conflict really involves supremacy, and glory is the objective of war, the very same reasons should neverthe-

---

[33] Perseus, last king of Macedonia, was defeated by Aemilius Paullus in 168 B.C.

[34] See *Glossary.*

less be present, the ones that I said a little while ago[35] were just grounds for wars. Wars in which the object is the glory of supremacy should be waged less bitterly. To draw an analogy: we fight with a fellow citizen in one way if he is a declared enemy, in another way if he is merely a rival. With the latter the struggle concerns honor and office, with the former it involves life and reputation. For example, we fought our wars with the Celtiberi and the Cimbrians on the level of enmity: each side's existence was at stake, not merely its supremacy. The wars with the Latins, the Sabines, the Samnites, the Carthaginians, and with Pyrrhus were wars for supremacy. [The Carthaginians broke treaties; Hannibal was cruel; the others were more reasonable.] Remember the well-known speech of Pyrrhus concerning the return of captives:

I demand for myself no gold; do not offer me ransom.
Neither side should be tradesmen of war, but warriors;
Let us not decide with gold who will live, but with steel.
Let us test with strength whether Lady Luck wants you
Or me to reign, or what she brings.
And listen to this saying, too:
Those whose strength the luck of war has spared
Will have their freedom spared by me for certain.
I release them; take them away; I present them with the god's
   good will.[36]

This is truly a regal speech, one worthy of a descendant of Aeacus.

[39] Even if individuals have made a promise to an enemy under compulsion of circumstances, they still must keep their word. For example, in the First Punic War the Carthaginians captured Regulus and then sent him to Rome to discuss an exchange of prisoners; he promised that he would return. As soon as he arrived in Rome he advised the Senate that the

---

[35] In section 35.
[36] Ennius, *Annales*. Pyrrhus addresses a Roman embassy that came to ransom prisoners.

prisoners should not be returned and later, when his relatives and friends were trying to dissuade him, he chose to return and submit to torture rather than to break the promise given to an enemy.[37] [40] [However, in the Second Punic War after the battle of Cannae, Hannibal sent ten prisoners to Rome, bound by an oath that they would return unless they succeeded in ransoming those who had been taken captive. Each successive censor[38] refused to include their names on the voting lists as long as they lived because they had been false to their oath. They treated in the same way one of the men who incurred guilt by breaking the oath. He was one who had left camp with Hannibal's permission but returned a little later because, as he said, he had forgotten something or other. Then he left the camp again, thinking that he had been freed from his oath. He was freed in a literal interpretation but not in substance. You should always, in a matter of trust, think of what you mean, not of what you say. The best example of honesty toward an enemy was provided in the days of our ancestors, when a deserter from Pyrrhus promised the Roman Senate that he would administer poison to Pyrrhus and kill him. The Senate and Gaius Fabricius returned the deserter to Pyrrhus. So our ancestors did not grant approval to the criminal killing even of a powerful enemy who was waging an aggressive war.] [41] I have undoubtedly said enough about the responsibility connected with warfare.

Let us remember also that justice must be maintained even toward inferiors. And both the condition and the fate of slaves are inferior. Those who urge that slaves should be put to use like hired hands give good advice: you should get work out of them, but you must treat them fairly.[39]

Now wrongdoing originates in one of two ways: either by

---

[37] The story of Regulus is discussed by Cicero at much greater length in III.99–113.

[38] See *Glossary.*

[39] Hired hands would expect to receive a minimum allowance of food, clothing, and shelter. Justice demands that slaves receive as much in exchange for their labor. Note the implication that the law did not demand as much.

force or by deception; deception is like a little fox, force like the lion. Both are most uncharacteristic of man, but deception should arouse greater contempt. Taking all forms of injustice into account, none is more deadly than that practiced by people who act as if they are good men when they are being most treacherous. Enough has been said about justice.

[42] Let our discussion next turn to generosity and liberality, as I planned. Nothing, of course, is more suited to man's nature than these qualities, but they contain many pitfalls. You must be careful, first, that your kindliness is not offensive either to those who you think are going to benefit from the kindliness or to others; second, you must watch that your generosity does not exceed your resources; and third, that the generosity is in proportion to each recipient's worth, for such proportion forms the basis of justice, and all these decisions have to be made in terms of justice. Men who do a favor that harms the very person they seem to want to help have to be considered harmful deceivers, not people of generosity and liberality. Those who harm some people in order to be generous toward others commit the same injustice as if they appropriated other people's property for their own use.

[43] There are also many, specifically those who crave display and notoriety, who steal from some what they shower on others, under the impression that they will get the reputation of being generous toward their friends if they enrich them by fair means or foul. But such a false reputation is so foreign to true generosity that it is the precise opposite. We must be careful to employ the kind of generosity that benefits friends and harms no one. For this reason, no one should think that Sulla and Caesar were being generous when they transferred funds from their legal owners to strangers.[40] Nothing is generous that is not also legal.

---

[40] Dictators regularly financed themselves and their friends by auctioning the confiscated property of the victims of their purges. See II.27 for another reference to these auctions.

[44] The second warning to caution was that generosity should not exceed your means. Those who try to be more generous than their means allow commit their first offense by being unfair to their dependents. In effect, they transfer to strangers those resources that with more justice they would make available or bequeath to their family. Furthermore, a temptation to seize and carry off property unlawfully often lurks beneath excessive generosity; the crime is necessary so that resources are on hand to give lavishly. It is quite clear that many individuals, who are not so much innately generous as they are swayed by the vain desire to seem generous, often indulge in gestures that apparently originate in ostentation rather than in genuine open-handedness. This kind of pretense is closer to vanity than to generosity or uprightness.

[45] The third warning was that acts of generosity should observe distinctions of rank. To accomplish this we should examine the character of the person toward whom we are directing our generosity, as well as his disposition toward us, his ties and social connections with us and the duties he previously carried out to our advantage. One would hope that all these conditions occur in one person; if not, the greater, more significant motives will have the preference.

[46] Since we do not live among men who are perfect and completely wise, but rather among men whose behavior is admired even if they only give the appearance of virtue, I think you should also realize that you must not completely despise any man who shows at least a trace of virtue.[41] The more an individual approaches perfection in his display of the finer qualities, in modesty, self-control, and in justice itself (I have said a great deal by now about this virtue), the more you should show him preference. These three virtues are the particular marks of a good man. As for the fourth virtue, a strong-willed and cou-

---

[41] An act of virtue, according to the Stoics, was truly virtuous only if performed by a completely wise man. The same act performed by an ordinary man would be merely the "appearance of virtue." See III.13 for a more complete analysis.

rageous temperament in a man who is not perfect or wise generally tends to be too reckless. So much concerning the character of those toward whom we are generous.

[47] Now concerning the good will that individuals display toward us: the main area of our responsibility is to devote the most good will to the person who loves us most.[42] Yet we should decide upon good will not by some passionate infatuation, like young people, but rather by firmness and self-possession. If you incur obligations and have to return a favor and not merely do one, then you must apply an extra degree of care: no duty is more necessary than to return a favor. [48] In fact if, as Hesiod orders,[43] you should return in larger measure what you borrow and use, provided that you can do so, what should we do when someone has obliged us by a favor? Perhaps imitate fruitful fields that produce much more than they receive? If we do not hesitate to carry out our obligations toward men we hope will be useful to us, how should we behave toward men who have already been useful? For there are two classifications of generosity: one of doing a kindness, the other of returning a kindness. Whether we do a kindness or not is up to us; but a good man is simply not permitted to neglect to return a kindness, as long as he can do it without injustice.

[49] Also, you have to discriminate among the kindnesses done to you: without any doubt your obligation is greatest to the largest favor. Here you have to determine first the spirit in which the person did the favor, or with what intention, or with what amount of friendliness. Many people act from a kind of indiscriminate rashness, excited by some chronic urge to be generous or by some sudden mental impulse, fickle as the breeze. No one should consider those favors to be equally as significant as those that men bestow with judgment, with deliberation, and with a system. In distributing favors and in returning obligations, when other considerations balance out, the

---

[42] Sections 47–49 show clearly that charity ranked low in Roman estimation and that *officium* was almost always to be regarded as a transaction.

[43] Lines 349–350 of Hesiod, *Works and Days*.

spirit of responsibility calls for you to prefer to help the person who needs the most assistance. People generally do the opposite: they put their all in the service of the man from whom they have the highest expectations, even if he does not need what they have to give.

[50] Now the society of men, their interrelationship, will be best preserved if the degree of kindness people show to each other is in proportion to the closeness of their relationship. I believe, however, that we should investigate more closely what the natural foundations of human community and society are. What one can observe in human society as a whole is fundamental. The bond of that society is reason and speech; they reconcile men to each other and join them in a sort of natural community by teaching, by learning, by communicating, by discussing, by judging. Nothing separates us farther from the nature of wild animals: we often say that animals possess bravery, horses and lions, for example; but we do not say they possess justice, a sense of equity or of goodness, because they do not participate in reason and speech.

[51] This is the society that extends most widely, joining men to men, all humans to each other. It must be the means by which men maintain the sharing of everything that nature has produced for the common benefit of men. The property assigned to individuals by statute and civil law must be maintained just as those laws prescribe. But we should regard everything else in the spirit of the Greek proverb: "all friends' property is common property." The common property of all men seems to be the kind of thing that Ennius mentioned: he gives one example that will apply to many other matters:

A man who kindly shows the way to a wanderer
Acts like one who lights another lamp from his own:
His own shines just as well after it has lit another's.[44]

----

[44] From an unknown tragedy of Ennius (fr. CLXV in Jocelyn; see note 20, p. 14).

This single example teaches well enough that one should share even with a stranger whatever can be shared without loss. [52] Such is the common theme of some precepts of ordinary morality: "Do not keep anyone away from flowing water;" "Permit a man to light his fire from yours;" "Give honest advice to anyone who is perplexed, if he wants it." These actions are helpful to the recipient and cause no trouble to the donor. You should therefore practice them yourself while constantly trying to contribute something to the common benefit. On the other hand, the resources of individuals are limited, while the mass of people who are in want is unlimited; so the popular concept of generosity must be restricted by the warning implied in Ennius' phrase, "His own shines just as well." We do not want to destroy the means of being generous toward those for whom we are responsible.

[53] Now there are several levels in human society. Apart from mankind as a whole, which we shall now leave out of the discussion, there is the more restricted level of belonging to the same race, the same tribe, and the same language: these join men together very closely. An even closer relationship is to belong to the same city; for fellow citizens hold many things in common: the forum, temples, colonnades, roads, laws, statutes, courtroom, voting rights, and, most important, customs and observances and the arrangements and agreements that thousands have entered into with thousands of others. Even closer are the ties among a group of relatives. From the all-embracing society of mankind as a whole, you see, the discussion narrows down to something small and circumscribed.

[54] We may assume that it is naturally common to living things to have the desire to procreate. The first stage of society, then, is in the basic man-wife relationship; a second stage is in the children of that union; and a third stage is in the single household where the members share everything. The household is the foundation of the city, what we might call the "seed-bed" of the state. There follow the relationships "brother" and

"sister" and then those of "cousin" and "second cousin." When a single house cannot shelter all of them, they migrate to other houses as if they were going out to colonies. Marriages and alliances of families deriving from those marriages follow, and they result in even more relatives. These propagations and offshoots are the beginnings of states. So blood relationship links men together in good will and affection; [55] for it is worth a great deal to have common ancestral monuments, to employ the same religious rites, and to possess common burial places.

[Yet of all associations none takes higher rank, none is more secure, than when good men who are alike in character have joined in fellowship. The moral goodness that I have mentioned so often stirs us even when we perceive it in a stranger; it makes us friends with a man in whom it is obviously present. [56] I grant that any virtue attracts us and causes us to love those in whom it appears to be present. Justice and generosity, however, have this effect beyond all other virtues.] Also, nothing is more conducive to friendship and intimacy than the similarity of character among good men. Men who have the same interests and the same outlook take satisfaction each in the other as much as in himself. The Pythagorean ideal of friendship takes on reality; one replaces the many.[45] Furthermore, the sharing that the reciprocal giving and receiving of kindnesses creates is great; as long as the exchange is mutual and acceptable, it binds those between whom it takes place by an unbreakable relationship.

[57] When you examine everything with your mind and spirit, no relationship is more important, none is more attractive than the relationship each one of us has with our country. Our parents are dear, our children are dear, our relatives, our friends; but the fatherland alone embraces all of our deep feel-

---

[45] Cicero has in mind such definitions of friendship as "one soul in two bodies," or "the friend is another self." An anecdote of Pythagorean friendship occurs in III.45. Note, however, the emphasis on reciprocity in the next sentence of this paragraph.

ings. What good man would hesitate to meet death for its sake, if he could be of any use to it? That is why I find so detestable the viciousness of those men who have torn their fatherland to pieces with every kind of crime, who have been and still are working for its complete destruction.

[58] If there should arise any need to estimate or choose by comparison those who are entitled to receive your highest duty, the fatherland and the parents should come first: our debt to their kindness is the largest. The children and the household in general come next: they depend on us alone and cannot look to any other refuge. The last place goes to the deserving friends: your destiny is often intertwined with theirs. For this reason, one owes the basic protections in life especially to those groups of people I have just enumerated; but it is especially in one's friendships that one finds the real strength of a shared life and households, advice, conversations, encouragements, consolations, and even occasional arguments. [A friendship that a similarity of character has cemented together is the most pleasant of all.]

[59] In carrying out all these obligations, you have to be cautious about what each person most needs, and what each person can accomplish or not, even without us. When you take this into consideration, the degrees of relationship are not going to be identical to those of circumstances. There are duties that one owes more to some people than to others. For example, you would help a neighbor take in his harvest more promptly than your brother or a friend. If a trial were underway, you would defend a relative or a friend rather than a neighbor. Such relationships and such considerations are what you have to examine whenever questions of responsibility arise, [and you must acquire this habit and discipline], so you can become accurate in calculating responsibility and by adding and subtracting find out what is the remaining total. By this calculation you can understand how far each individual is in your debt.

[60] Yet not even doctors, or generals, or public speakers can

accomplish anything that deserves much praise without experience or practice, even though they have learned by heart the rules of their profession. One passes on the "rules" for carrying out responsibility, of course, as I am doing right now, but the importance of the subject itself demands practice and experience also. I have discussed at sufficient length how morality develops from the justice necessary to human society and how duties depend on that morality.

[61] Although I proposed four categories that are the source of right action and duty, you still must realize that what seems most splendid are the accomplishments of a great, elevated spirit that despises worldly affairs. This fact explains why, if you want to insult someone, the appropriate thing to say is something like this,

You young men have women's souls, but she has a man's,

or something like this:

You son of Salmacis: you captive who cost no sweat or blood![46]
On the other hand, when we praise deeds that a man has accomplished nobly, bravely, brilliantly, we almost unconsciously speak our praise in a louder voice. That is the reason public speakers find fruitful themes in Marathon, Salamis, Plataea, Thermopylae, Leuctra. Because of this we hear so much about the Roman Cocles, the Decii, the two Scipios, Gnaeus and Publius, Marcus Marcellus, and countless others, and above all the Roman people themselves are remarkable for their heroism. The statues that we see every day also make clear how eager we are for glory in war: they are almost all in military uniform.[47]

---

[46] The author and source of the first quotation are unknown. The second is from an unknown tragedy of Ennius (fr. CLXXXI in Jocelyn; see note 20 on p. 14). "Son of Salmacis" means a coward; Salmacis was a legendary spring that weakened those who touched its waters.

[47] Romans preferred that full-length statues of themselves be in military uniform, not the *toga*, the official civilian dress. Cicero may also have in mind the contrast with the conventional nudity of much classical Greek statuary.

[62] The heroism that men display in dangers and difficult undertakings is faulty if it lacks justice and fights not for the common welfare but for its own comforts. Not merely are such actions uncharacteristic of virtue, but they are even more typical of a beastliness that rejects anything humane. The Stoics, therefore, define bravery with precision when they say that it is courage going to battle for justice. By this definition no one who has won his reputation for bravery by treachery and evildoing has won any praise, for nothing can be morally worthy that lacks justice.

[63] Therefore the following passage of Plato is outstanding: "Knowledge separate from justice should be called cleverness rather than wisdom. Not only that, but if the temperament, hardened to danger, is driven on by its private greed and not by the common benefit, the name we shall give that temperament is selfish recklessness, not bravery."[48] We therefore expect men who are strong and courageous to be good and straightforward as well, to be the friends of truth and completely trustworthy. These qualities are essential to the praise of justice. [64] Yet the following fact is distressing: aggressiveness and unrestrained lust to rule grow up too easily as accompaniments of this elevation and heroism. We read in Plato that "the lust to conquer inflames the whole Spartan character."[49] Similarly, insofar as a man surpasses all others by the scope of his character, to that extent he wants to be chief among his peers, or rather sole ruler. Unfortunately, it is difficult to preserve a sense of fair dealing when you have the urge to command everyone, and fair dealing is especially pertinent to justice. Such ambitious men do not allow discussions or any lawful and public statute to hinder them.[50] In the government they mostly turn out to be bribers and seditious elements who try to amass as

[48] Plato, Menexenus 246 E.
[49] Plato, Laches 182 E.
[50] Cicero's thoughts about Caesar may well color this passage. See I.26 above.

much wealth as possible, who want to be masters by force rather than equals in justice. But where the difficulty is greater, the glory is greater. There is no emergency that should compel a man to abandon justice.

[65] I conclude that we should consider strong and courageous not those men who inflict injury but those who protect others from injury. Moreover, a genuine, wise nobility of character decides that the moral excellence that nature requires above all consists of accomplishments, not of reputation; a man of such character prefers to be a true leader, not an apparent one. You cannot count among great men those who depend on the instability of an inexperienced mob. Also, insofar as a man has an ambitious character, his lust after a reputation easily drives him on to criminal acts. Reputation, of course, is a sensitive topic, because you can find hardly anyone who, once he has taken on hardships and broached dangers, does not desire a bit of fame as if that were the payment for his accomplishments.

[66] Two distinctive traits especially identify beyond doubt a strong and dominant character. One trait is contempt for external circumstances, when one is convinced that men ought to respect, to desire, and to pursue only what is moral and right; that men should be subject to nothing, not to another man, not to some disturbing passion, not to Fortune. The second trait, when your character has the disposition I outlined just now, is to perform the kind of services that are significant and most beneficial; but they should also be services that are a severe challenge, that are filled with ordeals, and that endanger not only your life but also the many comforts that make life attractive. [67] Of these two traits, all the glory, magnificence, and the advantage, too, let us not forget, are in the second, while the drive and the discipline that make men great are in the former. A certain quality exists there that breeds individuals of outstanding vigor who are not affected by ordinary concerns. Two signs help us to recognize this particular quality: if you de-

cide that only what is moral is good, and if you are free from
any mental turbulence. You must believe that it is characteristic
of a strong and heroic mind to consider trivial what most people think glorious and attractive, and to despise those things
with unshakable, inflexible discipline. To endure reverses that
seem bitter, the many varying events that happen during men's
life and fortune, to endure them so that you depart not one
inch from your basic nature, not a jot from a wise man's
self-respect: that is the mark of a strong spirit and of great
consistency.

[68] However, it is inconsistent for a man who is impervious
to fear to succumb to physical desire, or for a man who has
shown that hard work cannot destroy him to yield to pleasure.
So you must beware of desire and pleasure. You must also shun
the greed for money; nothing is as good an index of a narrow
and trivial spirit as the love of wealth; nothing is more upstand-
ing and glorious than the contempt for wealth if you are not
wealthy, or if you have wealth, to apply it to benefits and
generosity. Infatuation with a glorious reputation should be
avoided, as I said above; for that takes away freedom, and men
of great spirit ought to pursue independence by every means.
Of course you should not grasp military commands; you should
even try to evade them occasionally and sometimes submit
your resignation.

[69] You must also be free from any disturbance of the spirit,
both from lust and fear, as well as from anxiety or sensuality or
anger, so that you possess both mental tranquillity and calm;
with them goes self-control as well as self-esteem. There exist
and have existed many men who, in pursuit of the tranquillity I speak of, have withdrawn from public affairs and taken
refuge in retirement. Among them are the most distinguished
philosophers, the leading teachers, and certain serious and
thoughtful men. They could not endure the habits of the people or of the rulers, and a great many have lived in the country,
taking pleasure in their own private estates. [70] These men

had the same object as kings: to be in want of nothing what-soever, to be in no one else's service, to enjoy freedom, whose definition is to live in just the way you want. Those who desire power pursue this goal just like the retiring people I mentioned. The one group, however, think they can attain their aim if they possess great wealth; the others if they are content with their small private property. In this matter you can condemn neither group's convictions, of course, but the life of those who with-draw is both easier and safer and less harsh or harmful to others. On the other hand, the life of men who have devoted them-selves to government and to the administration of great enter-prises is more beneficial to the human race and more advan-tageous to their own fame and magnificence.

[71] For this reason perhaps you have to excuse those who have devoted themselves to their outstanding talent for philos-ophy and take no active part in government. Weak health or some more serious impediment has also incapacitated some men, and they have withdrawn from government, so leaving to others the opportunity to run it and to reap the praise. How-ever, I do not think anyone should praise men who have no such excuse. In fact, they deserve criticism if they say they de-spise the things that most people admire: commands and of-fices. Of course, it is hard not to approve their decision insofar as they despise fame and consider it meaningless; but they give the appearance of fearing the hard work and trouble and, I would say, the embarrassment, the humiliation of criticism and defeats. Some men are not very consistent with themselves as circumstances change; they utterly despise soft living, yet are rather sensitive about facing pain; they pay no attention to fame, yet they are crushed by a scandal; and they are not even very predictable in these weaknesses.

[72] Nature blesses some men with the talents for governing. They should cast aside any hesitation, take public office and help operate the government. There is no alternative way to rule the state, or to reveal a man's greatness of spirit. Men who

govern a state, no less than philosophers and probably even more than philosophers, should possess both greatness and the contempt for merely human affairs that I constantly mention, the tranquil spirit and the independence. These are the conditions of freedom from fear and they are necessary to a life of seriousness and self-control. [73] These attitudes are easier for philosophers to achieve insofar as their way of life is less exposed to the blows of fortune and insofar as philosophers do not feel the need of numerous possessions, and because they cannot fall very disastrously if anything evil happens to them. It is not without reason that men who govern the state are prone to stronger disturbances of the spirit and greater ambition for accomplishment than men who retire. Therefore statesmen require more greatness of spirit and freedom from annoyances. The man who undertakes the task of governing should also beware that he does not consider only the moral correctness of an action; he should also consider whether he has the ability to carry it through. At the same time he should remember not to despair uselessly through cowardice and not to be excessively confident through eagerness. In any transaction, he must apply hardheaded forethought before he begins.

[74] Although most people think that military deeds are more significant than civil government, the belief should be refuted. Many men have often pursued military careers merely because of their greed for fame. This greed infects mostly men of strong character and ability, especially if they are talented in military matters and are fond of waging wars. However, if we wish to make a true evaluation of these matters, there have been numerous civil events of more significance and better-known than events in war. [75] Although Themistocles might deserve the praise he receives, although his name might be far more famous than Solon's, although men might cite Salamis[51]

---

[51] Themistocles commanded the Greek forces in this sea battle against the Persians in 480 B.C.

as an example of an immortal victory and give it precedence over the policy of Solon's by which he first set up the Areopagus—still, Solon's program should not be thought any less outstanding than the victory. The victory was a single advantage, but the policy will always benefit the state; it is this policy that preserved the Athenian laws and their ancestral practices. Furthermore, Themistocles could not mention any action by which he helped the Areopagus, but the Areopagus could truly say that it helped Themistocles, because the Athenians waged the war with the advice of the body that Solon had constituted. [76] One can say similar things about Pausanias and Lysander.[52] Although people may think that the Spartan empire was expanded by their achievements, still those military deeds cannot begin to compare to the laws and discipline of Lycurgus. Indeed, it was precisely because of the Lycurgan institutions that the Spartans had stronger and more obedient armies.

It did not seem to me when I was a young man that Marcus Scaurus took second place to Gaius Marius, or, when I was taking part in public affairs, that Quintus Catulus was inferior to Gnaeus Pompey; for weapons have small value abroad unless there is good advice at home.[53] Africanus, that extraordinary man and general, was no more useful to the state when he destroyed Numantia than was Publius Nasica at the same time, when, as a private citizen, he assassinated Tiberius Gracchus. I grant that the assassination was not solely the result of domestic policy; in fact it came close to being military, since it was done by a violent attack. Yet the attack itself was made as a political measure, not with an army.[54]

---

[52] After the illustration from Athenian history comes a parallel example from Spartan history.

[53] Cicero now illustrates his argument with examples from recent Roman history. Scaurus and Catulus made contributions in civic affairs comparable to the military successes of Marius and Pompey.

[54] Scipio Africanus the Younger destroyed Numantia in 133 B.C.; this was a key event in the Roman conquest of Spain. In the same year Publius Cornelius

[77] I hear that some shameful and envious people continue to attack the following verse, but it cannot be surpassed in this context:

Let weapons give way to the toga, let the laurels yield to praise.[55] I will not mention other men's careers, but when I was steering the ship of state, did weapons not give way to the toga? Never did a more serious danger threaten the government, as you realize, and yet never was there a more remarkable absence of alarm. Through my policies and tireless work the weapons, struck from the hands of the most desperate citizens, fell to the ground voluntarily. What action in wartime was ever as significant? What military triumph was comparable? [78] I believe I may boast in your presence, Marcus my son, because you will inherit the fame I earned then and you may imitate my actions. In fact, a man who achieved vast renown for his military exploits, Gnaeus Pompey, paid me this tribute in the hearing of numerous people: he stated clearly that the third triumph he earned would have been an empty honor if he had not had a place in which to celebrate it, thanks to my services to the state.[56] I conclude that many civilian acts of bravery are no less important than military successes, and that you should devote even more energy and ambition to civilian than to military duties.

[79] Of course strength of character, not physical strength, produces the morality that I would like a man of outstanding and heroic character to have. Yet a man must exercise and discipline his body so that it can respond to advice and planning

---

Scipio Nasica led the group of Senators who killed Tiberius Gracchus in Rome. Cicero notes that because violence was used against Gracchus, the illustration is not perfectly similar to the previous example, but still permissable.

[55] A verse from a poem written by Cicero about his own suppression of the Catilinarian conspiracy; the verse was widely cited as a sample of Cicero's vanity.

[56] Pompey's third triumph was granted to him after his victories in the East in 61 B.C.; Cicero's consulate was in 63 B.C.

during the conduct of business and while undergoing hardships. The particular morality that I am pursuing, however, is
the result of the attention and application of men's characters.
In this area men who head the government as civilians bring
as much advantage as the generals who wage war. It is on the
advice of these civilians that military leaders have frequently
avoided or abandoned wars in the past or have declared war
when the occasion demanded. The advice of Marcus Cato led
to the declaration of the Third Punic War, and his persuasive-
ness was powerful even after he died.[57] [80] You should try
more earnestly to find a basis of negotiation than the bravery
to fight to the end, and yet you must be careful to negotiate
not because you are reluctant to fight but because you have
calculated what is advantageous. You should start a war, moreover, in such a way that you clearly have no other object than
peace.

It is the mark of a truly brave and unswerving character not
to be upset in difficult circumstances, or to be confused and
thrown off stride, as they say, but to preserve his presence of
mind and his ability to reflect and not to lose his reasonable-
ness. [81] Such consistency is an attribute of one's character,
but the following traits also involve one's intellectual capacity:
to anticipate the future by thought, and sometimes to have in
mind well in advance what might happen in alternative cases
and what reaction a particular turn of events will demand, and
never to find it necessary to say, "I had not thought of that."
Such are the operations of a great and elevated spirit, of one
that trusts its own wisdom and planning. To get involved
thoughtlessly in the front rank and to fight the enemy in hand-
to-hand combat is rather monstrous and rather like wild animals. Yet when the occasion and necessity demand, you should

---

[57] Cato the Censor is said to have advocated the destruction of Carthage
in all his speeches before the Senate, whatever the topic under debate. The
Third Punic War was declared in 149 B.C., the year in which Cato died.

fight it out hand-to-hand and you should prefer death to slavery and shame.

[82] [When it comes to defeating and pillaging cities you must be extremely careful that none of your actions is rash or cruel. It is the sign of a great man to punish only the guilty in a time of disorder, to protect the populace, to cling to what is upright and moral in any turn of fortune.] Just as there are men, as I said above,[58] who prefer military affairs over civil ones, so you can find many who consider dangerous and daring policies to be more attractive and impressive than policies that are restrained and carefully considered.

[83] We should certainly never make the mistake of allowing ourselves to be called cowards and men of fear by running away from danger. On the other hand, we should run away from it if we thereby avoid getting involved in perils for no reason; nothing could be more foolish than that. In dealing with danger, you should imitate physicians: they treat mild cases mildly, but they have to apply risky and doubtful cures to more serious illnesses. In the same way only a madman would desire a driving hurricane during a calm; but the wise man prepares to meet a storm with all the resources he commands. He fights more willingly if the good that he will receive when the danger ends surpasses the evil that will result if the crisis is postponed. The danger in performing great actions falls partly on the individuals who act, partly on the state as a whole. In the same way some men answer the summons to danger to save their life, some because of ambition and desire to serve fellow citizens. We ought to be more willing to put ourselves in danger than to endanger the public welfare; more prepared to wage war over honor and reputation than over advantages of other sorts.

[84] History records the careers of many men who were prepared to pour out not only money but even their life on behalf

----

[58] In section 74.

of the fatherland; yet the same men were not willing to sacrifice a small amount of their glory, not even when the state was imploring them. An example is Callicratidas. Although he had been a Spartan general in the Peloponnesian War and had many outstanding accomplishments to his credit, in the end he spoiled his whole career. He did not heed the advice of men who thought that the Spartans should withdraw their fleet from Arginusae and that they should not fight the Athenians. He answered that if the Spartans lost their fleet they could equip another one, but that he could not possibly retreat without personal disgrace. Yet for the Spartans Arginusae was only a slight setback. They sustained a disastrous blow when Cleombrotus, in fear of disgrace, rashly joined battle with Epaminondas and wrecked the power of Sparta.[59] Quintus Maximus' tactics were much more successful. Ennius writes about him,

> One single man by delaying restored our state.
> He did not rank fame higher than security;
> And so now afterwards the man's renown glows ever brighter.[60]

To rank your own glory higher than the needs of the fatherland is also wrong in civilian life. Some men do not have the courage to say what they think, even if their advice is the best; they are afraid that people will dislike them.

[85] Those who are going to be in charge of the government should most certainly remember two teachings of Plato. The first[61] instructs them to watch over the interests of the citizens in such a way as to refer to it in everything they do and to forget completely about their own interests. The second[62] tells them to minister to the entire body of the state so as not to

---

[59] Two Spartan defeats are attributed to the vainglory of the Spartan commanders. The naval defeat at the Arginusae Islands was in 406 B.C., the defeat of Cleombrotus on land at Leuctra was in 371 B.C.

[60] Ennius, *Annales*. Quintus Fabius Maximus was appointed dictator in 217 B.C. when Hannibal had defeated Roman armies very seriously in Italy. Fabius' strategy was to follow and harass Hannibal's army without risking a pitched battle; he thus won the *cognomen, Cunctator*, "The Delayer."

[61] Plato, *Republic* I. 342 E.

[62] *ibid*. VI. 420 B.

neglect the majority while they are vigilant for a particular sector. We may compare Plato's advice to legal guardianship: one should administer the estate for the advantage of the legal wards, not for the profit of the guardians. Men who take care of one group of citizens but neglect another group introduce into the state an extremely destructive circumstance, treason and discord. The result is that some appear to be leaders of the people while others appear to support the aristocrats, but there are few who lead the whole populace. [86] This situation caused great strife among the Athenians, and in Rome the result was not merely conspiracies but destructive civil wars as well. A self-controlled and courageous citizen, who conceivably could hold the highest rank in the state, will shun these things, will hate them, will devote himself entirely to government, will not pursue wealth or power, and will be guardian over the whole state so that he might work to everyone's advantage. Of course he will not involve anyone in hatred and blame by false criminal charges and, in general, will so cling to justice and morality that, as long as he upholds them, he would rather suffer any misfortune, however severe, and go to meet death rather than abandon the qualities I mentioned.

[87] Campaigning for public office and fighting for election are on the whole quite degrading. Again, Plato speaks brilliantly about this: "those who argue with each other about who should rule the state act like sailors who fight over who should steer the boat."[63] He also teaches that, "we shall regard as enemies only those who bear arms against us, not those who might wish to govern the state out of private conviction."[64] The argument, one without bitterness, that arose between Publius Africanus and Quintus Metellus concerned a similar question.[65]

---

[63] *ibid.* VI. 488 B.

[64] *ibid.* VIII. 567 C; cf. *Laws* IX. 856 B.

[65] Scipio Africanus the Younger and Metellus fell out over political questions, but their dispute was restrained because events might possibly have induced them to be allies again. Detailed discussion in A. E. Astin, *Scipio Aemilianus* (Oxford, 1967), pp. 312–315.

[88] Of course you should not listen to men who think you must be bitterly angry with your foes and who imagine this is the sign of a great and strong man. Nothing is more praiseworthy, nothing more worthy of a great and outstanding man than a reasonable and forgiving attitude. Among free peoples, where everyone enjoys equal rights, you must practice courtesy and what we might call detachment. Those qualities will prevent us from lapsing into profitless and repulsive bad temper if we become annoyed when people barge in at inconvenient times or pester us with irritating questions. Yet gentleness and mercy deserve approval only as long as strictness continues to be effective on behalf of the state: without such severity no one can run the government. Also, all criticism and correction ought to be free from insult and should be used for the benefit of the state, not the profit of the person who punishes or verbally corrects another. [89] One should also be careful that the punishment does not surpass the crime and that some people receive beatings while others do not even receive a reprimand, both for the same crime. In administering punishment, the most important thing to avoid is anger; for the man who attempts to mete out punishments in a state of anger will not maintain the balance between "too much" and "too little." The "mean" appeals to the Peripatetics, and so it should, if only they did not praise hot temper and say that it is a profitable gift of nature.[66] You should restrain your temper at all times, of course; one should hope that the men who head the state resemble the law, for the law does not punish because it is angry but because it is just.

[90] Let us shun haughtiness, arrogance, and especially overbearing pride, even when things go well for us, rolling along just as we wish. For it is only the changeable man who reacts violently to bad luck or to good luck. An even temper in every

---

[66] Aristotle, *Nicomachean Ethics* IV.v.3: "We praise the man who grows angry for the right reasons and against the right people and also in the right manner and at the right time and for the proper length of time."

phase of life, always the same expression, the same face: that is admirable, a quality we learn from Socrates[67] and Gaius Laelius as well. I note that even Philip, King of Macedonia, although his son outdistanced him in military exploits and renown, was never surpassed in adaptability and human feeling. Philip was unfailingly great, Alexander was frequently scandalous. So those who teach that the higher we rise, the more humbly we should conduct ourselves are clearly giving correct advice.

Panaetius says that Africanus, his student and friend, used to say, "horses that have become crazed to the point of violence because of repeated battlefield engagements are sent off to the trainers, so that the owners can manage them when they become more tractable. In the same way men who have become unbridled and excessively self-confident through prosperity ought to be led, as it were, into the ring of reason and philosophy, so they can see the fragility of men's circumstances and the changeability of luck." [91] Even when you are most prosperous, you should make the greatest possible use of your friends' advice, and you should allow their influence to be even greater than before. In those same circumstances we must beware of lending an open ear to flatterers and of allowing them to praise us excessively. It is easy to be trapped by flattery. We begin to think we are the type of person that men should really praise. That is the beginning of innumerable crimes, since men who overrate themselves because of other men's flattery expose themselves to shameless ridicule and get involved in the extremes of misjudgment. That is surely enough on these matters.

[92] The following conclusion is inevitable: those who rule states perform the most significant and boldest actions because nothing extends more widely or affects more people than an entire government. However, there are also many courageous individuals, past and present, who, although they live in retire-

---

[67] Socrates's wife Xanthippe was supposed to have said that no matter what emergencies arose in Athens, Socrates wore the same expression coming home at night that he wore leaving in the morning. Aelian, *Varia Historia* IX.7.

ment, carry out certain great inquiries or enterprises but content themselves within the boundaries of their own business.
They fall half-way between philosophers and those who conduct public affairs, and they take pleasure in their own private
estate, not expanding it by every possible means, not excluding
their relatives from its benefits, but rather sharing it with both
friends and the state if there is need. The first obligation is to
acquire such an estate honestly, not by some shameful or de-
spicable transaction. Second, its expansion should be the result
of planning, industry, and thrift. Lastly, it should prove itself
beneficial to as many as possible, as long as they deserve it;
it should not serve lust and dissipation in preference to generosity and usefulness. By observing these rules a man can live
richly, impressively, independently and yet also plainly, honestly, and as a true friend of man.

[93] It follows that I must speak about the one remaining
category of morality, the one where we find the sense of shame
and the qualities that we may say give shape to a life: restraint,
self-control, a complete conquest of anxieties, and moderation
in all things. This area deals with what Latin calls *decorum* and
what Greek calls *prepon*. It has the property of being insepara-
ble from morality. [94] What is moral is "becoming," and what
is "becoming" is moral. It is easier to understand the nature of
the difference between *decorum* and what is moral than to
explain it. Whatever is "fitting" appears only when moral correctness has preceded it. So *decorum* appears not only in the
category of moral correctness that I must talk about here but
also in the three preceding categories.[68] 1. To think and to
speak wisely and to carry out your actions prudently, and to see
the truth in every situation and to support it: these are signs of
decorum. On the opposite side, to be tricked, to be mistaken,

[68] That is, *decorum* is not only characteristic of moderation, which is the
last of the four cardinal virtues of the Stoics, and which Cicero is about to
discuss, but it is also characteristic of the virtues previously discussed: wisdom,
justice, and courage. These three virtues are very briefly discussed in the rest
of this section.

to hesitate, to go astray, are as "indecorous" as insanity or being simpleminded. 2. Also, everything just is becoming, while unjust actions, since they are degrading, are unbecoming. 3. The relationship with courage is similar. An action of manliness and great spirit seems worthy of a man and becoming; an opposite action is as unbecoming as it is degrading.

[95] That is why this quality that I call *decorum* surely pertains to every category of morality. The relation between them is such that *decorum* requires no tortuous reasoning process to grasp; on the contrary, it is as plain as day. *Decorum* is a distinct quality that can be traced in every kind of virtue. It is possible to detach it from virtue, but more in speculative theory than in fact. Just as it is impossible to separate loveliness and physical beauty from health so this *decorum* that I am discussing is thoroughly blended with virtue, and yet it is possible to separate them in the mind and in thought.

[96] It can, moreover, be divided into two groups: we understand a certain general *decorum,* which is connected with all types of moral correctness, and another subsidiary *decorum,* which relates to separate classifications of moral correctness. General *decorum* is usually defined in this way: *decorum* is a quality consistent with the superiority of man insofar as his nature surpasses that of other living things. The subsidiary part to the whole is defined like this: *decorum* is the achievement of a harmony with nature that reveals a man's moderation and self-control, together with that certain outlook that characterizes a free man.[69]

[97] We can see that this is the correct understanding of *decorum* from the *decorum* that dramatists strive to capture. Poetic *decorum,* of course, is usually the subject of more elaborate discussions in other places.[70] But we say that dramatists preserve *decorum* when the actions and the speeches of each

---

[69] This separation of *decorum* into general and special types is referred to again in section 98 below.

[70] A general reference to handbooks of rhetoric and poetry.

character are mutually suitable. Thus if either Aeacus or Minos[71] should say, "They can hate as long as they are in fear," or "The father is his own son's tomb," that would not seem fitting because we have learned that they were just men. When Atreus speaks these lines, however, the applause rises up because the speeches are consistent with his character. So playwrights will judge from the mask what is fitting for each man.[72] However, nature itself has made us wear a mask that indicates our great superiority, our primacy, in fact, over the rest of living creatures. [98] Consequently, dramatists will provide suitable and fitting speeches for a vast variety of characters, even for immoral ones. Nature has assigned us, however, the roles of faithfulness, temperance, self-control, and consideration; and since nature also teaches us not to be indifferent about our behavior toward other men, it gradually becomes clear how widely diffused the general *decorum* is that applies to every kind of moral correctness, and the other one that each separate type of virtue reveals.

Physical beauty delights the eyes by the fine proportioning of the limbs and gives pleasure specifically because all parts harmonize with each other to produce a certain attractiveness. Similarly, the *decorum* that radiates from a man's life wins the approval of the people among whom he lives by the regularity and consistency and restraint of everything he says and does. [99] For that reason one should show as deep a respect for men in general as for the few leaders. To be quite indifferent about people's opinion of you is an act of not merely an arrogant but

[71] As sons of Zeus who were extraordinarily just during their life, these two men were made judges of the dead in the underworld. It would be inconceivable that they would speak the violent phrases that follow, which are quoted from a Roman play about Atreus.

[72] The illustration drawn from the stage-mask is appropriate because once the actor had put on the mask, his character was fixed within certain limits by the expression and coloring of the mask. The playwright had to keep in mind what the mask would be for each character and compose appropriate speeches (he "judges from the mask"); so men must act and speak in conformity with the character that nature has bestowed on them.

of a completely depraved man. Moreover, in maintaining distinctions among men there is a degree of difference between justice and decent respect. The duty of justice is not to do violence to men. The duty of decent respect is not to insult them; this latter especially reveals the essence of *decorum*. Having expounded these things, I think it is clear what *decorum* is, or what we call "fitting."

[100] The duty that derives from *decorum* first puts us on the road that leads to conformity with nature and respect for it. If we use nature as a guide we shall never stray, and we shall follow what is naturally clear-cut and farsighted, what is adapted to the society of mankind, and what is forceful and strong. The greatest power of *decorum* is in the classification now under discussion; men should praise movements of the body that are in harmony with nature, but they should praise much more highly motions of the soul that conform to nature in the same way.

[101] Now the essence and nature of souls is two-fold. One aspect lies in passion (in Greek *hormē*): it pulls a man first one way, then another. The other aspect lies in reason; it teaches and makes clear what must be done or what must be avoided. [Hence reason ought to rule, passion should obey. Every action, moreover, ought to be free of rashness and carelessness; no one should do anything for which he cannot give a plausible explanation. This is practically a definition of morality.] [102] The passions must be made to obey reason and neither outrun nor lag behind it because of laziness or cowardice; they should be calm and free of every mental anxiety; this state of the soul will permit a display of complete stability and self-control. When desires stray any distance and either lust or cowardice stimulates them to the point of frenzy, so to speak, and reason does not hold a tight enough rein over them, they quite clearly pass beyond the boundary of moderation. They abandon obedience and kick it over; they do not obey reason to which they are subordinate by a law of nature. They throw both mind and

body into disarray.[73] All you need do is look at the faces of those in a rage, or of those who are excited by some lust or fear, or who are beside themselves with extreme pleasure. All of these people undergo a change in expression, in voice, in movement, and in appearance.

[103] Let us return to the outline of duty[74] and note that these facts force us to draw the conclusion that we must restrain all our passions and force them to subside. Attention and patience must stand vigilant, so that not one of our activities is impulsive or random, none of our actions are unreflective or careless. Nature shaped us not to give the impression that we were made for jokes and games, but rather for seriousness and all kinds of grave and important matters. Of course, it is permissible to enjoy relaxation and amusements, but we should enjoy them like sleep and other refreshing pastimes, after we have devoted enough energy to important and serious affairs. The particular type of amusement must be neither disordered nor immodest but refined and sophisticated. We do not give children unlimited permission to play but extend permission only so far as it does not interfere with the activities imposed by right behavior. Just so even during relaxation some sign of upright character should remain visible.

[104] In general, there are two classes of play: one is slavish, annoying, vicious, and obscene; the other is elegant, witty, resourceful, and urbane. The Roman Plautus and the Old Comedy of the Athenians abound in this latter type, of course, but so do the writings of the Socratic philosophers.[75] The Socratic dia-

---

[73] A slightly different image of training animals was quoted from Panaetius in section 90 above. This passage seems to be based on the image of horses yoked to a chariot, an image of the soul made famous by Plato's *Phaedrus*.

[74] Begun in section 100 but interrupted by the digression on the passions vs. reason in section 101 and 102.

[75] It is perhaps surprising that Cicero ranks Plato along with Plautus and Aristophanes. He is clearly comparing the aura of sophistication and the polished expression of these authors, rather than the content of their works.

logues contain numerous acute remarks by various speakers, the kind that Cato the Elder collected and called *apophtheg-mata*. So the distinction between respectable humor and low-life comedy is easy. The one is worthy of the most distinguished man if the occasion is appropriate, as when men are relaxing. The other is not worthy of any free man if it employs disgusting material or an obscene vocabulary. Even during relaxation we should retain a certain moderation. We must avoid indulging ourselves to excess and slipping into vile behavior when pleasure gets the better of us. [105] Both the Campus Martius and the pursuit of hunting furnish acceptable examples of recreation.

It is pertinent in any inquiry into duty to maintain constant awareness of how far mankind surpasses the cattle and other beasts. Animals have no feelings except for gratification, and their impulses drive them toward that. What nourishes the human mind is learning and thinking; it is always investigating something or acting on something and is strongly influenced by its enjoyment of sights and sounds. Even if someone is more in-clined than usual to physical pleasures, as long as he is not a member of the race of beasts (there are some men who are men in name but not in fact)—even if, as I say, someone is rather bent in that direction, although sensuality may snare him, he conceals and glosses over his hunger after pleasure for de-cency's sake. [106] This impulse to conceal lust reveals clearly that physical pleasure is not sufficiently worthy of man's pre-eminence. It should be held in contempt and rejected. Yet if any person exists who has some interest in pleasure, he should maintain a strict limit to its enjoyment. It follows that food and care of the body should pertain to health and strength, not to pleasure. Furthermore, if we agree to contemplate the pre-eminence and dignity of man's nature, we shall begin to realize how shameful it is to amass wealth, to live in luxury and in sensuality, and how correct it is to live frugally, chastely, mod-estly, soberly.

[107] You must also understand that nature has clothed us,

as it were, with two characters. One of them is universal, deriving from the fact that we all participate in the intelligence
and superiority by which we surpass other animals. This intelligence is the origin of all morality and *decorum,* and it supplies
the means to discover duty in a rational way. The other is the
character bestowed separately on each individual. We may
think of the large variations in physiques. We know that some
men are outstanding in speed and run well, others are strong
and can wrestle; appearance shows the same variations: some
men possess impressiveness, others possess attractiveness.
There are similar variations in human character, perhaps even
more wide-ranging. [108] Lucius Crassus' endowments were
brilliant, as were those of Lucius Philippus; Gaius Caesar, the
son of Lucius, possessed an even greater and more cultivated
brilliance. Marcus Scaurus and the young Marcus Drusus, who
lived in the same period, were men of great seriousness; Gaius
Laelius was a man of great gaiety, while his friend Scipio was
a man of more ambition and of a more austere way of life.[76] Of
the famous Greeks we learn that Socrates was pleasant and witty
and companionable in conversation, and that in all his talk he
was the kind of tantalizing speaker that the Greeks called
"ironic."[77] On the other hand we learn that Pythagoras and Pericles attained the highest power without any humor whatsoever. We learn that among the Punic leaders Hannibal was
clever. Among Roman leaders so was Quintus Maximus, hiding
easily, keeping silence, tricking, laying ambushes, anticipating
the plans of the enemy. In cleverness the Greeks rank Themistocles and Jason of Pherae before others. They place foremost the ingenious, shrewd accomplishment of Solon: he pre-

[76] These seven Romans who illustrate the possible variety of character are
all taken from Republican history.

[77] Socrates' "irony" is revealed in Plato's dialogues; to draw his companions
into discussion Socrates pretended to know less than they and to be less
capable of pronouncing expertly on some topic. Cf. section 104 above.

tended to be mad so that his life might be safe and so that he would be of considerably more use to the state.[78]

[109] There are others far different from these, men of open character, without guile, who believe that no action whatsoever should be secret or concealed. They are worshippers of truth, enemies of deceit. At the same time there are others who would endure anything or subject themselves to anyone, so long as they attain what they wish. We saw examples in Sulla and Marcus Crassus. Among this group we learn that the most wily and persistent was the Spartan Lysander. But Callicratidas, the very next fleet commander after Lysander, was the opposite. Likewise we learn that in his manner of speaking a man can make himself seem to be quite ordinary, even though he is very influential. This we have seen in Catulus, both father and son,[79] as well as in Quintus Macius and in Mancia. I have heard from older people that such deception was also characteristic of Publius Scipio Nasica;[80] yet on the contrary his father, the one who avenged the desperate attempts of Tiberius Gracchus, was not a facile speaker, and for that very reason was great and famous. [Xenocrates, that most austere of philosophers, did not converse easily.] Other differences in character and habits among men are countless but hardly the kind one would blame.

[110] However, on the whole, each man should retain his particular qualities, though not the harmful ones; that will make it easier for him to preserve the *decorum* that we are seeking.

---

[78] During the struggle between Athens and Megara over control of the island of Salamis in the late 7th Century B.C., the Athenians became convinced that they would not succeed and passed a law to prohibit further encouragement of the campaign. Solon strongly believed in the importance of Salamis for Athens, pretended to be deranged (and therefore immune to legal punishment) and recited a poem urging the Athenians to seize the island, which eventually came under their domination.

[79] The abilities of the Catuli are further discussed in section 133 below.

[80] This Scipio died during his consulship in 111 B.C., five years before Cicero's birth.

We have the obligation to act in such a way that we do not put ourselves in opposition to nature in general, and yet we must follow our particular nature without violating the general one. Even if other pursuits are more important and attractive, we should nevertheless measure our own ambitions against the yardstick of our own nature. It is not profitable to fight against nature or to pursue something that you cannot attain. From this the essence of *decorum* emerges more clearly, insofar as nothing is fitting "Minerva unwilling,"[81] that is to say, with nature opposed and fighting back.

[111] Certainly whatever else *decorum* is, it is essentially balance in one's entire way of life as well as in individual actions. A man cannot preserve this balance if he imitates other people's nature and neglects his own. Just as we should use the language we know to avoid the kind of laughter that people quite justifiably direct against men who sprinkle their conversations with Greek phrases, so we must not allow any dissonance between our actions or in our life as a whole. [112] This difference between characters is so powerful that sometimes one man recognizes an obligation to commit suicide, while another man in the same circumstances does not. Was Marcus Cato in one situation, while the others who surrendered to Caesar in Africa were in a different one? Yet perhaps the others would have incurred blame if they had killed themselves; precisely because their life had been less severe than Cato's, their characters were more easygoing, whereas nature had endowed him with a seriousness passing belief. He strengthened it consciously with unremitting inflexibility; he remained completely faithful to a planned and commenced enterprise; he had to die rather than look upon the face of a tyrant.[82]

---

[81] Minerva, the Roman goddess of wisdom, in this proverb stands for a man's native endowment of intelligence.

[82] Cato's suicide in 46 B.C. was a recent and significant event. Cicero's lost pamphlet *Cato* (see C. P. Jones, "Cicero's *Cato*," *Rheinisches Museum*, vol. 113 (1970), pp. 188–196) assessed the meaning of Cato's career in favorable

[113] How much Ulysses endured in the course of his long wandering! He even enslaved himself to women, if Circe and Calypso can be called women! And he tried to be pleasant to everyone everytime he spoke. In fact, at home he even tolerated insults from slaves and serving-girls in order to arrive eventually at what he wanted.[83] Ajax, however, would have preferred to die a thousand times rather than endure such insults; such was the haughty spirit that legend attributes to him.[84] By contemplating these examples, each man will see his duty to weigh well the individuality he possesses and to regulate it. He will not wish to discover how far other men's characteristics might suit him. What suits a particular man best, you see, is that particular man's individuality. [114] Therefore let each man come to know his own ability. Let him judge himself strictly on his own good points and bad points. If that is done, then it will not seem that actors are more sensible than the rest of mankind. They do not select the best plays but the plays most suited to themselves. Actors who rely on their voice play *Epigoni* or *Medus;* those who excel in mime play *Melanippe* or *Clytemnestra.* I can remember Rupilius, and he always played *Antiope.* Aesopus seldom played *Ajax.*[85] Will an actor respect his native abilities on the stage and the wise man not do so in life? If we have a choice, we shall work faithfully at those things that are most suitable to

---

terms, and it was answered by Caesar's *Anticato* (also lost), which was hostile to the memory of Cato. Cato came to serve as a symbolic figure of the lost Republican cause, and the beginnings of that inspiration may be seen here.

[83] The last part of Homer's *Odyssey* narrates the victory of Odysseus (=Ulysses) over the hostile suitors of his wife Penelope, a victory which he achieved by appearing in the disguise of a beggar in his own household and patiently biding his time until the right moment for revenge.

[84] The most famous illustration of Ajax' haughty spirit occurs in the *Odyssey* XI. 541–567, where the ghost of Ajax refuses to answer a conciliatory speech of Odysseus.

[85] Antiope, we can guess, would have been a role that called for the male actor to play a female part of great pathos and suffering. Ajax was a part that would have called for a display of truculence and insanity.

us. If from time to time necessity pushes us into affairs that are alien to our character, complete care, forethought, and application must be brought to bear. In such circumstances we should act with as much fitness as possible, since complete *decorum* cannot be expected. One must strive not so much to accomplish good results that may not be granted to us as to avoid bad faults.

[115] A third role exists in addition to the two I explained above,[86] the role that chance or opportunity thrusts upon the individual. A fourth exists also, the one that we freely adopt for ourselves by a personal decision. When it comes to kingdoms and commands, nobility and high offices, wealth and property, chance governs all and accidents rule the world. The same is true of their opposites. The role we ourselves might wish to play, however, begins with our own will. Accordingly some men apply themselves to philosophy, others to civil law, others to oratory. As for the virtues, different people prefer to excel in different ones. [116] Those whose parents or ancestors were pre-eminent in a particular field are mostly eager to reach for the same kind of praise. Examples are Quintus Mucius, the son of Publius, in civil law, and Africanus, the son of Paullus, in military affairs. Certain sons, however, add their own glory to what they received from their fathers. For example, the Africanus I just mentioned added eloquence to military glory. Timotheus, the son of Conon, did the same thing; although he was not inferior to his father in military renown he added to it praise for his learning and the fame of his intelligence.[87] Another case involves the numerous men who find it quite impossible to imitate their parents: they pursue their individual goal. It is particularly men born of humble ancestors who mark out ambitious lives for themselves and most exert themselves here.

---

[86] The first two roles (see section 107 above) were the duty to preserve the general superiority of humans in the scale of nature and the duty to preserve one's individual character.

[87] Timotheus studied with Isocrates, the orator.

[117] When we inquire into what is "fitting," we ought to embrace all these things in our spirit and thought. But primarily we must decide who we want to be, what kind of man we want to be, and what sort of life we want to lead. This decision is the most difficult of all. For it is at the beginning of young manhood, when the ability to plan is weakest, that each man chooses the kind of life he will lead, and he chooses the kind that he finds most alluring. As a result he is caught up in a certain pattern and course of living even before he can judge what is best.

[118] Prodicus says (as we read in Xenophon)[88] that when Hercules became a young man, he went out into the wilds, sat there, and debated long and hard with himself. Young manhood is the time that nature appoints for each person to select the path he is going to follow in life. Now Hercules saw two paths, one of pleasure, the other of virtue, and debated which would be better to traverse. It was perhaps possible that such a choice could fall to the lot of Hercules, to him sprung from the seed of Jove, but the same kind of choice is not ours. We imitate those who seem best to each of us, and we are urged on toward their pursuits and goals. We generally absorb the teachings of our parents also and incline toward their habits and characteristics. Others are influenced by the judgment of the mob and set their highest hopes on what seems most attractive to the majority; and many men have followed a straight path in life without discipline from their parents, either through luck of some sort or because of simple goodness of nature.

[119] There is one extremely rare class of men, those who have had the opportunity to consider what course of life they most wish to follow, either because of an unusual degree of intelligence, or because of a splendid education in philosophy, or because they possess both these advantages. In this deliberation every thought must bear a relationship to each man's particular natural character. Since in every separate action we look

---

[88] Xenophon, *Memorabilia* II.121.

for what is fitting in each man's innate disposition, as we stated above,[89] so in arranging his whole life a man must exercise much greater caution. The result we seek is stability within ourselves for the whole duration of life and no failure in any duty whatsoever.

[120] Since in this choice nature is the primary influence on us and fortune the second, it is certainly necessary to take both into consideration when the pattern of life is chosen. Nature must receive the greater consideration, because it is far more stable and consistent. Fortune is so much weaker than nature that she seems to have to fight against nature, and she struggles like a mere mortal matched against a god. The man, therefore, who has adapted his whole plan of living to his own natural type (as long as the type is not evil) should cling to his decision, for to do so is eminently fitting. He will have to make an exception, however, if he has realized that he made a mistake when choosing his pattern of life. If such a mistake should happen, for it can happen, there has to be a change in habits and goals. If circumstances encourage this change, we can make it more easily and comfortably; if not, it will have to be made gradually and step by step. For example, wise men think it is more fitting that friendships that cease to be pleasing and become less valued should be dissolved gradually rather than broken off suddenly. [121] When you have changed your way of life, you must use every resource to make people believe that you did it for a very good reason.

Since I asserted a little while ago[90] that men should imitate their ancestors, I must point out two exceptions: first, there is an obligation not to imitate faults; second, imitation is sometimes impossible when a man's character prevents him from being able to imitate certain traits. For example, the son of the older Africanus who adopted our Africanus, the son of Paullus,

---

[89] In section 110 above.
[90] In section 116 above.

because of weak health was not able to resemble his father to the same extent as the younger Africanus resembled his father. If a man does not have the ability to defend clients in court, to command the electorate's attention with his speeches, or to conduct military campaigns, he should nevertheless practice the qualities that are within his power: justice, faithfulness, generosity, modesty, restraint. The result will be that the absence of what he lacks will attract less notice. The best heritage that descends from fathers to sons is the fame for honesty and great deeds. Such fame surpasses any legacy. We must judge it a crime and a shame to disgrace it.

[122] The same duties are not pertinent to different times of life, because some belong to young men, others to older men, and something must be said about this distinction, too. It is a young man's duty to respect his elders and to select the best and most virtuous among them, on whose advice and authority he may place reliance. The practical wisdom of older men should stabilize and guide the inexperience of younger men. It is very important to warn young men away from carnal pleasures and to see that they devote themselves to hard work and endurance, both mental and physical. The object is to insure that their attention to both military and civic duties will be unflagging. Even when young men wish to relax their spirits and devote themselves to enjoyment, they should beware of excess and remember their sense of shame. To learn moderation will be easier for them if their elders will consent to take an interest in their relaxations.

[123] As for older men, they must obviously diminish their bodily exertions, but the employments of their minds must actually be increased. In fact, they must exert themselves to help their friends as much as possible with advice and wisdom, to help also young people, and especially the state. Older men must direct their greatest vigilance to one failing: surrendering themselves to laziness and neglect; self-indulgence, of course, is shameful at any age but is most disgusting in old age. If un-

restrained indulgence in carnal pleasures is also added, the disgrace is doubled, because old age itself commits a disgrace while it contributes to more open licentiousness in young men.

[124] It is not at all out of place to speak about the duties of magistrates, private citizens [citizens], and foreigners. It is the particular responsibility of the magistrate to realize that he represents the character of the state and that he ought to maintain its dignity and distinction, to preserve its laws, to define rights, to remember the things entrusted to his care. A private citizen ought to live under equal and similar laws with other citizens, neither submissive and cringing nor with a domineering spirit. Next he ought to desire conditions in the state that are undisturbed and honorable. It is a man like that whom we customarily consider and designate a good citizen. [125] Foreign residents and settlers have the duty not to engage in anything except their private business, not to pry into another's affairs, and to meddle as little as possible in a state that is not their own. That is approximately how the duties will appear when one inquires what is fitting and what is appropriate to individuals, to situations, and to ages. There is nothing so fitting, however, as to remain consistent in managing affairs or in making plans.

[126] The *decorum* we seek is evident in every deed, every speech, and ultimately in the movement and posture of the body. Our physical impression consists of three things: attractiveness, tact, and a style of dress suitable to the business at hand. These are things difficult to describe, but it is enough if people understand them. Our anxiety to obtain the approval of those with whom or among whom we live is linked with these three things, so a few points should be made about them, too. In the first place, nature itself seems to have had a master plan for our physique; it placed out in the open our face and the other parts of our figure that can be displayed with propriety. It covered and concealed those parts of the body, however, that were intended only for necessity and that would convey an in-

different appearance or even ugliness. [127] The feeling of shame in men has imitated this very careful natural arrangement. All men of sound mind hide from other eyes what nature has hidden. They deal with necessity as unobtrusively as possible. They do not call by their real names certain parts of the body or the necessary functions of those particular parts. It is indecent to discuss those things that are not shameful to do as long as they are done in private. The open performance of those things is immodest, as is the vulgarity of talking about them. A custom among actors that is dignified by ancient practice forces them to be so modest that no performer would step onto the stage without something covering his waist. Actors are afraid that if certain parts of their person were by some accident exposed, they would present an obscene spectacle. In fact, it is our custom that sons past puberty do not bathe with their fathers, nor sons-in-law with their fathers-in-law. Therefore we must cling to this feeling of shame, especially when nature itself is our instructor and guide.

[128] Of course, no one should pay attention to the Cynics, or to those few Stoics who were nearly Cynics.[91] They scold and mock because we consider damaging the words for acts that in fact may not be shameful, and yet we call undoubtedly criminal things by their proper names. To rob, to deceive, to commit adultery are criminal acts, but to speak of them is not obscenity. To undertake the task of begetting children is a moral action, but its name is an obscenity. They advance a host of similar arguments against modesty. Let us follow nature and take flight away from anything that the eyes and the ears will not approve. Our posture, our walk, our sitting or our reclining at meals, the expression, the eyes, the movement of the hands: let them all maintain the *decorum* we seek.

[129] In these areas you must especially avoid the two ex-

[91] Some Stoics advocated that "every object should be called by its proper name." Cicero summarizes their arguments in the following sentences, without approving them.

tremes: manners should not be womanly and delicate, nor should they be rough and coarse. These extremes are suitable for actors and public speakers, but that fact does not therefore make them permissible for us.

[130] Now there are two categories of beauty, one the category of attractiveness, the other of nobility. We should think of attractiveness as being feminine, nobility masculine. Therefore any allurement unworthy of a man should be eliminated from his appearance, and we should guard against comparable faults in our gestures and movements. The movements seen at gymnasiums are frequently rather repugnant, and most of the gestures of actors are filled with affectations. In both gesture and movement praise goes to the direct and simple. A healthy complexion helps maintain an impressive appearance, while physical exercise helps maintain the complexion. Besides this, one must display grooming that is neither offensive nor excessively nice, but simply the kind that avoids crude and vulgar carelessness. You should adopt the same moderation in your clothing: here, as in most things, a middle course is the best. [131] We have to beware also of practicing the languid, slow movements in walking that make us look like the men who carry litters in processions. When we hurry we should avoid indulging in excessively rapid movements. These cause heavy breathing, they distort the face, they twist the expression. All these phenomena indicate that self-control is absent.

We must be careful that the movements of our soul do not diverge from nature, and the care must be all the greater as the soul is greater. We shall achieve this if we are careful not to reach states of extreme excitement or alarm and if we keep our minds intent on the preservation of *decorum*. [132] The movements of our souls are of two kinds: some involve thought, others involve passion. Thought is mostly expended in seeking out the truth, passion urges men to action. Therefore we must take care to expend thought on the best objects and to make clear that our passions are obedient to our intellect.

The effective range of speech is great. It is twofold, being applied to oratory and to conversation. Men use oratory in arguments before judges, in public assemblies, and in the Senate. They use conversation in small gatherings, in discussions, in interchanges among friends, and it even has a place during festivities. Rhetoricians offer instruction in oratory but none in conversation, although I rather think it could also exist.[92] The interests of those who want to learn produce teachers; no one is interested in studying conversation, while great throngs surround the teachers of rhetoric. Yet their rules for words and arguments will apply unchanged to conversation.

[133] Since our voice carries our speech, we should cultivate two characteristics in it: that it be clear and that it be pleasant. Both these qualities should take their origin in nature, of course, but exercise will increase clarity, while the imitation of those who speak smoothly and with careful enunciation will improve its pleasantness. The Catuli did nothing to make you think that they possessed a refined taste in literature, although they were men of high education. Others, of course, were also educated, but people thought that the Catuli spoke Latin perfectly. The sound was sweet, the syllables were neither muffled nor forced, so their speech was neither indistinct nor offensive, their enunciation was not strained, it was neither soft nor loud. The richer speech of Lucius Crassus was no less polished, but the general high opinion of the speech of the Catuli never diminished. Caesar, the uncle of Catulus, surpassed everyone in wit and sophistication. Even when speaking in the courts of law Caesar could demolish the formal arguments of other lawyers merely by talking in a conversational style. We must work at all these skills if we are to discover what is fitting in all things.

[134] As for conversation, in which the Socratics especially

---

[92] That formal study of conversation should be available may seem rather extraordinary, but Cicero has in mind philosophical conversations such as the ones composed by Plato and Xenophon. See section 134 below, where Cicero offers some rules of his own about conversation.

excel, it should be gentle and only mildly aggressive; there should be something attractive in it. Of course, a man should certainly not exclude others from a conversation as if he had taken private possession of it. He must remember that turn-and-turn-about is not a bad policy, both in general conversations and in all other activities. To begin with, he should notice what the topics of the conversation are; if they are serious, let him display seriousness; if they are lighthearted, let him display charm. He should take special care that his way of talking does not indicate some defect in his politeness. This fault is especially likely to appear when someone deliberately says something about those not present to malign them, something said jokingly or seriously, either malice or slander. [135] Most everyday conversations concern household affairs, the government, or the pursuit and knowledge of the professions. You must make an effort to recall the conversation to these topics, even if it has begun to wander to other matters. Remember who is present, for we are not all delighted with identical subjects at all times or in the same way. You also have to notice to what extent the conversation is holding people's attention: there was a reason for beginning it and so there should also be a natural way of ending it.

[136] Throughout a man's life the most correct advice is to avoid agitations, by which I mean excessive commotions in the soul that do not obey intelligence. The same advice applies to our conversation. It should be free of vacillations of that kind so that we avoid the appearance of anger or strong desire, of indifference or cowardice, or of any such fault. We should take the greatest care to seem to respect and admire those with whom we join in a conversation. Not infrequently unavoidable quarrels arise during which we perhaps have to use a more argumentative tone and more penetrating and severe words, and we may even have to act as if we were speaking in anger. Just as cauterization and amputation are not frequently required in medicine, we will use this type of scolding rarely and unwill-

ingly, and only when it is necessary because no alternative cure is available.

All things considered, you should avoid anger; nothing good or courteous happens when men are angry. [137] Yet in many cases it is permissible to administer a mild scolding as long as you add seriousness to it. The object is to apply severity but to avoid violence, and you must make clear that the trace of bitterness that your criticism contains is there to benefit the person you are criticizing. It is correct, even in those arguments that we conduct with our worst enemies, even if we have to listen to things unworthy of us, to retain our self-possession in spite of that and to avoid anger. Whenever passionate feelings disturb our activities, we are, of course, not acting with self-control and those around us cannot approve what we do. It is also in bad taste to boast about yourself, especially about falsehoods, and to amuse bystanders as you imitate the "Braggart Soldier."[93]

[138] Since we are following everything through—or at least want to do so—I also must speak about the kind of house I consider appropriate for a man who has held high rank, a leading citizen. Its object is usefulness. The plan of the building should be adapted to this, but at the same time some care should be spent on making it comfortable and impressive in appearance. I know that people thought Gnaeus Octavius, who was first in his family to become consul, reaped much honor because he built a distinguished and stately house on the Palatine. When the common people saw it, they thought that it had helped its owner to the consulate, since he was the first of his family to hold a curule office. Scaurus demolished it to build an addition to his mansion. Thus Octavius was the first man in his family to bring the consulate into the house, while Scaurus, who was the son of an important and widely known father, enlarged his house but brought back to it not only defeat but

---

[93] The vain, boastful soldier was a stock character in Graeco-Roman comedy, the prime example being Pyrgopolynices in the *Miles Gloriosus* (The "Braggart Soldier") of Plautus.

shame and ruin, too.[94] [139] A house may enhance a man's dignity, but it should not be the only source of dignity; the house should not glorify its owner, but he should enhance it. As in other matters, you should consider other people as well as yourself. A popular man must see to it that his house is spacious. Many guests have to be received in it, and it has to admit crowds of people of every rank. On the other hand, a large house is frequently an embarrassment to its owner if it contains only empty rooms. Such a thing is especially likely to happen if another owner sometime earlier used to keep the house crowded with guests. It is annoying when passers-by repeat:

> Oh! ancient house, alas! A different kind of
> Owner owns you now!

That can be said these days about many houses.[95] [140] You have to beware, however, especially if you are going to build your own house, that you do not exceed a certain limit of expense and ostentation. In this kind of thing there is a lot of evil merely in the example set. Most people, you see, feverishly copy what the leaders of society do, especially in this direction. Take the case of Lucius Lucullus, that greatest of men. How many people have copied the sumptuousness of his country houses! But who imitated his virtues? There is certainly a need to apply a limit to villas at least and to set the limit within a moderate scale. You should apply the same moderation to every habit and endeavor of your life. But enough of these things.

[141] When we undertake any action, we must obey three rules: first, desire should obey reason; nothing is more apt to help moral duties. Second, we should notice the scope of the undertaking we intend to complete, so that the attention and effort involved are neither larger nor smaller than reason demands. The third rule is that we should be careful to keep within

---

[94] When he ran for consul in 54 B.C., Scaurus was accused of bribery and extortion; two years later he was sent into banishment.

[95] The quotation is from an unknown poet. The contemporary reference seems to be to the houses once belonging to followers of the defeated Pompey that fell into the hands of Caesar's supporters.

limits those things that affect our status and self-esteem as free men. The best limitation is to cling to precisely that *decorum* that I explained earlier and to go no farther. However, of these three rules the most important is that the desires obey reason.

[142] Next I must discuss orderliness in actions and appropriate circumstances for actions. These topics are discussed by the Greeks under the branch of knowledge they call *eutaxia*, a word that means "the preservation of good order." The Latin word for this branch of knowledge should not be *modestia* ("self-control") because that word is a derivation from *modus* ("moderation"). I am nevertheless going to use *modestia* as the equivalent of *eutaxia*, having in mind a Stoic definition of the word. *Modestia*, say the Stoics, is the knowledge of how to arrange all words and actions in their right place. [So apparently the words "orderliness" and "arrangement" are taken to mean the same thing, because they define "orderliness" as the "location" of things in proper and suitable places.] The Stoics have another definition, in which they say that to "find the place for an action" means to "find the appropriate circumstances." Now the Greek word for "the appropriate circumstances" is *eukairia*, the Latin word being *occasio*.[96] If we understand *modestia* ("self-control") according to the Stoic definition I mentioned above, it becomes a suitable equivalent for *eutaxia*, that is, the knowledge of what circumstances are suitable for what actions.

[143] The same definition may also apply to practical knowledge, which I discussed in the beginning.[97] In this section, however, I am discussing temperance and moderation and comparable virtues. Accordingly, the essential points about prac-

[96] Cicero, in other words, says that he cannot translate *eutaxia* by *occasio*, which might appear to be the appropriate word. To translate *eutaxia* he will have to use *modestia* but attach an unusual definition to it.

[97] Cicero discussed the duties related to knowledge in sections 18 and following. Here he suggests that "practical knowledge" might be defined as "the knowledge of what should and should not be done in particular circumstances." The earlier discussion stressed the moral obligation to pursue knowledge, whereas the present discussion will investigate the discipline that underlies social intercourse.

tical wisdom were discussed previously in their own place, and now is the time to discuss the properties of these other virtues, which I have mentioned frequently and which relate to considerateness and the approval of the people with whom we live.

[144] One must therefore strive to preserve the kind of order in one's activities that causes all the elements of life to be balanced and under control, like the elements in a well-made speech. During a serious piece of business it is shameful and a great fault to let anyone introduce remarks that are appropriate to a party or some sophisticated conversation. Pericles once reacted commendably when he and the poet Sophocles were colleagues in the generalship.[98] They had met to discuss the military command they shared, and by chance a handsome boy walked past. Sophocles said, "What a pretty boy, Pericles!" "But no, Sophocles! A general should remove lust from his eyes the same way his hands are free from greed!" If Sophocles had made this same remark during an athletic competition, no one could have justly criticized him. So great is the importance of place and occasion. For example, if someone is about to conduct a trial and on a journey or during a walk should begin to meditate silently on the arguments he will present, or if he should think about something else very deeply, no one can criticize him. But if he should lapse into a thoughtful silence during a banquet, he would appear unsocial in his ignorance of appropriate time. [145] Suppose someone should break into song in the Forum,[99] or imagine some other startling example of bad behavior. Such actions differ so greatly from accepted

[98] Sophocles and Pericles were both members of the board of ten generals at Athens in 440 B.C.

[99] Romans of the upper classes thought that singing and dancing in public by a Roman were extremely improper; only foreign slaves (Greek especially) who were professional entertainers would engage in such activities. The Forum, the center of civic and religious activity, would be an unthinkable location for an unthinkable act. See the case discussed in III.93.

conduct that they stand out clearly and do not require any special advice or warning. However, it demands more alertness to
avoid what seem to be small defects, not the sort most people
can recognize. In lyre playing or in tibia playing,[100] for example,
the instruments may be only slightly out of tune, but musical
experts can usually notice the fact. In the same way one must
conduct one's life so that there is no accidental discord, or even
more importantly, so that the harmony of one's activities is
greater and more pleasing than that of music.

[146] Just as in lyre playing the ears of musicians perceive
even the smallest details, so we should acquire the habit of
making important deductions from trivial details if we want to
become sharp and untiring critics. From the stare, from the
raising or lowering of the eyebrows, from sadness, from joviality,
from a laugh, from a spoken phrase, from a significant silence,
from a raised voice, from its lowering, from other similar indi-
cations we shall begin to judge quickly which of these actions is
in tune, which of them clashes with moral duty and nature. In
this respect it is appropriate to observe other men and to judge
the quality and character of their actions so we ourselves can
avoid actions that are not to be suitable in other men. I am
rather afraid, you see, that we notice faults of all kinds in other
people more readily than in ourselves. So in teaching: when the
teachers imitate the faults of students in order to correct them,
the students find it very easy to improve themselves.

[147] When trying to reach a decision about matters that
create doubt, it is not really inappropriate to consult wise men
or merely men of wide experience and to ask their opinion
about each area of moral duty. The majority usually drifts along
pretty much to wherever nature herself provides the lead. In
consulting these men you must examine not only what each one
says but also what each one thinks and even the reasons why
each one has his particular opinions. Consider painters and

---

[100] For *tibia* see *Glossary*.

sculptors and even poets too: each artist wants the public to inspect his individual work so he can correct whatever the majority criticizes. They painstakingly question themselves and others, trying to learn what faults there might be in their work. In the same way there are many, many things we should do and should not do, should change and should correct, based on the judgment of other people.

[148] Of course, no instructions have to be given about actions performed according to traditions and customs of a state. The traditions and customs themselves are instructive. Socrates and Aristippus acquired their freedom of action in exchange for great, almost superhuman services. No one should fall into the mistake of assuming that he has the same permission because those men did or said something contrary to the custom and usage of their country. Of course, the philosophy of the Cynics has to be thrown out completely; for it is the enemy of considerate behavior, and nothing correct or honest can exist without that. [149] We also ought to respect and cultivate men whose lives are conspicuous for great and good accomplishments, men who are true patriots, and men of true service, in the past or present. We should treat them like men appointed to some public office or military command. Also we ought to pay high respect to old age, to defer to men who hold a magistracy, and to make a distinction between a citizen and a foreigner and, in the particular case of the foreigner, whether he came in private or in public capacity. I do not want to enumerate every item, so in short, we ought to develop, preserve, and defend the common interrelations and the social frame of all mankind.

[150] Now the following is the gist of my understanding about professions and trades, those that free men can think of entering and those that are contemptible. First, no one can approve professions that arouse people's dislike, for example, collectors of harbor duties or usurers. Similarly, the work of all hired men who sell their labor and not their talents is servile and

contemptible. The reason is that in their case wages actually constitute a payment for slavery.[101] Another disreputable class includes those who buy whole lots from wholesalers to retail immediately. They would not make a profit unless they indulged in misrepresentation, and nothing is more criminal than fraud. All mechanics work in contemptible professions because no one born of free parents would have anything to do with a workshop. The employments least worthy of approval are those that pander to pleasure: "Fishmongers, butchers, cooks, sausage-makers, fishermen," as Terence says.[102] Add to this list, if you like, perfume makers, stage dancers, and the whole musical stage. [151] However, those professions that require greater knowledge or that result in more than ordinary usefulness, for example, medicine, architecture, teaching in respectable subjects: these are reputable callings for those whose rank they suit. Commerce should be considered vulgar if it is a rather small affair. If it is extensive and well-financed, importing many products from all over the world and distributing them to many customers honestly, one should not criticize it severely. In fact, there seems to be every justification for praising it if a merchant who has had his fill of trade, or I should say is satisfied with his profit, retires from the quayside to his farmhouse and estates, just as he sailed so many times from the deep ocean to harbor. Of all pursuits by which men gain their livelihood none surpasses the cultivation of the earth. Farming is the most pleasant livelihood, the most fruitful, and the one most worthy of a free man. Since I have said enough about this in my *Cato the Elder*, you may refer to it for remarks that apply to this topic.

[152] I think the foregoing is an adequate description of how moral duties are developed from the various categories of virtue. However, the possibility of conflict and comparison often arises even among those acts that are virtuous: which of

[101] The resemblance of the status of slaves and that of hired hands was mentioned in another context in section 41 above.
[102] Terence, *Eunuchus* II.ii.26.

any two virtuous actions is the more virtuous? Panaetius over-looked this topic. Remember that every virtuous act develops from one of four categories, either wisdom or mutual benefit or courage or temperance. It is therefore unavoidable that these categories should often be compared with each other when a man is deciding what his duty is.

[153] Now I contend that the duties developed from the category of mutual benefit are more in keeping with nature than those derived from wisdom. The following argument proves this: Suppose a wise man should get the chance to live in the midst of unfailing abundance of all necessities and sup-pose that that man, in the greatest comfort, could meditate and contemplate in solitude everything worth knowing; still, if his loneliness were so great that he never saw another human be-ing, his existence would be intolerable.

Furthermore, wisdom is the leader of all the virtues. The Greeks call it *sophia*. (Do not confuse it with another kind of wisdom, which the Greeks call *phronesis*, that is, simply the practical knowledge that some things should be done and other things avoided.) But the wisdom that I have just called the "leader" is the knowledge of things divine and things human, which implies the concepts of mutual benefits between gods and men and social unity among them. If that is the greatest virtue, as it undoubtedly is, it necessarily follows that the moral duty that develops from the category of mutual benefit is the most important one.

Mere wisdom and contemplation [of nature] is somehow lame and imperfect if no practical action results from it. Such action is seen at its best when it helps preserve human interests; and so it deals with the social unity of the human race. There-fore it should be preferred to mere intellection. [154] All very good men demonstrate this and prove it in reality. Suppose that a man were studying and contemplating subjects that were worth knowing beyond all others, and suppose that he were suddenly made aware of some danger or emergency in his own country that he could relieve or remedy. What man would be so absorbed in examining and contemplating the heavens that he would not discontinue and abandon all his investigations under such circumstances, even if he thought he could count the stars or measure the size of the universe? Surely the same man would act in the same way in case of danger to a parent or during a friend's crisis.

[155] From these arguments it becomes clear that moral duties developed from justice must rank higher than those concerns and duties based on knowledge. Those based on justice contribute something useful to mankind, and nothing ought to be more important to a man than that. Even those men who devoted their entire energy and life to the intellect still did not hesitate to increase the stock of knowledge about things useful and beneficial to mankind. They undertook the instruction of numerous men to make them better citizens and more useful to their respective governments. Examples are Lysis the Pythagorean who taught Epaminondas of Thebes, Plato who taught Dion of Syracuse, and many others and their pupils. Whatever useful services I personally rendered to my country, if I performed any worth mentioning, I undertook them after receiving intellectual and literary training for them from the lessons of my teachers. [156] It is not only living contemporaries who instruct and teach those eager to learn, but teachers fulfill the same task after death by their literary records. Philosophers have covered every topic as far as laws, customs, or management of a government are concerned. As a result they seem to have dedicated their retirement to the business that tires us. These men above all, then, immersed in the pursuit of philosophy and wisdom, most notably applied their own knowledge and insight for the benefit of mankind. For the same reason it is better to speak eloquently, provided you speak intelligently, than to have the most clever thoughts without the ability to express them. The

reason is that speculation begins and ends with itself, while the ability to speak directs itself toward those who are linked to us by mutual benefit.

[157] Just as swarms of bees do not congregate in order to construct honeycombs, but devise honeycombs because they are by instinct swarming creatures, in the same way men apply their industry to actions and thought after they have formed communities according to an instinct much more powerful than that of bees. It is therefore clear that factual knowledge will be solitary and barren of results unless it is accompanied by the virtue that consists of protecting mankind, or, in other words, of promoting the social unity of the human race. The same condition holds true for courage. If courage does not function in a context of mutual benefit and human intercourse, it is hardly better than brutality and savagery. [Thus it turns out that man's sense of mutual benefit and community is stronger than his desire to pursue knowledge.]

[158] Some philosophers[103] argue that men exchange mutual benefits and form social groups because of the harsh necessity to maintain life. They argue that we could not obtain or create those conditions that nature requires for life unless we acted in groups. If everything that contributes to nourishment and comfort were supplied to us with the proverbial magic wand, then, they say, all the most talented men would abandon all their responsibilities and would devote themselves completely to contemplation and learning. This is not so. The wise man would flee his solitude and look for a companion for his interests; he would want to teach sometimes, sometimes to learn, to listen and to speak alternately. I conclude that any moral duty that works toward preserving the common fellowship and the society of man must be preferable to the moral duty that is developed from the category of wisdom and knowledge.

[159] Perhaps the next necessary inquiry is whether this

---

[103] The principal allusion is to Plato, *Republic* II. 369 B.

mutual helpfulness that is so harmonious with nature should also be ranked ahead of moderation and sense of tact. I do not think so. Some acts are so disgusting, some of them so violent, that a wise man would not perform any of them even to preserve the fatherland. Posidonius has enumerated quite a few such acts, but some are so depraved, so shocking that it seems shameful even to mention them. A wise man, therefore, will not undertake these on behalf of the state, nor will the state require any one to perform them on its behalf. Because no emergency can possibly arise where it would benefit the state if a wise man were to perform any of these actions, there is a direct relation between public benefit and individual self-control.

[160] So let this be the conclusion: when we choose among moral duties, the group that takes precedence is the one based on the idea of social harmony. [For a well-considered action will follow thought and wisdom. Acting thoughtfully is worth more than thinking abstractly.] But enough of these things. The essential point is clear: when evaluating moral duties, it is not difficult to see what rank each one should have. The concept of mutual helpfulness provides a ranking of duties, and that ranking makes it possible to see which duty takes precedence over another: first duties are owed to the immortal gods, second duties to the fatherland, third ones to the parents and so on down the list of the ones remaining. [161] From these arguments, as I have briefly set them forth, it is evident that usually men not only ponder whether an action is honest or criminal but also, when two courses of action are both honest, which of them is more so. This point, as I have said,[104] was one that Panaetius overlooked. Now let us proceed to other matters.

[104] In section 10 above

BOOK TWO

[1] I think Marcus, my son, that the preceding book presented an adequate explanation of how moral duties develop from virtue, or rather from each category of virtue. It follows that I should complete my exposition by examining the classes of responsibilities that contribute to the conditions of life and to the acquisition of those things that are useful to men, especially wealth and property. [I said that the subject of this inquiry would be things that are useful, things that are not useful, and the greater or lesser usefulness of the objects in the former category.] I will undertake to analyze these topics after I have briefly discussed the work I have begun and the principles that lie behind it.

[2] Although my books have aroused in numerous people the desire for reading and, more importantly, for writing, still, I fear sometimes that even the subject of philosophy is obnoxious to certain worthy men and that they are amazed that I spend so much time and energy on it.[1] Let me say that I devoted all my care and thought to the Republic as long as the men who governed it were those whom the Republic had asked to be its rulers. But when the tyranny of a single man[2] got control of everything, when there were no further opportunities to give advice or to provide leadership, and finally, when I had lost those great men who were my companions in preserving the

[1] For a previous expression of Cicero's feelings about the effects of his literary activities on the Romans, see I.1 and section 5 below. See also the important discussion of the relationship between the philosopher's life and his public life in I.70–73. Cicero here applies that discussion to his own life.
[2] Julius Caesar.

Republic, I did not surrender to moods of depression, which would have destroyed me if I had not resisted them, nor did I devote myself to trivial amusements unworthy of an educated man. [3] Yet I wish that the Republic had remained standing in its original condition and had not fallen into the power of men who want to revolutionize the government rather than to reform it! To begin with, I would now be expending more energy on public affairs than on literature, as I used to do when the Republic was flourishing. Not only that, but I would be putting down on paper not the essays that now occupy me but my public speeches, as I have often done before. But now that the Republic, to which all my care, thought, and effort were once devoted, has completely ceased to exist, my writings both legal and senatorial have become silent, as you can understand.

[4] Because my mind could not bear to be completely idle, I reached the conclusion that the most honorable way to banish my troubles would be to return to philosophy, since I had already steeped myself in it from the beginning of my maturity. As a young man I had devoted a lot of time to philosophy for the sake of my education. But after I began to assume public offices and devoted myself entirely to the Republic, there was only as much time for philosophy as remained from the crises of my friends and of the state. However, I exhausted all available time in reading; there was no leisure for writing.

[5] Therefore, even though the times could not be worse, I still believe that I have attained at least this much good: to commit to writing matters that were not sufficiently familiar to the Romans but were well worth knowing. What is more desirable than wisdom or more remarkable? What is better for men or more worthy of them? Those who pursue wisdom have earned the title "philosophers," and philosophy is nothing more or less, if you translate the word, than the "devotion to wisdom."[3] This is how some older philosophers[4] define wisdom: it

---

[3] Cicero translates the Greek roots of the word "philosophy."
[4] The definition is Stoic and probably goes back to Zeno.

is the knowledge of everything about both gods and men and what causes underlie nature. Some men denounce that as a subject of inquiry, but I am at a loss to imagine what subject they think should replace it. [6] If you want intellectual amusement and relaxation from cares, what can be compared with the studies of men who are always trying to find a relevant and effective way to live well and happily? Or if someone is developing a plan of self-control and virtue, he attains it by means of philosophy; there is no other way. To say that there is no discipline in the most significant affairs when nothing of the least importance exists without a discipline, is a statement by men who speak with little reflection and who are vague about extremely important matters. Moreover, if there is any discipline in virtue, where would you look for it if you had completely abandoned philosophical thinking? However, when I am urging people to take up philosophy I usually make these points with greater accuracy, and I have done so in another book.[5] At this juncture the only thing I have to say is why, once deprived of my functions in the Republic, I turned my interest especially to this particular endeavor.

[7] Now some people raise an objection against me, and those who raise it are learned and studious men.[6] Their objection concerns the apparent consistency of what I argue. Although I assert that absolute knowledge is impossible, I still cling to my practice of discussing numerous topics, and at this very moment I am reviewing instructions about responsibility. I wish these men were sufficiently well acquainted with my position. I am not one of those people whose minds wander illogically, the kind who never understand the nature of their assumptions. What kind of intellect would be left if the very

[5] Cicero here refers to his lost dialogue *Hortensius*, whose subject was the praise and defense of philosophy.

[6] In sections 1–6 Cicero answered the criticisms raised against him by average Romans. Now he turns to deal with the criticisms of those familiar with philosophy who charge that because Cicero is an adherent of the New Academy, he is inconsistent when he sets out to lay down fixed rules of duty.

basis of reasoning were removed? I might even ask, what kind of life would there be without a rational foundation?⁷ Just as other writers speak of things as being either certain or uncertain, I say some things are probable and others not probable. This is where we disagree.

[8] What prevents me from pursuing statements that seem probable to me or from rejecting improbable statements? By so doing I avoid the violence of flat assertion and escape the dogmatism that is the precise opposite of wisdom. I raise arguments against all points of view because, when the explanations on both sides of a question have been forced to compete, then the probability that I wish to establish can reveal itself. But I think I have explained this position exhaustively enough in my *Academics.* I want you to become familiar with my general outlook, which is similar to yours, my Cicero, in spite of the fact that you are studying a very old and distinguished philosophy under the guide of Cratippus, who so resembles the men⁸ who formulated those famous doctrines. But now let us proceed to the goals laid down.

[9] In the preceding book I established five divisions of investigation into man's responsibility.⁹ Two of them pertain to honesty and right action. Two pertain to the necessities of life, property, wealth, and power. The fifth pertains to the judgment exercised in selection if the principles I have mentioned are ever apparently in conflict with each other. The part about

⁷ Cicero asserts that although he believes with the Sceptics that absolute knowledge is impossible, he denies that this belief removes the possibility of inquiring into philosophical and ethical problems.

⁸ Aristotle and his followers (the Peripatetic School). Cicero does not refer to his and his son's personal conclusions, but to his own generally Platonizing position (Academic) over against the Peripatetic doctrines that Cratippus was presumably teaching young Cicero. See I.1 above, with note.

⁹ These were established in I.10. The inquiries into what is good and which of two competing goods is better pertain to honesty and right action. The inquiries into what is useful and which of two competing expedient actions is better, pertain to the necessities of life, etc.

honesty is now complete, and I want you to know that best of all, of course. But the topic that concerns me now is the particular quality that men call "useful." The everyday use of this term has lost the way and strayed from the correct path. Ordinary thinking has gradually decayed to the point where people distinguish between a right action and a useful action. Men have decided that something can be right that is not useful, and something can be useful that is not right. No one could have introduced anything more destructive into human life than the habit of making such a distinction.

[10] Philosophers of the highest authority distinguish in theory between justice, usefulness (or personal advantage), and right action, although these three things are essentially interrelated. Whatever is just they also consider advantageous, and they identify justice with right action; hence they conclude that right action is also advantageous. Of course the philosophers are logical, and their motive is irreproachable. But those who do not understand the philosophers very well, yet admire them as sophisticated and clever men, often reach the conclusion that evil is wisdom.[10] Those who do so should rid themselves of their mistake and should change their whole point of view. One should hope that they attain what they desire by honest planning and by deeds of justice, not by deceit and evil intentions.

[11] Now the commodities that contribute to the support

[10] The argument at this point depends on equivocal meanings of the Latin *utile*. The two meanings in question here are "profitable" in the narrow, selfish sense, and "advantageous" in a neutral sense. The two arguments may be schematized thus:

    a.)   Justice is advantageous.
           Justice is right action.
    ∴ Right actions are advantageous.
    b.)   Justice is profitable.
           Justice is right action.
    ∴ Right actions are profitable.
Cicero paraphrases the last conclusion as "to act like a just man is personally, selfishly profitable," i.e., "wisdom is evil."

of human life are partly inanimate, for example, gold, silver, other products from the earth, and other things of the same class. They are partly animate and possess their own particular instincts and physical appetites. One method of subdividing animate creatures is to note that some do not use reason and others do. Horses, oxen, other cattle, [bees] whose work produces something for man's use and welfare, do not employ reason. We assume that there are two divisions of creatures that use reason, one, the gods; the other, men. Religion and purity will ensure propitious gods. However, next to and closely following the gods is man who can be most useful to other human beings.

[12] There is also a similar division in the sources of harm and frustration.[11] But since no one thinks that the gods do harm, we can withdraw them from consideration, and the conclusion imposes itself that the greatest source of harm to men is other human beings. The very objects that I have called inanimate, you see, are mostly produced by human effort; we would not possess them if the skill of human hands had not helped; we would not be using them without the hard work of other men. Without the industry of men there could have been no curing of sickness, no seamanship, no cultivation of fields, no harvesting and storage of grains and other crops. [13] And unless men performed such services, there would certainly be no export of those products of which we have a surplus, no import of those products we lack. By the same agreement there would be no quarrying of stones necessary to our use nor would there be mining of iron, bronze, gold, or silver, which is hidden so deep, without the toil and resourcefulness of men. Consider houses: they repel the force of cold weather and reduce the annoyances of hot weather. How could the human race originally have

[11] That is, harmful agents are either inanimate or animate. Animate harmful agents would be divided into divine and human if the division in section 11 were followed; but it cannot be followed because no one believes in divine harmful agents.

built houses, unless the life men shared had taught them to seek help from each other in these matters? And men helped each other later if the houses collapsed in the violence of a storm or an earthquake or through aging. [14] Add to these aqueducts, the canalization of rivers, the irrigation of fields, the breakwaters set against the waves, the harbors dug out by hand: how could we get such works without the industry of men? These and other possible illustrations make it clear that whatever benefits and advantages we may derive from inanimate objects, we could not possibly possess them without the skill and industry of men. And finally, what profit or what benefit could be derived from animals unless men helped them? The original discoverers of the possible benefits we might obtain from each beast were undoubtedly men. Even in this age we could not pasture the animals or tame them or guard them or take the seasonal products from them without the industry of men; and it is men who kill harmful beasts and capture those that can be useful.

[15] Why should I enumerate the variety of skills without which life simply could not proceed? By what skill would the sick be helped? What diversion would the healthy have? What would our nourishment or clothing be like if this variety of skills were not at our service? Is it not this range of comforts that civilizes human life and separates it so far from the subsistence and shelter of the beasts? Of course, if men had not formed communities, cities could not have been built or occupied. Only after that stage were laws and customs established, as well as the equitable division of rights and a fixed pattern of living. The civilization of temperaments and the respect for others have achieved these improvements, and as a result life is more secure; by giving, receiving, and exchanging resources and advantages, none of us lack anything.

[16] I am dwelling on this topic longer than is necessary. Who does not clearly understand the facts when Panaetius recounts at great length how no man, neither a general on the

battlefield nor a leader at home, could accomplish anything significant or useful without support from other men? Panaetius discusses Themistocles, Pericles, Cyrus, Agesilaus, and Alexander, and he denies that they could have completed their ambitious projects without the cooperation of other men. He produces unnecessary proofs of an assertion that no one doubts.

But just as we gain great advantages through cooperation and agreement with other men, so there is no plague, however disastrous, that some men have not brought on other men. There is a book by Dicaearchus, the great and prolific Peripatetic, *On the death of men.* He lists numerous causes of death: floods, epidemics, exposure, even sudden hordes of wild beasts, whose attacks, he teaches, exterminated certain races of men. He goes on to compare to those the attacks by other men, wars and uprisings, for example, and shows how many more men have perished by these than by all other forms of disaster.

[17] Since the argument permits no doubt that men are both the greatest benefit and the greatest harm to each other, I therefore assert that it is the essence of virtue to win over the minds of men and to harness them to their own advantages. Those advantages that men secure for human life from inanimate objects and the benefits that they obtain by employing and training dumb animals are owing to hard work and skill. But where other human beings are concerned, it is the wisdom and virtue of outstanding men that set in motion men's ready and dependable efforts to increase our human advantages.

[18] It might be said that three elements are the constituents of virtue.[12] One is to see clearly what is true and honest in each different matter, what is appropriate to each matter, what is implied, the origin of each matter's existence, and the reason behind each separate thing. The second is to restrain the disturbed impulses of the spirit, which the Greeks call *pathe,* and to force

---

[12] These may be summarized as wisdom, moderation, and good will. Cicero explains each one without attaching a name to it.

those desires that they call *hormai* to obey reason. The third is to act reasonably and wisely toward those people with whom we come in contact, people whose efforts will help us to attain all the objects we desire, or perhaps even more. The same people may help us to ward off whatever annoyance may happen to us, to take revenge on those who might attempt to harm us, and to exact the degree of punishment that our sense of justice and human feeling allow.

[19] I shall say in a short while by what means we can attain this ability to engage and retain the services of other men. But I must mention a few points beforehand.[13]

All men know that the power of fortune is great and that it can work in opposite directions, either to favor or to obstruct our affairs. When we benefit from fortune's favorable breeze, we sail along toward the success we desired; but when fortune blows against us, we are stricken. Some of the accidents that fortune holds in store are rather infrequent, for example, (to mention physical ones first) windstorms, storms at sea, shipwrecks, collapsing buildings, and fires; and second the injuries that animals cause: kicks, bites and attacks. [20] Accidents owing to bad fortune alone, as I said, are not very frequent. But there are other kinds of disasters. Armies are slaughtered; there have been three examples recently[14] and many others at various times. Generals are assassinated; a recent example involved an eminent and unusual man.[15] And then the crowd begins to hate citizens who have rendered excellent service, and the result is numerous exiles, ruin and flight. On the opposite side are favorable events like election to offices, military commands, and victories. All of these events involve luck, to be sure, but neither the lucky nor the unlucky events can happen without the aid

---

[13] He resumes the discussion in section 21 below, after the digression on fortune and luck.

[14] The three armies defeated in the victories of Julius Caesar at Pharsalus (48 B.C.), Thapsus (46 B.C.), and Munda (45 B.C.).

[15] The murder of Pompey the Great in Egypt after his defeat at Pharsalus.

and efforts of other men. Once this is made clear, it may be pointed out how we can rouse and attract the efforts of other men to our advantage. If this topic is rather prolonged, compare its length with the amount of usefulness in it; perhaps then it will seem all too short.

[21] Now whatever men bestow upon another man to enrich and promote him,[16] they bestow either because of good will when they like someone for whatever reason; or because of the man's achievement if they respect his character and think that he deserves the greatest good fortune; or because they put their trust in someone and think that he takes a great interest in their affairs; or because they fear someone's wealth or, conversely, expect something from someone, as when kings or demagogues make various lavish gifts; or finally because they are enticed by bribes or rewards. This last is undoubtedly the most sordid motive and the most unfair one, both to those who are ensnared in it as well as to those who try to use it. [22] It is an evil business when one tries to do something with money that should be done by virtue. But because such subventions are frequently unavoidable, I shall discuss how a man should use them, once I have discussed topics that are more relevant to virtue.

[Men go so far as to subject themselves to the rule and power of another man for a variety of reasons. They are influenced by good will, or by the extent of benefits received, or by the glamor of the other man's prestige, or by the hope that submission will be advantageous to themselves, or by fear that they might be compelled to obey force; or they are enticed by the hope of largesse and by promises, or finally, as we often witness in our government, seduced by a bribe.]

[23] However, among all qualities there is no more appropriate way to preserve and defend one's resources than to be

---

[16] There are six reasons why one man promotes another's interests, which may be listed as affection, respect, trust, fear, and its opposite, expectation, and lastly cash inducements.

well-liked, nothing less appropriate than to be feared. Ennius
has an excellent verse,

> They hate the man they fear; and when one man hates
> Another, he hopes to see him dead.[17]

Recently men realized, if they did not know it before, that
no power can resist the hate of the multitude. *The death* of a
recent notorious tyrant is not the only one *that makes clear*
how relentlessly the hatred men feel works toward destruction;
the citizens oppressed by weapons endured this tyrant. . . .[18]
But comparable assassinations of other tyrants also make this
clear, and hardly one of them avoided such an end. To arouse
fear in others is a bad guarantee of longevity, while on the
other hand good will is faithful into eternity. [24] Men who
dominate and command other men, whom they have subju-
gated by force, have to apply some harshness, just as the owner
uses harshness toward his slaves if he cannot control them any
other way. But it is completely senseless for men in a free city
to act in such a way that it causes others to live in fear: no one
could be more insane. Although an individual's wealth and
power may circumvent the laws, although he may threaten
liberty, nevertheless laws and liberty eventually rise to the sur-
face again, either by anonymous expressions of opposition or
by secret arrangements to secure election to important offices.
But the wounds caused by the suspension of freedom hurt
worse than those caused by maintaining it. So let us embrace a
rule that applies widely and that is extremely effective not only
in maintaining safety but also in acquiring wealth and power,
namely, that there should be no fear, that one should hold affection dear. This is the easiest way for us to attain what we
want both in private affairs and in the government.

[17] The quotation is from Ennius (fr. CLXXXII in Jocelyn; see note 20, p. 14),
from an unknown tragedy.
[18] The "recent notorious tyrant" was Julius Caesar. The manuscripts have
not transmitted this sentence in an understandable shape; the italicized words
are an approximate translation.

Men who want to be feared must necessarily fear the very people who fear them. [25] What should be our opinion of the elder Dionysius, for example? The agony of fear was a daily torment for him. He was afraid of the barber's razor and used to have his beard singed with a glowing coal. What conclusion should we draw about the state of mind in which Alexander of Pherae lived? He loved his wife Thebe very much. And yet we read how, when he went from a feast to her in the bedroom, he used to order a foreign slave, a man actually covered with tattoos, as the story goes, to precede him with a drawn sword. He sent men from his bodyguard ahead to inspect his wife's closets and to make sure that no weapon was concealed in her clothing. What a wretched man he was, to think that a barbarian with a slave's brand mark was more trustworthy than his wife! And she did not disappoint him; for it was his wife and no other who killed him because she suspected him of adultery.

In fact, no dominant power is so great that it can last forever under pressure from fear. [26] We have the example of Phalaris, who was an exception among other bloodthirsty men in that he did not die by assassination, as did Alexander of Pherae, whom I just mentioned, nor did he suffer death at the hands of a few men, as did our Roman example. No, the entire population of Agrigentum attacked Phalaris.[19] Consider this: did not the Macedonians abandon Demetrius and turn in a body to Pyrrhus?[20] Consider this: did not nearly all their allies suddenly desert the Spartans when they began to rule unjustly and later, did they not come and watch without concern while the Spartans were being crushed at Leuctra?[21]

On a topic such as fear I mention foreign examples more

---

[19] He is said to have been stoned to death.

[20] Demetrius Poliorcetes had established himself as the ruler of Macedonia in 293 B.C. but desired to regain the empire of his father Antigonus in Asia Minor. When he left to campaign in the East, Macedonia was invaded by Pyrrhus, and the people accepted him as ruler in 288 B.C.

[21] See I.84.

willingly than Roman ones. But it is true that as long as Roman rule was maintained by good deeds, not by crimes, as long as the Romans waged wars either to protect allies or to settle power struggles the measures they took after the wars ended were either humane or, if not that, the steps that necessity dictated. The Senate was the port and refuge of kings, of peoples, and of nations. The only rule our magistrates and commanders followed in their attempts to win the highest praise was to protect the provinces and the allies with justice and dependability. [27] So one could more truly call Roman domination the protector of the world, not the ruler.

Even at an early stage we slowly began to relax this ingrained discipline of forbearance, and since the triumph of Sulla we have let it slip from us completely. When so much cruelty toward Roman citizens had occurred, whatever we did to our allies no longer seemed unjust. In the case of Sulla, his policies may have been acceptable, but the kind of victory he celebrated was not. He put out the auctioneer's sign and proceeded to sell in the Forum the confiscated property of decent and prosperous people who no one doubted were Roman citizens. He also dared to say that he was selling his "booty."[22] He was succeeded by a man who, in an offensive cause and in an even less acceptable victory, offered for sale not the goods of individual citizens, but thought it was his privilege to inflict disaster on entire provinces and districts.[23] [28] So it was that, after he oppressed and destroyed foreign nations, we saw a model of Marseilles carried in triumph as proof that its power was lost,

[22] The sign of an auction in this case was a spear stuck in the ground. One of Sulla's shocking actions was to apply the term "booty," a word used of spoils taken legitimately by a victorious commander from a non-Roman enemy, to the goods confiscated from citizens who were political victims.

[23] Cicero refers to Julius Caesar's confiscations after the defeat of Pompey in the Civil Wars. Cicero's sympathies lay with Pompey, needless to say. In this war Marseilles sided with Pompey, refused to help Caesar, and was besieged and taken; it had been a faithful ally of the Romans in their campaigns in Southern Gaul.

and a triumph thus celebrated over the one city without which Roman generals never celebrated a triumph after their Trans-alpine wars. I would mention many other crimes against our allies, except that the sun has never looked down upon any-thing more reprehensible than that particular act. We are being punished justly. If we had not tolerated and left unpunished the crimes of many men, such enormous lack of restraint would never have appeared in this one man. He left a legacy of family possessions to a few, but a legacy of greed to many other shameless men.[24]

[29] Naturally the seeds from which civil wars grow will never disappear as long as men of no principle remember and want that bloodied spear. Publius Sulla had brandished it when his uncle was dictator, and he did not shrink from an even more criminal use of the spear thirty-six years later.[25] Another Sulla,[26] who had been a secretary during the older dictatorship, was a *quaestor urbanus* in the recent one. The obvious conclusion is that civil wars will never disappear as long as such rewards are available. The house walls of Rome are still standing, but even they are fearfully expecting the final disasters and, as for the government, we have lost it completely. We find ourselves sur-rounded by these calamities (for I must return to my subject) because we prefer to be feared rather than to be gracious and to win respect.

If these things could happen to the Roman people when they ruled unjustly, what conclusion should individuals draw? Since it is absolutely clear that the power of good will is strong but

[24] This estimate of Caesar's career may be compared with the judgment in I.26.

[25] The spear is the auctioneer's sign of section 27 above, symbolizing the greed of dictators. P. Cornelius Sulla was a nephew of the dictator. He con-ducted auctions of confiscated property in 82 B.C. and in 46 B.C.

[26] Probably a freedman of Sulla who took his name; Caesar increased the number of quaestors. Cicero is showing the continuity between the dic-tatorships of Sulla and Caesar in order to prove that fear will always produce demoralization in similar circumstances. For *quaestor urbanus* see *Glossary.*

the power of fear is weak, it follows that we should discuss the means by which we can most easily attain that combination of affection, public honor, and trust that we desire. [30] Not all of us feel to an equal degree a need for such things. The question whether a man requires the affection of many or whether he is satisfied with the affection of a few must be measured against each person's plan of living. Therefore let the following at least be taken as proved, and it is important and extremely necessary: that we enjoy the steadfast closeness of those friends who love us and who admire our achievements. In this respect there is no great difference between the most important men and average people, and both classes of men have to work almost equally hard to gain that closeness. [31] Perhaps not all men feel the same need for prestige and glory and the good will of their fellow citizens. Nevertheless, if one has these advantages in good measure, they will help a great deal in gaining friendships and other benefits.

But I have discussed friendship in another book[27] [entitled *Laelius*]. Now let me discuss glory, although on this subject as well there exist two books[28] by me; still, let me touch on it since above all it helps in carrying out affairs of importance. The best and perfect glory consists of three elements: the admiration of all the people; the trust of all the people; and their opinion that certain men are worthy of office accompanied by a degree of affection. These three elements, moreover, to put it plainly and concisely, can be won from the people as a whole by practically the same means employed to win them from individuals. But there is a certain additional approach that has to be made to the people so that we can penetrate the awareness, so to speak, of every person in the state.

[32] With regard to the first element of the three I men-

[27] *Laelius* or *De Amicitia (On Friendship)* written earlier in the same year as *De Officiis (On Duties)*.

[28] *De Gloria* (one work in two books, as *De Officiis* is in three books) is a lost work of Cicero's.

tioned just now, let us inspect the rules concerning good will.[29] The chief way to gain good will is by good deeds. Next to that, good will is aroused by the intent to do good deeds, even if by chance a man's resources do not come up to the intent. Also merely a widespread reputation for generosity strongly stimulates the respect of the crowd as does a reputation for justice, for trust, and for all of those virtues that result in gentleness and easiness of manners. There is a particular quality that we call excellence or *decorum* because we approve it for its own sake, because it moves the hearts of all men both by its essence and its appearance, and because it shines through, as it were, most clearly in the virtues I listed. For these reasons nature itself compels us to love those in whom we believe those virtues to be present. These virtues are the most important reasons for loving someone. There can be many other reasons for love that are not so important.

[33] People's trust can be won in two ways: first, if we possess the reputation of having acquired wisdom that is combined with justice. We trust those men who, we think, understand more than we and who, we believe, can foresee the future, who improvise an action and who can produce a plan quickly when an event is underway and has reached a crisis; for men think that such abilities are useful and genuine wisdom. Second, people put their trust in honest [and dependable] men, that is, in good men, for the reason that no one has the least reason to suspect them of deceit and wrong-doing. We conclude quite correctly that we should entrust to them our safety, our fortunes, and our children.

[34] Therefore, of the two qualities that produce trust, justice is the more powerful, especially since it has enough influence by itself without wisdom; but wisdom without justice has no power to inspire trust. The cleverer and more sophisticated a person is, the more disliked and distrusted he becomes once

[29] That is, the "admiration of the multitude."

his reputation for trustworthiness has disappeared. For this reason justice combined with wisdom will have all the force it could want to inspire trust. Justice without wisdom can do many things, wisdom without justice will be powerless.[30]

[35] It is agreed among all philosophers, and I myself have often agreed, that whoever possesses one virtue possesses all virtues. This being true, someone may have wondered why I should now separate the virtues, as if anyone could be just who is not at the same time wise. My answer is that one degree of subtlety is used when philosophers debate and try to grasp abstract truth, and another when a writer adjusts his whole exposition to the average reader's understanding. For this reason I am using the language of ordinary people at this point, and I say that some men are courageous, others are good, others are wise. When I speak about popular conceptions, I must work with the people's vocabulary, with the words in use; Panaetius did the same. But let us return to our topic.

[36] The third of the three elements that constitute glory was this: that men judge us worthy of holding public offices and grant us their affection at the same time. The general rule is that people admire everything they notice that is impressive or beyond their expectations. But when they become aware that certain individuals possess good qualities whose existence they did not suspect, then they feel a particular affection. They respect and acclaim with the loudest praises those men in whom they believe they perceive certain outstanding and incomparable virtues, and conversely they reject and despise men whom they believe to possess no virtue, no spirit, no energy. They do not, you must remember, condemn all those of whom they have a bad opinion. Men whom they consider shameless, slanderous, of bad faith, and prepared to commit crimes they do not necessarily reject, although they have a bad opinion of

---

[30] The third way to capture glory (after good will expressed by good deeds, and the ability to inspire trust) is delayed until section 36.

them. So, as I said just now, people condemn those men who, as they say, are no good to themselves or to others, who make no effort, who do not work, who do not care.

[37] However, people regard with admiration men who have the reputation of surpassing others in virtue and of not merely being completely free of corruption but more particularly of resisting the faults that others cannot easily resist. Physical pleasures, those most seductive mistresses, turn the attention of most men away from virtue. And when the burning agony of pain approaches, most men are terrified beyond reason. Concern about life and death, riches and poverty upsets all men greatly. Everyone admires those men of impressive and noble character who pay no attention to these exterior circumstances, either the good or the bad. And who does not stand amazed at the splendor and beauty of virtue when he becomes aware of some magnificent and virtuous act that attracts and commands his complete attention? [38] This spiritual nobility, then, arouses great wonder in others. And justice in particular seems to the mass of people something amazing, and they are not wrong: good men achieve their reputation for goodness from that one virtue alone, and no man can be just who lives in fear of death, pain, exile, or poverty. If a man shuns fair-dealing in order to avoid these evils, he cannot be considered just. People especially admire the man who is not concerned with money because they think that anyone who is clearly indifferent to money has survived an ordeal by fire. Justice, in summary, creates all three of the conditions that are necessary to achieve glory: good will, because justice wants to benefit as many as possible, and for the same reason trust and admiration, because justice spurns and disregards those things toward which most men, enflamed with greed, are always rushing.

[39] In my opinion, at least, every plan and arrangement of living requires the help of other men, mainly so that a man might have other men with whom to carry on relaxed conversations. This is difficult unless other men look upon you as a

good man. Therefore the reputation for justice is indispensable even to the solitary man and to the man who lives his life in the countryside. It is even more necessary to them because, if men have no such reputation [they will be considered unjust], they will be the victims of much wrongdoing because they are not protected by any guardians. [40] Even retail merchants, employers, and contractors find that justice is indispensable in their dealings. The power of justice is so great that not even men who gain their living by treachery and crime can live without any trace of justice at all. The man who steals or seizes the possessions of one of his fellow thieves disqualifies himself even from belonging to a band of robbers. Even the companions of the so-called pirate king will kill him or abandon him unless he divides the booty fairly. So the saying goes: there are laws even among thieves, and they respect and obey those laws. Because of his evenhanded distribution of booty the Illyrian pirate Bardulis (Theopompus mentions him) came to wield great power. Viriatus of Lusitania acquired much greater power. In fact, even Roman armies and generals retreated before him. Gaius Laelius the praetor, the one known by the name "The Wise," broke and defeated him. Laelius so reduced the terror inspired by Viriatus that he left an easy war to other commanders to finish.[31] Since the power of justice is so great that it strengthens and increases even the influence of bandits, how much power should we believe it has where courts of law exist, in a legally constituted state?

[41] I believe it was once the custom among our ancestors (and not only among the Medes, as Herodotus reports[32]) that

---

[31] Bardulis and Viriatus were native leaders. Bardulis organized a kingdom in Illyria, north of Macedonia, came into conflict with the Greeks, and died in battle against Philip II in 358 B.C. Viriatus organized and led native Spaniards against Roman forces in 148–146 B.C. and later; the Romans procured his assassination in 139 B.C.

[32] In his *Histories* I.96, Herodotus reports the origin of kings among the Medes. A man named Deioces acquired a reputation for justice and worked

the individuals who were made kings were men of good character. The purpose of this custom was to assure the enjoyment of justice. When during peacetime the common people suffered under the oppression of men who were stronger, they used to turn to some single man who was preeminent in virtue. That man would protect the weaker from wrongs, and by legislating equality would treat the greatest and the lowest with the same justice.

People made laws for the same reason they created kings. [42] The justice men sought was always based on equality; it would not be justice otherwise. If men received that kind of justice from a single just and good man, they were content with him. When that did not happen, written laws were invented to speak always to all men with one and the same voice. So one conclusion is clear: men whom the crowd considered great in matters of justice were the men they usually elected to rule. If they also regarded these same men as wise, they believed there was nothing they could not accomplish with these men as their governors. Justice, therefore, should by all means be nurtured and maintained for its own sake (otherwise it would not be justice) as well as because it increases a man's dignity and eminence.

Now just as plans exist not simply to earn money but also to invest it so that the money will pay for all expenses without diminishing, and not only for necessary expenses but also for luxuries: in the same way you should earn and invest your glory according to a plan. [43] Yet Socrates used to say brilliantly that it was the nearest path, a kind of shortcut, to glory if a man

---

tirelessly to make the whole country dependent on his decisions. He then abruptly refused to serve any longer as a dispenser of justice. Crime and injustice began to increase suddenly, the people decided they needed a strong leader and chose Deioces to be their king. Cicero generalizes the story to explain the origin of kings at Rome.

tried to be the same person he wanted people to think he was.[33]
If anyone thinks he can attain lasting glory by mimicry, by empty
shows, by pretense in his looks and his conversation, he is far
from correct. Genuine glory puts down roots and even sends
out new growth; any pretense dies down quickly, like fragile
flowers. Nothing simulated can be long-lasting. There are many
examples of this on both sides,[34] but for brevity's sake I shall be
content with a single family. Men will praise Tiberius Gracchus,
the son of Publius, as long as the memory of Roman history
lasts. But no reputable person praised Tiberius' sons while they
lived, and in death they rank among those who were justly
killed.[35] Therefore, whoever wishes to acquire true glory [for
justice] should practice the obligations of justice. What those
are I explained in the preceding book.

[44] I must formulate a few rules to save us trouble when
we attempt to make our real character match our outward image, even though the main point is that we should be the person we want others to think we are. The eyes of the whole
world turn toward a person who from the beginning of his life
has reason to anticipate that he will inherit fame and a good
reputation from his father (which I believe is your situation,
my son), or who anticipates that he will have them because of
some other circumstance or piece of good luck. People are
curious about what this young man does and about his way of
life. He seems to move within a brightly illuminated circle, and
nothing he says or does can be kept in the dark. [45] Boys who
in their formative years remain hidden from people's recogni-

---

[33] Xenophon, *Memorabilia*, II.39.

[34] That is, many examples occur to Cicero of both true and false glory.

[35] Tiberius Gracchus, the father of the tribunes, distinguished by lasting
accomplishments in all phases of Roman public life, is the example of true
glory. Cicero consistently regards the sons, the tribunes, as disruptive revo-
lutionaries and therefore examples of false glory. See I.76, where Cicero expresses approval of the assassination of Ti. Gracchus the tribune.

tion because of their low rank and obscurity ought to fasten their eyes on greatness as soon as they enter young manhood and work toward it with unswerving endeavor. They will work with a more resolute spirit because young manhood does not attract envy; on the contrary, men encourage youth. Now the first kind of praise people give young men on the way to fame is the praise they are able to earn in military service.[36] Many of our forefathers won such praise because they were almost always at war. However, your youth coincided with a war[37] that had too much crime on one side, too little good luck on the other. Nevertheless when Pompey put you in charge of [one of the] cavalry squadrons in that war, you earned a great deal of praise from the great man and from the soldiers by your horsemanship, your spear-handling, and by enduring every military hardship. Of course, your fame disappeared along with the Republic. However, I undertook this exposition not to write about you but about young men in general: so let us press on to what remains.

[46] Just as in other areas the accomplishments of the spirit are much greater than those of the body, so the results that we achieve by intelligence and planning are more satisfying than those we owe to our muscles. A chief source of praise, therefore, is courtesy and respect toward one's parents and good will toward one's relatives. But young men become well-known most easily and most favorably if they apprentice themselves to outstanding men of wisdom who are good counsellors to the government. If they spend a lot of time with such men, they create an expectation in people that they will be comparable to the men they selected for imitation. [47] Residence and study with Publius Mucius endowed the young Publius Rutilius with

---

[36] In Cicero's time service in the army was no longer compulsory, but it was still the most usual way of entering into public life.

[37] The Civil War between Pompey and Caesar; the younger Cicero served with Pompey in Greece in 48 B.C.; he was sixteen.

a nascent reputation for integrity and legal knowledge.[38] Lucius Crassus, as you know, did not borrow praise from someone else when he was still a young man but won the highest praise for himself through an impressive and famous prosecution. At the same age when those who practice hard usually begin to reap praise, as we know in the case of Demosthenes, Lucius Crassus showed that he could already perform outstandingly in the law-court in matters that would have won praise even if he had still been practicing them at home.[39]

[48] There are two divisions of speaking. One embraces conversation, the other argument. Of course, there is no doubt that argument makes the greater contribution [of speaking] to glory, for that is what we call eloquence. Yet it is not easy to explain the extent to which gentleness and courtesy in speaking will win over other men's minds. We possess letters of Philip to Alexander his son, of Antipater to Cassander, of Antigonus to Philip. These were three of the wisest men we know. In their letters they teach their sons how to turn the minds of the people toward good will by kind speech and to captivate their soldiers by addressing them gently [in conversation]. On the other hand, a public speech that presents an argument often achieves widespread fame. People greatly admire a man who speaks fluently and wisely; those who hear him even believe that he knows and understands more than other men. In fact, there is nothing more admirable than a speech in which unassuming intelli-

---

[38] Young Romans customarily attached themselves to an older man in a sort of apprenticeship in law and public life. See I.122 above. There were no professional schools of law or rhetoric at Rome. Cicero argues that the quality of the man to whom a youth attaches himself demonstrates something about the abilities of the youth.

[39] L. Licinius Crassus made his debut as an orator at the age of twenty-one in 119 B.C. when he successfully prosecuted C. Carbo. To prosecute an eminent man was an established way of making one's reputation early, although Cicero himself preferred to defend. Demosthenes argued a case at age eighteen.

gence is blended with impressiveness, especially when those qualities are found in a young man.

[49] Although there are several kinds of occasions that require eloquence, and although many young men in Rome have won praise by speaking before judges, the people, and the Senate, the greatest admiration is won for speaking in a court of law, and there are two branches of that. Legal eloquence is divided into prosecution and defense. Even though defense is the more praiseworthy of these two, nevertheless, prosecution has frequently attracted praise, too. A moment ago I mentioned Crassus; Marcus Antonius likewise conducted prosecutions as a young man. A prosecution also made the eloquence of Publius Sulpicius famous when he called to judgment a treasonable and harmful citizen named Gaius Norbanus.[40]

[50] You must not conduct prosecutions very frequently and only in the interests of the government (like those men I just mentioned), for compensation, as the two Luculli did, or to provide protection, as I did for the Sicilians, or as Julius did in the case of Albucius for the Sardinians; and the energy of Lucius Fufius was displayed in prosecuting Manius Aquillius.[41] So one may prosecute once, or a few times, but very infrequently; or, if someone does have to prosecute rather often, let him perform this service for the government: to punish its enemies frequently should not attract criticism. However, there should be some limit. It seems characteristic of a harsh man, or rather of

----

[40] The date of Antonius' earliest speech is not known; Sulpicius prosecuted Norbanus in 95 B.C., when he was perhaps twenty-nine years old.

[41] A list of prosecutions undertaken for apparently generous reasons. The Luculli sought to avenge their father by prosecuting an augur who had prosecuted him. Cicero successfully and brilliantly prosecuted Verres, governor of Sicily, in 70 B.C., in response to complaints by Sicilians that Verres had pillaged them. Julius was an orator whom Cicero admired; he prosecuted T. Albucius on complaint of the Sardinians. Fufius prosecuted Aquillius unsuccessfully in 92 B.C.

someone scarcely human, to put a large number of people in danger of capital[42] punishment. This is not only dangerous to the prosecutor himself, it also lowers his reputation to allow himself even to be called an accuser. This happened to Marcus Brutus, a man born into a great family,[43] the son of a man who was among the leading experts in civil law.

[51] You must also carefully observe the following rule of duty: never charge an innocent person with a capital offense. There is no possibility that such an action is not a crime. What is so inhuman as to pervert eloquence, which nature bestowed for the salvation and preservation of people, into the plague and destroyer of good men? However, just as we should avoid that, neither should we be excessively reluctant to defend a guilty man from time to time, as long as he is not depraved or sacrilegious. The people want this, custom condones it, and our sense of humanity even compels it. The judge's function in trials is always to pursue the truth; the defender must sometimes maintain what resembles the truth[44] even if it is not strictly true. I would not dare to write this, especially since I am writing about philosophy, except that Panaetius, the most serious of the Stoics, is of the same opinion. Still, you gain the greatest prominence and gratitude by conducting a defense. The prominence is still greater if you ever happen to come to the aid of a defendant who apparently is surrounded and hard-pressed by the resources of some powerful man. I have often done precisely

---

[42] "Capital" here means loss of civic rights and exile, not execution.

[43] M. Brutus is said to come from a great family because it was a Brutus who expelled the kings from Rome in legendary times.

[44] That is, when defending the guilty. Cicero weighs his words carefully when he discusses this possibility. The previous sentence, which lists the three sanctions of the act, would seem to summarize the reasons that Panaetius gave for his opinion, although this is not certain. Note the implication that if he were not writing philosophy Cicero would give more straightforward advice.

that in various cases, and as a young man I defended Sextus Roscius of Ameria against the power of Lucius Sulla the over-lord.[45] This speech, as you know, is published.

[52] Having set out those obligations of young men that are useful in achieving glory, I must next discuss kindness and generosity. There are two kinds; a man behaves with generosity toward those in need either by an act or by a gift of money. The latter alternative is the easier one, especially for a wealthy man; but the former is nobler, more impressive, and worthier of a strong and famous man. Although a generous desire to please is present in both alternatives, nevertheless one act of generosity takes from the money chest, the other from one's personal abilities, and a payment made out of one's private means exhausts the very source of generosity. So generosity with cash destroys its own source, and the more you have spent on some people, the less you have to spend on many others. [53] But those who are generous and openhanded with acts, that is, with their talents and with hard work, will have helpers in doing charitable deeds in proportion to the number of people they benefit. Also, because of the habit of doing good deeds they will be better prepared and more experienced, as it were, in bestowing favors on many people. Philip does well to scold his son Alexander in one of his letters because Alexander was trying to win the good will of the Macedonians by making large gifts. "You fool," he says, "what train of thought led you to expect that men you have corrupted with cash would be faithful to you? Or are you trying to cause the Macedonians to hope that you will not be their king but their servant and supplier?" He did well to say "servant and supplier" because it points up the degradation for a king. He did even better to say that a large gift was a "corruption" because a man who accepts gifts is somewhat tainted and more prone to expect constantly to receive the same again.

---

[45] Cicero was twenty-six when he defended Roscius in 80 B.C.

[54] Philip wrote this warning to his son, but let us consider it a rule for everyone. Consequently one thing at least is not in doubt: the type of generosity that consists of service and hard work is more honest, has wider application, and can be useful to more people. Sometimes, however, one cannot avoid having to make gifts, and there is no reason to reject this type of generosity completely. Often one must disburse from one's private means to other men in want who deserve the gift, but one must do so carefully and in moderation. Many people have wasted their inheritance by dispensing charity thoughtlessly. What could be more pointless than to devote your effort to making it impossible to do any longer what you really want to do? Excessive bounty even results in theft. When hands begin to be empty because of generosity they are compelled to dip into other men's property. So, although men wish to be generous in order to accumulate good will, they are not as successful in captivating the devotion of those to whom they have given as in exciting the dislike of the men they have robbed.[46] [55] For this reason, you should not lock up your private means so tightly that they are not accessible to generosity, or on the other hand guard them so carelessly that everyone has access to them. To set a limit is necessary, and it should be determined by your ability to give. Certainly we ought to remember a phrase that has become a proverb for us Romans through frequent use: "Bounty has no bottom." After all, what moderation is possible when those who have become used to accepting gifts want something, and new claimants want precisely the same thing?

In general, there are two sorts of liberal people: some are spendthrifts, some are generous. The spendthrifts are those who pour their cash into feasts and distributions of meat,[47] into shows

---

[46] Obviously Cicero is not thinking here so much of generosity between individuals as of the wholesale use of cash and gifts to secure and retain followers by such contemporaries of his as Sulla and Caesar.

[47] Public feasts were held on certain religious holidays and sometimes as part of the funerals of the wealthy and eminent. Fresh meat was scarce in the

of gladiators and the equipment of wild-beast shows, and into the kind of spending that will leave behind either no memory of it or only a short one. [56] Generous men, on the other hand, are those who, with their own resources, ransom prisoners from bandits, or underwrite the debts of their friends, or help the daughters of friends to marry with dowries, or help friends in acquiring or in expanding property. So I am amazed at what Theophrastus had in mind in his book *On Wealth,* where among many brilliant things he argues one absurdity. This absurdity is his prolix praise of costly display and the providing of games for the people; he thinks that the ability to provide such expensive shows is one advantage of being wealthy.[48] To me, however, it seems that a much greater and more genuine advantage is the generosity of which I just gave a few examples.

How much more serious and truthful is Aristotle's criticism! He blames us for not being disturbed about those outlays of wealth that men make to captivate the populace. He says, "Suppose men who are besieged by an enemy are compelled to buy a pint of water for a *mina*.[49] At first this would seem unbelievable to us, and we all would wonder at it; but when people considered the circumstances, they would excuse it with necessity. In the case of the enormous expenditures and limitless outlays on shows, however, we do not feel any great amazement. Yet they do not relieve any need, they do not increase anyone's importance, the crowd itself gets amusement only for a brief and limited time, only the most thoughtless elements feel amused, and what is more, their memory of being amused starts fading the moment they have had enough of it." [57] He deduces correctly that "these expenditures are attractive to chil-

---

average Roman's diet, so distributions of it were an acceptable way to capture the crowd's favor.

[48] Theophrastus' book *On Wealth* is lost, so it is not possible to recover the arguments that supported this "absurdity."

[49] See *Glossary.*

dren and housewives and slaves and free men of slavish instincts, but a truly serious man could not possibly approve of
them, a man who weighs whatever happens with strict judgment."[50] In spite of this I realize that it has long been the custom at Rome, even in the good old days, to expect leading men
of the state to finance magnificent displays during their aedile-
ships. So Publius Crassus, a rich man both in *cognomen*[51] and
money, spent unlimited amounts of money while holding the
aedileship. Somewhat later Lucius Crassus together with Quintus Mucius, the most moderate of all men, served an aedileship
of extreme splendor. Then came Gaius Claudius the son of
Appius and many others afterwards, the Luculli, Hortensius,
Silanus. However, Publius Lentulus surpassed all those older
men when I was consul. Scaurus imitated him. The most truly
magnificent games were those of our Pompey in his second
consulate.[52] You can see which of all these examples meet with
my approval and which do not.

[58] However, you must avoid the suspicion of stinginess.
His decision not to seek election to the aedileship later caused
Mamercus[53] to lose the consular elections, although he was an
extremely rich man. Therefore you must undertake these expenditures if the people demand them; reasonable men will
agree to them even if they do not like them. You should only
spend according to your resources, however, as I did myself.
Occasionally you may gain a rather significant and useful advantage by offering distributions to the people. For example,
Orestes recently reaped great honor with his public feasts in

[50] This translation or paraphrase of Aristotle does not match any passage
in his preserved writings.

[51] See *Glossary* for *aedile* and *cognomen*.

[52] In 55 B.C., when he was consul for the second time, Pompey opened the
theater that he had built. This was the first permanent theater building in
Rome, and the theatrical, athletic, gladiatorial, and animal shows lasted many
days. For Cicero's own aedileship see the end of section 59 below.

[53] But he was consul in 77 B.C.; the date of his earlier defeat is not known.

the streets, which he gave under the pretense of making a tithe offering.[54] Of course, no one blamed Marcus Seius because during a scarcity he sold grain to the people at the price of one *as* per *modius*.[55] By this outlay he rid himself of a deep, long-standing prejudice against him and because he was aedile, the gesture was neither blameworthy nor excessively expensive.[56] My friend Milo recently reaped the greatest honor when he purchased gladiators to protect the government, whose preservation depended on my personal safety; he completely suppressed the intrigues and violence of Publius Clodius.[57] Therefore large financial outlays are justified if they are either necessary or useful. [59] Even with necessary expenditures the rule of moderation is best. Lucius Philippus the son of Quintus, a very well-known man of great intelligence, used to boast that he had attained all the most eminent public offices without spending any money at all. Cotta and Curio used to say the same thing. I also am in a position to boast about this to a certain extent.[58] My expenditure on the aedileship was rather trifling in comparison to the impressiveness of my offices, which I attained by unanimous vote in the very first year I was eligible.[59] None of the men I mentioned just now achieved such a record.

[60] To proceed: those expenditures that provide for the needs of the state of all preferable to outlays on public enter-

---

[54] See *Glossary*.

[55] See *Glossary*.

[56] The reason for the disgrace or unpopularity in which M. Seius found himself is not known. On the price of grain see section 72 below, with note.

[57] The last example of personal expenditure involves Cicero himself. It seems more likely that the gladiators of Milo were intended to oppose the gangs of Clodius than that they were to protect the state.

[58] Unlike L. Philippus and Cotta, Cicero never became Censor.

[59] An important law known as the *Lex Villia annalis* fixed the order of magistracies by defining the minimum age (later modified) when they could be held: quaestor (30), aedile (36), praetor (39), and consul (42). Cicero won all these offices at the minimum age.

tainments. I have in mind such projects as city walls, dockyards, port facilities, and aqueducts. I grant that a direct gift, right into the hand, as it were, is more attractive; however, public works are more pleasing to posterity. As for theaters, porticoes, new temples: I criticize such projects rather reluctantly because of Pompey,[60] but the most learned men do not approve them. For example Panaetius himself, whom I have largely followed (not translated), in these books, does not approve them. Demetrius of Phaleron scolds Pericles, the leader of Greece, because he expended so much wealth on those famous Propylaea.[61] But there is a thorough discussion of this entire topic in the books I wrote *De re publica.*[62] In sum: the whole concept of large public expenditures is basically harmful but necessary in some circumstances, and even then they must be tailored to one's financial abilities and moderated by restraint.

[61] In the other category of expenditures, the one that has its origin in generosity, we should not let one single rule bind us in differing cases. The case of the man overwhelmed by bad luck is quite different from that of the man who, although his affairs are not in immediate danger, is trying to improve his position. [62] Generosity will feel the obligation to be more helpful to victims of misfortune, unless by chance they deserve their misfortune. In the case of men who wish to help themselves advance a step higher and not merely to save themselves from ruin, we should not be without generosity either. But we must use caution and judgment in selecting suitable people. Ennius has an excellent line:

I think that good deeds in a bad place are bad deeds.[63]

---

[60] Pompey's building program was extensive. See the end of section 57 above.

[61] See Index of Names.

[62] Cicero's treatise *On the State* survives in large fragments. The section dealing with expenditures on public works does not survive.

[63] The source of this verse in the writings of Ennius is not known (fr. CLXXXIII in Jocelyn; see note 20, p. 14).

[63] When you invest in a good and grateful man, you reap profits both from him and from other people. Except for indiscriminate charity, you see, generosity is very pleasing; most people praise it even more eagerly because kindheartedness in any eminent man offers all men common protection. For this reason we must work hard to help as many people as possible with our acts of generosity, acts that will stay in the memory of their children and descendants and will make it impossible for them to be ungrateful. Everyone dislikes a man who fails to remember a good deed. People believe that this lapse of memory causes an end to generosity toward themselves and that the person who forgets a good deed is a common enemy of the less wealthy. Some types of charity are even useful to the government, such as ransoming prisoners from slavery and providing for the poor. In a speech of Crassus, in fact, we can find an eloquent discussion of how these are quite common and usual practices of our senatorial class.[64] Consequently I much prefer this habit of charity to the expense of public entertainments. Charity belongs to men of dignity and greatness; but public spectacles seem to be the mark of those who fawn on the people, those, it seems, who use pleasure to encourage the frivolity of the crowd.

[64] Just as it is proper to be generous in giving, so it is proper not to be petty in exacting one's due. It is proper to be fair and courteous in any transaction involving contracts, in selling or buying; in renting or hiring; in matters of adjoining houses and property lines. You should yield to others a considerable share of your own rights; you should certainly avoid litigation to the extent that you feel you can reasonably do so, or perhaps even more than that. It is the mark of a generous man to retreat slightly from his own rights at times. Not only

---

[64] In 106 B.C. Crassus spoke in favor of a bill whose contents are not certain, but which was possibly a law to restrict the membership of juries to Senators.

that: sometimes it is even profitable.[65] A man must keep an account, however, of his private means; to let them go to waste would be shameful. But the accounting must be such that no suspicion of harshness and greed arises. Unquestionably the greatest advantage of wealth is the ability to be generous while not depriving oneself of one's inheritance.

Theophrastus was also[66] correct when he praised acts of hospitality. It seems extremely appropriate to me, at any rate, that the homes of distinguished men stand open to distinguished guests. It is also an advantage to the state that men from foreign countries do not lack this kind of hospitality in our city. To have influence with foreign peoples and to earn their gratitude by acts of hospitality are also exceptionally useful to men who wish to acquire power legitimately. Theophrastus indeed writes that at Athens Cimon was a host even to members of his own deme, the Laciadae. He had made this arrangement and ordered his servants to provide everything to any of the Laciadae who stopped off at his country estate.[67]

[65] Now the advantages that come from services and not from outlays of money are directed both toward the state as a whole and toward individual citizens. To be useful to as many people as possible by protecting their legal rights, by giving legal advice, and by legal knowledge in general, is strongly effective

[65] The Latin word *fructuosum* hints at monetary profit, not just moral gain. But for once Cicero gives no illustrations.

[66] This implies that Cicero is again referring to Theophrastus' book *On Wealth*. See section 56 above.

[67] The preceding paragraph reflects the constant ancient emphasis on hospitality both as a means of prestige and as a convenience. In the absence of a developed hotel industry, the traveller depended on lodging in private homes. The wealthy or eminent expected to entertain guests from abroad or to be entertained when travelling abroad themselves. In either case the act of hospitality could express political power and prestige. Cimon went to the extreme of opening his country estate to his fellow demesmen, presumably without regard to their rank or ability to reciprocate. On the duties associated with maintaining a house see I.138.

in increasing one's influence and popularity. Our ancestors were distinguished in many ways, but their most remarkable trait was that they always had the highest respect for the study and interpretation of our well-constructed body of civil law. In fact, leading men kept this knowledge in their exclusive possession up to the present confused times, but now the glory of the legal profession has died, along with public honors and all positions of eminence.[68] This is all the more lamentable because it has happened in an era when one man[69] was alive who easily surpassed his predecessors in legal knowledge and who was equal to them in honor. Legal help, then, is acceptable to many and is a suitable means of putting other men under obligation for favors received.

[66] Closely related to the legal discipline is a more crucial, pleasing, and honored ability: public speaking. What ranks higher than eloquence? Nothing, when you consider the fascination of the audience, the hope that it arouses in the needy, or the gratitude of the people that you defend successfully. For this reason our ancestors [also] reserved the highest rank in civil life for men with ability in oratory. The good deeds and the protection provided by an eloquent man and a willing worker, by one who defends many people's cases both cheerfully and without fee (this was one of the customs of our forefathers),[70] extend far and wide.

[67] This subject would remind me to lament on this occasion, too, the decline, I should say the demise, of eloquence,

---

[68] Law was not a highly organized profession at Rome and there were no professional schools. On the custom of learning by associating with older men see sections 46 and 47 above. Cicero naturally associates law and oratory (see sections 66 through 68 below) and repeatedly expresses his belief that they died as effective forces along with the free Republic; see sections 2 and 3 above and III.1–4.

[69] Cicero refers to Servius Sulpicius, consul in 51 B.C., a close friend of his who was renowned for his legal knowledge.

[70] The Lex Cincia of 204 B.C. prohibited advocates from receiving fees; however, the law appears to have been evaded easily and regularly.

except that I should be afraid to seem to be complaining a little on my own behalf. And yet, since certain orators have died, we can observe how few men show promise, how even fewer show ability, how many of them show nothing but presumption. Although not all men, not even many men, have the ability to be learned in law or to be eloquent pleaders, they can still help many people by various activities: helping to campaign for small offices, giving character testimony to judges or to magistrates, being watchful on another's behalf, making inquiries of the particular men who are either giving advice or conducting a defense. Men who do these things earn the highest gratitude and their hard work has a very wide impact. [68] It is obvious and therefore not necessary to warn them to be careful not to offend one group when they are trying to help another. Frequently they insult men whom they should not insult or men whom it is disadvantageous to insult. This is due to carelessness if they do not know better; to sheer folly if they have their eyes open. Under these circumstances they must offer the best excuse possible to those whom they accidentally offend. They should explain that what they did was unavoidable and that there was no other way they could have done it; they should say that they will make up for the apparent offense by performing other helpful services in the future.

[69] Now in helping people we usually examine either their character or their wealth. Most of us find it extraordinarily easy to repeat what everyone else says: that the only decisive factor in bestowing favors is the other man's character, not his wealth. This is a worthy affirmation. But who does not actually prefer to put his effort into winning the gratitude of a wealthy and powerful man, rather than be bothered by the difficulties of someone who may have a very good character but who has no money? On the whole, our choice leans more toward the man who, as far as we can tell, will repay us more certainly and more promptly. But we must reflect more thoroughly on the true state of affairs. That poor man I mentioned just above, if

he is a good man, can surely display gratitude even if he can not return the favor equally. Whoever said the following spoke to the point: "The man who keeps his money has not repaid it; the man who has repaid it does not have it; but when he expresses his feelings of gratitude, he still has them after he has expressed them, and when he has them, he expresses them."

Men who consider themselves wealthy, distinguished, and fortunate do not even want to feel that they have been even obligated by a good deed. In fact, when they have willingly accepted even a considerable favor, they think that they have bestowed it. They even suspect that it will allow someone to have a claim on them or to expect something in return, and they would as soon die as make use of someone else's protection or be known to be dependent on someone else. [70] But the man of modest means whom I mentioned assumes that his own character and not the amount of his wealth was the motive for whatever you did. Consequently he tries very hard to seem grateful not only to the man who helped him but even to men whose help he anticipates, for he needs many benefactors. This man does not exaggerate his service with fine phrases if he ever happens to render some service in return; on the contrary, he minimizes it. You should also remember the following point: if you defend a wealthy and prosperous man, his feeling of gratitude only lasts for his lifetime and possibly that of his children; but if you defend a man who is not wealthy but is honest and humble, all men of the lower ranks of society who are not ingrates realize that your action has provided a bulwark for them, and there is a large number of such persons among the lower classes. [71] For this reason I think that a good deed is better invested in good people than in prosperous people.

We must, of course, try to act well toward every class; but if circumstances force a choice, Themistocles is undoubtedly the counsellor to follow. When someone asked him whether he would marry his daughter to a good but poor man or to a wealthy man who was not respectable, he said, "I prefer a man who lacks money to money that lacks a man." Admiration for wealth has spoiled and depraved our characters. What does an accumulation of wealth signify for us as individuals? Perhaps it might help the man who possesses it. Not even that is always true, but assume that it helps him; more resources are at his disposal, of course, but how is he really a better man? Yet assuming that he is both wealthy and good, his wealth should not deter you from helping him just as it should not attract you. Let the entire decision rest on each man's character, not on how wealthy he is. My final advice about doing favors and offering help is never to try to accomplish something unfair or criminal by those means. Justice is the basis of unending praise and good reputation; nothing can deserve praise without justice.

[72] Since I have spoken about the category of good deeds that applies to individuals, I must next discuss the category that applies to all men and to the state. In this group belong two kinds of services, those that affect the whole body of citizens and those that affect particular groups. The latter create more popularity than the former. If possible, you should, of course, pay attention to both kinds, not so that you show less concern toward particular groups but so that the transaction either benefits the state or at least does it no harm. For example, the distribution of grain by Gaius Gracchus was on a large scale, but it threatened to exhaust the treasury. The restricted distributions by Marcus Octavius were something the government could afford and were indispensable to the people: consequently they were healthy both to the people and to the state.[71]

[73] The man who administers the state will have to see, as

---

[71] Since the city of Rome depended on imported grain, it was necessary for the government to intervene in the free market in times of scarcity or in emergencies. C. Gracchus, as part of his reforms in 123 B.C., passed a law that offered grain to citizens at a subsidized price. The date at which M. Octavius revised the law is not known; possibly it was in the 90's B.C. or later. The price was fixed by Gracchus' law at six and one-third *asses* per *modius*. See section 58 above.

his most important task, that each citizen keeps possession of his own property and that no public action causes a reduction in private property. Philippus acted destructively in his tribunate when he proposed an agrarian law. But he allowed it to go down to defeat without causing trouble and thereby showed himself to be extremely mild-tempered. However, when he was advocating the measure, much of what he said was calculated to appeal to popular taste. The following quotation is especially evil: "There are scarcely two thousand men in the state who own property." The speech is perfectly criminal, advocating as it did the equal distribution of property, and what plague can be worse than that one?[72] Men founded states and cities primarily on the principle that private property may be retained. Even if men first formed groups because of a natural impulse, still, they sought out the protection of cities in the hope of guarding their private possessions.

[74] An effort must also be made not to levy a property tax. Our ancestors often imposed one because of the low state of the treasury and the frequency of wars. One should make plans long in advance so that this does not happen. I prefer to speak in general terms rather than to threaten Rome with a bad omen. However, I am not arguing about Rome alone but about governments in general. So, if anywhere in any state an emergency arises that makes such a tax unavoidable, an effort must be made to make all men understand that they must submit to this necessity if they want to survive. In addition, all men who govern a state will have to take steps to assure a good supply of the commodities necessary to sustain life. It is not necessary to enter into details about the kind of provision governments usually make and ought to make for these things; it is an obvious matter; the topic merely had to be mentioned.

[72] Philippus was tribune of the people in 104 B.C. The purpose of his proposal is not known, but presumably it had in view the use of publicly-owned land to benefit the poorer classes. Cicero's strong reaction to a law defeated sixty years before is remarkable. See section I.21, with note.

[75] In administration of any public office or private business the chief requirement is to evade clearly even the smallest suspicion of greed. Gaius Pontius the Samnite said, "I wish it had been my luck to wait and not to have been born until the times when the Romans began to accept bribes! I would not have allowed them to rule a day longer." Well, he would have had to wait many generations, for it is only recently that this evil has crept into the Roman government. It is no grief to me that Pontius lived long ago, if in fact he was a character of such strength. Not a hundred and ten years have passed since Lucius Piso introduced an extortion law; there had been no such law before.[73] Since then, of course, there have been many laws, and the more recent ones are more severe. So many people were accused, so many were guilty, a lengthy Italic War stirred up because of the fear of extortion courts, and once the laws and judges were removed, so much looting and robbing of our allies took place that we remain strong because other men are weak, not because of our own strength.

[76] Panaetius praises Africanus because he was not greedy. Why should he not praise that quality? But Africanus had greater virtues. Praise for lack of greed applies not only to that man but also to his era.[74] Paullus, who gained possession of all the vast wealth of the Macedonians, brought so much money into the treasury that the booty of this single general put an end to

[73] In 149 B.C. Piso passed a law providing for a permanent court to investigate and prosecute cases of extortion by provincial governors. The penalties had to be increased by new laws as time passed. The Italic (or "Social") War of 90–88 B.C. resulted from the attempts of Rome's Italian allies to secure the full rights of Roman citizenship. Legislative measures to provide these rights were introduced, but they included the establishment of courts to investigate maladministration, which roused the fears of the ruling oligarchy. They bitterly opposed the measures.

[74] The booty in a conquered city was at the disposal of the victorious commander. The commander usually took the best, then allowed the soldiers to plunder at will. Scipio was inclined to be more generous to his men than other commanders.

property taxes.[75] He brought nothing into his own home, however, except the undying remembrance of his name. Africanus imitated his father: he did not become a bit wealthier because of his conquest of Carthage.[76] What do you think about Lucius Mummius, who was his colleague in the censorship? Was he any richer after he had completely destroyed the richest city of all?[77] He chose to decorate Italy rather than his own home. Yet the home also seems better decorated to me because Italy was decorated.

[77] Let my argument return to where my digression began.[78] No vice, I conclude, is more destructive than greed, especially greed in leaders and those who govern states. To use the government as a source of profit is not merely a matter for criticism, it is criminal and sinful. The oracle delivered by the Pythian Apollo, that Sparta would not suffer defeat for any reason except greed,[79] seems a prophecy directed not merely to the Lacedaemonians but in fact to any wealthy state. The men in charge of a state can win the good will of the multitude by no other quality as easily as by self-restraint and by personal moderation. [78] In fact, those who wish to be known as champions of the people and therefore try to pass agrarian laws so that tenants are driven from their land, or who propose that money out on loan should be remitted to the debtors[80] are undermining the foundation blocks of the state. Those foundations are, first, harmony among classes, which cannot exist when money is taken away from some people and turned over as a gift to others, and, second, fair dealing, which disappears completely

[75] In 168 B.C., after Aemilius Paullus' victory at Pydna.

[76] Scipio Africanus' father was Aemilius Paullus; he was adopted by Scipio and took his name. He destroyed Carthage in 146 B.C.

[77] Corinth, also in 146 B.C. See I.35.

[78] In section 21 above.

[79] The oracle said that love of money would destroy Sparta. A law in Sparta is said to have condemned to death anyone who amassed a fortune.

[80] Proposals to change the status of public land, with the possible result of driving tenants from it, and proposals to cancel all debts were measures repeatedly brought forward by popular leaders as solutions of economic crises.

if the laws do not allow each man to retain his private property. As I have said previously,[81] it is the basis of a state and city that each man has free and undisturbed possession of his own property.

[79] Besides, while working this destruction on the state, demagogues do not even achieve the popularity they crave. The man whose property they confiscated is their enemy. The man who receives the property goes so far as to pretend he did not want to accept it. He hides his joy, especially in a case where he owed money, so that he does not seem to have been bankrupt. Conversely, the man who suffers an injustice never forgets his misery; in fact, he tends to advertise the fact. If those who receive property as an illegal gift are more numerous than those who had it taken from them illegally, it does not follow that they are also more important. The standard of judgment in these matters is not arithmetic but significance. How can it be fair when a person of no property gets possession of land that has been occupied by a family for many years or even many generations, while the former owner loses it? [80] Because of this kind of wrongdoing the Lacedaemonians drove out Lysander, their ephor; they killed their king, Agis, an unprecedented event in Sparta's history. From that time on such upheavals followed that tyrants began to spring up, the best people went into exile, and this most excellently organized state crumbled to pieces. In fact, not only did Sparta itself fall, but it even brought ruin to the rest of Greece with infections from its evils, which started with the Spartans and spread even wider.[82] Is another example

---

[81] In section 73.

[82] Cicero illustrates the bad consequences of attempted wholesale economic reform with an incident from Spartan history. Agis IV became one of the kings of Sparta in 244 B.C. Sparta was underpopulated; much of the land was heavily mortgaged or had been amassed into large holdings by a few owners. Agis introduced reforms that would have had the effect of restoring the ancient constitution of Sparta. But he pressed the reforms too quickly and too violently and was eventually killed. Within about forty years Sparta had lost its independence, and within a century the Romans controlled all of Greece.

needed? Did not strife over agrarian reforms prove to be the loss of our Gracchi, the sons of that great man Tiberius Gracchus and the grandsons of Africanus?[83]

[81] Aratus of Sicyon of course deserves to receive praise. After tyrants had held his city for fifty years, he set out from Argos[84] to Sicyon, got the city in his power by using a secret entrance, and after he had overcome the tyrant Nicocles by surprise restored six hundred exiles, who had been the richest citizens, and freed the government by his return. But then he noticed that there was great difficulty about property and possessions. He concluded that those men he had restored himself, whose property other people had come to possess, were suffering most unjustly; yet he thought it was not very fair that the possessions of fifty years should be disturbed, especially because in such a long period of time many things had legally passed into ownership by wills, by purchase, or in dowries. He decided that nothing should be taken away from present owners and that restitution ought to be made to those who had owned the property at one time.

[82] Therefore, realizing that he needed money to carry out this decision, he announced that he wished to journey to Alexandria. He said that he did not wish the state of affairs to change until he returned. He went immediately to his guest-friend Ptolemy, who was then reigning as the second king after the founding of Alexandria. After Aratus had explained to Ptolemy that he wished to free his country from debt and had stated the difficulty, he, impressive as he was, easily persuaded the wealthy Ptolemy to help him with a large sum of cash. When he had brought this back to Sicyon, he summoned to council fifteen leading men. He reviewed the state of affairs with them, and by estimating the amount of property that belonged to

---

[83] See I.76 and II.43 and 72 for further references to the Gracchi.

[84] Aratus had been living in Argos some thirteen years in exile from his native Sicyon. He was twenty years old when he gained control of Sicyon in 251 B.C.

those who owned others' property, and the amount that had belonged to those who had lost their own property, he managed to persuade some people to accept cash and to return their possessions to the original owners. He persuaded some of the exiles to think it more convenient to have the value of their property paid to them in cash than to recover the actual property. So it came about that they reached an agreement and everyone went away without complaint.

[83] What a great man! He would have been worthy to be born a Roman! That is the way to deal equitably with citizens, not, as we have already seen twice, to set up a spear in the Forum and to place the property of citizens at the mercy of the auctioneer's voice.[85] But Aratus, a Greek, thought that all interests should be consulted, a policy that showed he was wise and unusual. It also shows the unsurpassed insight and wisdom of a good citizen: not to deprive some citizens of benefits but to treat everyone with equal justice. "Let them live free in someone else's house!"[86] Why so? So that when *I* have purchased and built, when *I* maintain and repair, *you* might enjoy my property against my will? What else does it mean, when you seize the belongings of one set of people and bestow gifts of confiscated property on others?

[84] In fact, what meaning do "new ledgers"[87] have unless this: that you, the debtor, buy an estate with my cash, and you have the estate, but I no longer have the cash? For this reason one must take care that indebtedness does not reach a point where it might harm the government. There are many ways to avoid it. If debt does reach high levels, the solution should not cause the wealthy to lose their property while debtors grow

[85] Both Sulla and Caesar auctioned confiscated property. See sections 27 through 29 above.

[86] Cicero quotes the appeal of an imaginary interlocutor to an edict of Caesar that granted remission of rents.

[87] "New ledgers" implies cancellation of debts, a repeated promise of Roman popular leaders.

rich on others' money. Nothing else supports a government more strongly than its credit; there can be no credit unless the repayment of debts is mandatory. There was never a more vigorous campaign to excuse debtors from repayments of debts than when I was consul.[88] Armed camps were formed by every kind and class of men to force the adoption of these proposals. I put up such a fight against those men that the whole evil disappeared from the state. Never was debt greater, never was it liquidated more completely or more easily; once the hope of evading debts vanished, the necessity of payment followed. On that occasion, at least, Caesar[89] lost, although by now he has won, since he secured the adoption of measures that he dreamed up when they were crucial to his career, although by the time he enacted them they were no longer so essential. He had such a lust for crime in him that he found it attractive by itself, even without a motive.

[85] Those who are going to govern will therefore refrain from that strange kind of generosity that consists of depriving some to give to others. Principally, they will strive for this: that under fair administration of the law and of the courts every man securely owns his own property; that the less well-to-do are not cheated because they have no power; that envy does not prevent the rich either from keeping or recovering their property. Government leaders especially should enrich the state with power, territory, and revenues by whatever means they command, military or domestic. These are services of great men; they were the kind that our ancestors performed. Those who perform such duties will render the highest service to the state and will earn for themselves great admiration and praise.

[86] Antipater, the Stoic from Tyre, who recently died at

---

[88] Catiline promised cancellation of debts if he gained power.

[89] Julius Caesar. Cicero charges that before Caesar became dictator, he thought up plans to rid himself of debt by proposing general cancellation of debts. After his victories in Gaul and in the Civil Wars Caesar was wealthy but clung to the same proposals.

Athens, thinks that Panaetius overlooked two points in the rules about useful advantages: care of health and care of money. I suppose that the lofty philosopher overlooked these items because he thought them quite obvious. They are most certainly beneficial. Health can be maintained by observation of one's constitution; by noting what things are usually helpful or harmful to it; by being moderate in one's diet; by care for the body through abstinence from sensuality to keep it healthy; and lastly by the skill of medical men whose knowledge includes these matters.

[87] A man's private means ought to derive from those employments that do not involve dishonesty. These means should be maintained by watchfulness and thrift, and those same qualities should also serve to increase them. Xenophon, Socrates' disciple, offered skillful arguments in support of these points in his book *Oeconomicus,* which I translated from Greek into Latin when I was about the same age as you are now. On all these topics, on acquiring money, on investing, I hope even on putting money to good use, a discussion by some of the outstanding men who frequent the Stock Exchange[90] is more appropriate than a lecture by a philosopher in any academy. These topics deserve to be well understood, for they pertain to advantages, and this book is on that topic.

[88] A comparison of advantages is frequently unavoidable. This is my fourth topic, the one Panaetius overlooked.[91] It is not unusual for people to compare physical advantages with acquired advantages, and acquired advantages with physical, as well as comparing physical advantages with each other and acquired advantages with each other. Physical advantages are

[90] An approximate translation of *ad Ianum medium,* "at the middle of Janus [street?]", a location in the Forum where bankers gathered to transact business.

[91] Refer back to I.10 for the original outline. The question now is, when two advantages present themselves, which one is better? Cicero deals with the topic very hastily and sketchily.

compared with acquired advantages by stating, for example, that you prefer being healthy to being rich. [The acquired advantages are compared with bodily advantages in this way: people prefer to be rich rather than to enjoy the greatest bodily strength.] Physical advantages are compared with each other: good health is preferred to pleasure; strength is preferred to speed. Acquired advantages are compared like this: glory is preferred to wealth; income from urban property is thought preferable to that from country estates. [89] A famous anecdote about Cato the Elder[92] belongs to this last class of comparisons. Someone asked him what was most profitable on an estate. He said, "Good herds." What next? "Fair herds." What next? "Poor herds". What next? "Crops." When the man who had asked these questions asked, "What about usury?" Cato answered, "What about murder?" From this and many other examples you ought to conclude that comparisons of advantages are nothing out of the ordinary and that it is correct to have included them as the fourth category in the discussion of responsibilities.

[90] Let us follow up the remaining topics.

---

[92] The Elder Cato collected famous anecdotes and sayings (see I.103), and his own laconic speeches were evidently remembered by others. His attitude toward the relative merits of farming and business is characteristic of many Roman writers; see I.151.

BOOK THREE [1] Marcus, my son, Cato wrote
down the following typical saying of Publius Scipio, who was
the first to bear the name Africanus and who was nearly the
same age as Cato.[1] Scipio said he was never less "away from
business" than when he was "away from business," nor less
"alone" than when he was "alone." The saying is admirable
and reflects the character of a great and wise man! It means that
he used to ponder his affairs when he was away from them,
and used to converse with himself in solitude; he never relaxed
and never felt [occasionally] that he would like to talk with
someone else. The two things that cause most people to become lazy, solitude and freedom from business, used to make
Scipio more alert.

I rather wish I myself could truly say the same thing. But if I
cannot attain such heights of genius by imitating Scipio, at
least I have come very close to it in my aspirations. I pursue
leisure because I have been shut out from the government and
from public transactions by violence and the weapons of
criminals. For that reason, having abandoned Rome, I am often
alone as I wander about in the country.

[2] No one should compare my leisure with that of Africanus,
however, or my solitude with his. It was while relaxing from the
most splendid duties of government that he found some leisure

---

[1] The saying is an example of the *apophthegmata* that Cicero mentions in
I.104. Scipio took the name Africanus following his victory over Hannibal in
the battle of Zama in Africa (202 B.C.). Scipio and Cato the Censor were
born within two years of each other, in 236 B.C. and 234 B.C. respectively.

for himself from time to time, and occasionally he would remove himself from the crush and crowd of men to solitude, like sailing into a port. My leisure, by contrast, is the result of the lack of something to do, not of any eagerness on my part to take a rest. What work worthy of me can I do, either in the Senate or in the Forum, now that the Senate is snuffed out and courts of law are eliminated? [3] So I, who once lived at the height of popularity and was always in the public eye, have gone into retirement to avoid seeing those criminals who now flock everywhere. I have hidden myself as far away as possible, and I am often alone.

But I am enjoying my leisure. That is because philosophers have taught me not only that one ought to choose the lesser evils but also that even from them one ought to gather whatever good they might contain. It is not the kind of leisure, of course, that the man who once produced leisure for Rome ought to enjoy.[2] I do not permit my solitude to be a lazy one, even though force and not my own choice bestows it on me.

[4] I am convinced, of course, that Africanus won more significant praise. You see, no works of his genius are in existence that are committed to writing, no result of his leisure, no product of his solitude. From this fact it is evident that, because of the activity of his mind and the steady examination of the topics he pursued in his thinking, he was never really at leisure or alone. However, I do not have enough strength to be drawn out of solitude by silent thought, and so I have turned all my effort and devotion to this work of writing.[3] As a result I have written more in a short time, now that the Republic has been overturned, than during the many years when it was in existence.

[2] Cicero produced "leisure" for Rome in the sense that he crushed the Catilinarian conspiracy. The Latin *otium* means both personal leisure and absence of strife in public affairs.

[3] Cicero's expression of modesty is very tortured. The paradox he advances is that because Scipio produced no writings during his absences from public life, he was therefore superior to the prolific Cicero.

[5] While philosophy as a whole, my Cicero, is fruitful and productive, and while no part of it is arid or uncultivated, still no section of it is richer or more vigorous than the one dealing with moral obligations. From this section the rules of consistent and honest living are derived. Although I am certain that you are constantly hearing and learning about these topics from my friend Cratippus, the chief philosopher of the age, nevertheless, I think it is profitable to make these rules ring in your ears from all directions. You should listen to them and nothing else if that were possible. [6] Although everyone who contemplates setting out on a respectable life has to absorb these teachings, still I am inclined to think no one needs them more than you. The reason is that you are bearing the burden of expectation. People expect you to match my hard work, even more my civil career, and perhaps also my fame.[4] Besides, by going to Athens and Cratippus, you have assumed a heavy responsibility. Since you went there as if you were going to a marketplace of culture, it would be very unworthy of you to return empty-handed and thereby display contempt for the eminence of the city and of your teacher. For that reason apply your mental powers as much as you can and strive to work as hard as you can, if hard work rather than pleasure is involved in learning. Work hard enough to succeed and do not be guilty of making people think that you have failed yourself after I have supplied all your necessities. But enough about these things, for I have written you often and at length to urge you on. Now let us go back to the remaining part of the scheme I laid out.

[7] Panaetius presented without doubt the most thorough arguments about moral obligations, and I have followed him for the most part, adding certain corrections.[5] In his first three books he set forth his views about two of the three proposed categories that people usually take as the basis of discussions and advice on obligations: one, when they deliberate whether the

---

[4] The same ideas were more elaborately expressed in II.44.
[5] In I.9 and 10.

action in question is good or evil; two, whether it is profitable or not; and three, what decision men ought to make when an apparently honest action conflicts with an action that seems profitable. He said he was going to write about this third category, but did not carry out his promise. [8] I find this all the more puzzling because his disciple Posidonius records that Panaetius lived thirty years after he published those books.[6] I am also amazed that Posidonius touched on this topic only briefly in a few annotations,[7] especially since he wrote that there was no topic in all philosophy as indispensable as this.

[9] There are some who assert that Panaetius did not overlook the topic. They say that he deliberately abandoned it and was not going to write about it at all because a profitable action could never come into conflict with a good one. I completely disagree with them. There can be doubt whether Panaetius should even have included this division (the third in his scheme), or should simply have left it out. But it cannot be doubted that Panaetius included it but did not take it up. Surely the man who has completed only two parts of a three-part plan must still be faced with the third. Besides, at the very end of the third book he promises that he is going to write in sequence.

[10] Posidonius comes forward as a reliable witness to this same point. He writes in one of his letters that Publius Rutilius Rufus, who had been a student of Panaetius, liked to say that no painter had ever been found to finish the parts of the Coan Venus that Apelles had left only in sketches. This was because the beauty of the face destroyed any hope of matching it in the rest of the body. He used this illustration to explain why no one had completed those topics that Panaetius had passed over [and not finished]: because of the excellence of the topics that he had finished.

---

[6] This dates Panaetius' books *On Duty* to about 139 B.C. It is not known why he never completed his outline.

[7] Summaries of these were supplied to Cicero by Athenodorus; see *Introduction*, p. xix.

[11] Consequently there can be no doubt about the intention of Panaetius. Perhaps there can be some doubt whether he was correct to add this third division in discussing moral duty or whether he was wrong. The Stoics, of course, state flatly that virtue is the only good. Your Peripatetics believe that virtue is the highest good, so that if you bring together all other goods and weigh them against it, they will move the scales a trifle, although you will hardly be able to detect the counterweight.[8] Whichever doctrine one follows, there can still be no doubt that advantageousness can never conflict with right conduct. That is why we learn that Socrates used to curse those[9] who in their speculation had first forced apart these concepts that naturally belong together. In fact the Stoics have agreed with Socrates insofar as they believe that whatever is right conduct is advantageous, and that nothing is advantageous that is not right conduct. [12] If Panaetius were the type of thinker who says that virtue ought to be cultivated primarily because it produces advantages, he would be like those[10] who gauge the desirability of actions by the amount of pleasure in them or the extent to which pain is absent. If he thought like that, it would be all right for him to say that expediency sometimes comes into conflict with right conduct. But he is a man who judges right conduct to be the only good and who judges, moreover, that anything that conflicts with this good because it appears to be an advantage does not make life more pleasant by its presence nor more painful by its absence. For this reason I believe

[8] On the resemblance between Stoic and Peripatetic doctrines, see I.2, with note. Here Cicero refers to the Stoic doctrine that virtue (or right conduct) is the only good and to the Peripatetic doctrine that virtue is the highest (but not the only) good; other good things, according to the Peripatetics, all put together have some measurable importance when weighed against virtue.

[9] Presumably Socrates did not know precisely who these thinkers were but assumed that the justification of the separation of expediency and right action began with particular individuals.

[10] Epicureans.

Panaetius was under no obligation to introduce a discussion of the conflict between an apparently advantageous action and right conduct.

[13] What the Stoics called the *summum bonum,* "to live according to nature," has this meaning, in my opinion: always to agree with virtue, and to select all other things that might be "according to nature" only if they do not conflict with virtue. Since this is so, the Stoics think that it was not correct to introduce the comparison between advantage and right conduct. They think that no one should ever have attempted to give advice on this question. The right conduct that is the result of strict and correct philosophical discussions exists only in perfectly wise men, and it is never possible to separate it from virtue. Those, on the other hand, who do not possess perfect wisdom cannot conceivably achieve the same absolutely right conduct: at most they are able to imitate it."

[14] The Stoics call the duties that I am discussing in this book duties of "the middle category": they are ordinary and widely applicable duties, the kind that numerous people achieve by goodness of character and progress in education. The duty that the Stoics identify with the good, however, is perfect and absolute, and, as these men say, it has "all numbers"¹² and can belong only to the wise man. [15] When someone performs an action in which duties of "the middle category" are involved, it can appear to be absolutely perfect, but only because the common man does not generally understand how far it falls short of being perfect. Insofar as he does understand, he thinks that nothing has been omitted. The same failure in understanding commonly occurs with poems and paintings and many other works of art. The uninitiated take delight in and praise those works they should not praise. The reason, I believe, is that such

---

¹¹ On this distinction see I.46, with note.

¹² That is, has attained perfection. The metaphor may derive from Pythagorean numerology or from another more ordinary source unknown to us (a dice game?).

works possess a measure of integrity that attracts the inexperienced, the very people who cannot judge the faults that
are present in the details. As a consequence, when they receive
instruction from the experts, they abandon their opinion without protest.

The performance of the duties, then, that I am discussing in
this book are certain "second category" acts of virtue according to the Stoics, not the ones that belong exclusively to wise
men but ones widespread among the entire human race. [16]
All men who have a disposition toward virtue are encouraged
by these acts. The two Decii or the two Scipios are frequently
cited as brave men. Either Fabricius or Aristides is called "The
Just." But it is not true that the ones provide an example of
bravery, or the others of justice, as if they were perfect. I say
this because none of these was a wise man in precisely the way
we want "wise man" to be understood. Those who are considered and specifically called wise men,[13] Marcus Cato and
Gaius Laelius, were not truly wise men; neither were the well-
known Seven Sages. Because of the large number of "second
category" duties they performed, they bore a certain resemblance to wise men and appeared to be such.

[17] For these reasons it is not permissable to compare ideal
good conduct with expediency. What we ordinarily call good
conduct, the trait that men cultivate who want to be known as
good men, should never be measured against its rewards. We
should respect and preserve the standard of right conduct as we
understand it just as carefully as wise men observe their standard, which is right conduct by the strict and rigid definition.
Otherwise whatever progress we have made toward virtue cannot be maintained. But this is enough about those who are considered to be good men merely because they preserve their
moral duties.

---

[13] Both Cato and Laelius had the cognomen *Sapiens*, "the Wise." But the
Stoics nevertheless would not regard them as "perfect" wise men.

[18] Those who measure everything by rewards and profits and who do not assign more importance to right conduct than to profit constantly weigh right conduct against what they consider profitable when they are making a decision. Good men never do this. For this reason I think that when Panaetius said that men usually debate this question with themselves, he meant precisely that: he said only that they "usually" do it, not that they "ought" to do it. It is extremely shameful not only to value what seems profitable more highly than what is right conduct, but also to compare these with each other and to debate inwardly about them.

The question is, then, why do situations constantly arise that cause discussion and that make us hesitate about our course of conduct? They arise whenever there is hesitation about the essential nature of the action under consideration. [19] It often happens in particular circumstances that what people usually consider a shameful act turns out to be not shameful at all. For the sake of example, let me mention a single case that has applications beyond itself. What crime could possibly be greater than the slaying of a man, or, worse, of a man who is your close friend? But has anyone who has killed a tyrant, no matter how close he was to him, stained himself with a crime? It does not seem so, of course, to the Roman people, who think that this is the most attractive of all remarkable deeds.[14] In this case does benefit outweigh right conduct? Far from it: benefit resulted from right conduct.

Therefore, we must set up a rule; then we will not make any mistake if it ever happens that something we consider profitable seems to be in conflict with what we know is right conduct. If we follow this rule when we compare actions, we shall never desert our moral duty. [20] As far as possible, this rule will be consistent with the thought and learning of the Stoics. Indeed,

---

[14] Another allusion to the recent assassination of Julius Caesar. Tyrants are discussed further in section 32 below.

I am following that system closely in this book because the Stoics explain things more attractively. I grant that the Old Academy and your Peripatetics (who were once the same as the Academics[15]) make genuine right conduct preferable to an apparently profitable act. But the Stoics believe that right conduct is identical with expedient conduct and that no action whatsoever is expedient that is not also right conduct. This Stoic position is more attractive than the one taken by those who say[16] that right conduct is inexpedient and that expedient actions are not right conduct. In any case, since I adhere to the New Academy, I have a wide discretion and I am within my rights when I support the position that seems to me most probable.

But let me return to the rule. [21] To deprive another man of something, to increase your own comfort by making another man miserable, is more against nature[17] than death, poverty, pain, and any other misfortune that can happen to one's body or one's possessions. In the first place, such an act does away with human society and social cooperation. [If we are so demoralized that a man will rob or injure another man to achieve a private advantage, it necessarily follows that what is preeminently "according to nature," the social structure of the human race, will disintegrate.]

[22] For example, if each separate limb of the body had the ability to think and believed that it would be able to strengthen itself by drawing out the strength of a near-by limb, it necessarily follows that the whole body would grow weak and perish.[18]

---

[15] On the relationship between the Academy and the followers of Aristotle see I.2, with note. Here Cicero adds the distinction between the Old Academy (Plato and his immediate followers) and "my Academy," i.e., the New Academy.

[16] The Academics and Peripatetics.

[17] Nature is the ultimate standard of the Stoics; see section 13 above.

[18] The image of society as a living organism recurs in section 32 below. See Livy, *History of Rome*, II.32.

In the same way, if every one of us should seize the possessions of others, should drag off what he could for his private advantage, it follows necessarily that society and cooperation among men would be destroyed. One can grant that as individuals men prefer to acquire the things that make life enjoyable for themselves, rather than for strangers. That is completely natural. But nature does not allow us to increase our own resources, property, and wealth by plundering other peoples'.

[23] It is forbidden to harm another person for one's own private benefit. This idea is established not only by nature, that is, by the law of nations, but also similarly by the laws of peoples, the laws that support the government in various individual states. Laws look to this end, they have this purpose: that the society of citizens remain undisturbed; whoever disrupts this society is punished with exile and death, with fines and prison. The very plan of nature itself demonstrates this much more effectively. That plan is law for both gods and men; whoever wishes to obey that law (and everyone obeys who wants to live according to nature) will never go so far as to attack another man and to appropriate for himself what he has seized from someone else. [24] Greatness of soul and high courage and courtesy, a sense of justice and generosity are far more in accord with nature than sensuality, existence itself, or wealth. In fact, it is the mark of a great and exalted spirit to weigh these things against the common benefit and then reject them and count them as nothing. [To rob another man for one's private advantage is more against nature than death, pain, and similar things.]

[25] By the same argument, it is more "according to nature" to take upon yourself enormous work and trouble in order to preserve and aid all the nations, if that is possible, and to imitate the renowned Hercules: his fame among men kept alive the memory of his good deeds and earned him a place in the council of the heavenly gods. These actions are preferable to living for yourself, not merely apart from every trouble, but also

in the midst of all kind of delicacies, amid the most refined pleasures, surpassing all others in beauty and strength. For this reason, every person of the greatest and most brilliant talent infinitely prefers a life of action to the alternative.[19] A result is that the man who obeys nature is quite unable to harm another man.

[26] Next consider the man who injures another man in order to secure some advantage for himself. He either believes that he is not doing anything against nature or he thinks that to harm another human being is not worse than death, poverty, pain, or even the loss of children, relatives, or friends. What kind of discussion can you hold with him if he believes that wronging another man is not an action against nature? His concept of "man" simply does not include what is essentially human. If he thinks doing harm should in fact be avoided but believes those other things like death, poverty, and pain are much worse, he is wrong. He falsely assumes that any injury to the body or any loss of property is more serious than injuries of the soul. So there ought to be one single rule for everyone: that what benefits each individual and what benefits all mankind should be identical. If any individual seizes an advantage for himself, the whole of human society will break apart.

[27] Furthermore, if nature demands that a man be willing to help another man, whoever he might be, for the simple reason that he is a human being, it necessarily follows that, according to the same nature, the advantage of all men is shared. If this assumption is correct, one and the same law of nature[20] binds all of us. If this last assertion is also correct, we are certainly restrained by a law of nature from harming another human being. [28] The first assertion is true and so, therefore, is the last. The contention that some people advance is absurd, of course: they argue that they would not deprive a parent or

[19] A similar argument has already been used in a slightly different context in I.153.

[20] In section 23 above Cicero identified "nature" and the "law of nations."

brother of anything for their own advantage but that there is another standard applicable to all other citizens. These people do not submit themselves to any law or to any obligation to cooperate with fellow citizens for the common benefit. Their attitude destroys any cooperation within the city. In the same way, those who say that one standard should be applied to fellow citizens but another to foreigners, destroy the common society of the human race. When that disappears, good deeds, generosity, kindness, and justice are also removed root and branch.

We must draw the conclusion that people who do away with these qualities are disrespectful even against the immortal gods. They destroy the cooperation among men which the gods instituted.[21] The strongest bond in this cooperation is the thought that it is more against nature if one man deprives another for his own advantage than if that man himself suffers destruction of any kind, either to his property, or to his person, or even to the spirit itself.[22] . . . that are not characterized by justice, because this one virtue is the mistress and queen of all the others.

[29] Perhaps someone might say, "But consider a wise man who is dying of hunger. Will he not take food from another man, a man who is quite useless for anything?" [Not true at all. For my life is not more useful to me than that particular disposition of mind that prevents me from harming anyone for my own advantage.] "Second: suppose a good man could steal clothing from Phalaris, that cruel and monstrous tyrant, to keep himself from dying of cold. Should he not do it?" These hypothetical cases are extremely easy to decide. [30] If you take something for your private use away from another man who is useless to anyone, you act inhumanly and against the law of nature. However, if you are the kind of person who can bestow a great benefit on the state and human society by remaining

---

[21] See the definition of philosophy given in I.153.

[22] The beginning of the following sentence has dropped out of the manuscripts.

alive,[23] then there is no blame if you deprive another man of something to sustain your life. Yet if this is not the situation, each man should endure his own suffering rather than reduce the benefits of another person. In summary, neither disease nor dire want, nothing of that kind is more contrary to nature than coveting and stealing another man's belongings. Disregard of the common benefit is against nature because it is unjust.

[31] The same law of nature preserves and defines the benefits common to all men. It will ultimately decree that commodities necessary to life may be transferred from a slothful and useless man to a man who is wise, good, and strong, one who would greatly reduce the common good if he should die. However, the law should act in such a way that the good man does not use this as an excuse for doing wrong because he has a good opinion of himself and loves himself. Thus he will always perform his duty while considering the benefit of men and, as I always repeat, that of the human society.

[32] The case involving Phalaris is extremely easy to decide. We have nothing in common with tyrants; on the contrary, we feel an extreme hostility toward them. It is not against nature to steal from one of them, if you can: after all it is good conduct to assassinate one. The whole loathsome and unholy breed of tyrants ought to be wiped out from the human community. Just as doctors amputate certain limbs when they have shown a lack of blood and what we might call vitality and begin to harm other parts of the body, in the same way the bestial wildness and enormity that in a tyrant masquerade as a human being should be segregated from what might be called the common body of humanity.[24]

---

[23] This condition is explained further in the next paragraph. It is against the law of nature to take from other men; it is also against the law of nature to reduce the common human advantages, which some individuals may do by allowing themselves to die although they could prevent it.

[24] The image of society as a living organism has already been introduced in section 22 above.

All inquiries about moral duty in particular circumstances follow this pattern. [33] I believe Panaetius would have completed his outline with similar arguments if some accident or preoccupation had not destroyed his plans. In respect to the deliberations themselves, he produced in his previous books many rules that state clearly what one should avoid because of its immorality, and what one does not have to avoid because it is always moral under any circumstances.

Since I am putting what you might call the capstone on an incomplete but almost finished project, I request you, my Cicero, to concede to me, if you can, that nothing should be sought out for its own sake except right conduct. My request is like that of geometricians; they do not always demonstrate everything but ask that certain axioms be conceded to them so they can explain what they want more easily. If Cratippus[25] does not permit this, you will certainly grant that right conduct more than anything else should be sought for its own sake. Either one of these axioms is sufficient: first one, then the other seems more probable, and nothing except these two seems probable at all.

[34] The first point on which one must defend Panaetius is that he did not say that expediency sometimes comes into conflict with right conduct. For him that would have been impossible. But he did say that a conflict arises in the case of actions that seem to be expedient. He often affirmed that nothing is expedient in the true sense that is not also right conduct, and nothing is right conduct that is not also expedient. He said that no greater plague has overwhelmed the life of men than the thinking that separated these concepts. Panaetius introduced

---

[25] See section 20 above. Cratippus represents (and teaches the younger Cicero) the Peripatetic doctrine that virtue (or right conduct) is the highest good, but that others must be taken into account. The Stoic view is that virtue should be sought to the exclusion of all else, without exception. Cicero's characteristic New Academic weighing of what seems probable emerges at the end of the paragraph.

this apparent, but not real, conflict, not so that we could occasionally prefer expediency to right conduct but so that we could judge between them without mistake if they ever conflicted. I will therefore fill out the part he abandoned, not with a group of helpers but with my own weapons, as they say. In all the books that have come into my hands, there is really nothing written on this topic later than Panaetius, at least nothing that meets with my approval.

[35] Now when some apparent advantage offers itself, we are inevitably attracted to it. But when we examine it closely, when we see that immorality is involved in the circumstances that present an appearance of expediency, then we are not forced to relinquish the advantage; we merely have to realize that expediency cannot exist in the same place as immorality. If nothing is as contrary to nature as immorality, since nature desires the right, the appropriate, the consistent, and shuns their opposites; and if nothing is so much according to nature as expediency, then surely expediency and immorality cannot exist in the very same set of circumstances. However, Zeno thought that we have been born for right conduct and that it alone should be sought out. On the other hand, Aristotle thought that men should consider right conduct more important in any calculation than anything else.[26] From both opinions it necessarily follows that what is right conduct is either the only good or the greatest good. What is good is doubtlessly expedient, and so whatever is right conduct is expedient.

[36] The false reasoning of unscrupulous men, once it has seized on something apparently expedient, immediately distinguishes between that and right conduct. That is the origin of assassins' daggers, of poisonings, of forged wills, of thefts and

---

[26] These two sentences restate the two propositions involved in section 33; see note. Zeno founded Stoicism; Aristotle founded the Peripatetic school. In this paragraph Cicero proves by two syllogisms the essential point of Book Three: expediency and wrong conduct (immorality) cannot exist together in the same act; right conduct must always be expedient.

embezzlements, of plunderings and lootings of allies and fellow citizens. That is the source of desire for excessive wealth, for intolerable power, ultimately even the desire to act like a king in states that have self-rule. Nothing more shocking, nothing more repulsive than such desires can be imagined. Men draw the wrong conclusions and envisage rewards for these actions, they do not see the penalties. I do not mean punishment by the law, which men often evade, but the punishment of degradation itself, which is extremely harsh.

[37] This group of vacillators should be whipped out of society; they are completely criminal and ungodly. They debate with themselves whether they should follow what they see to be right conduct, or whether, with full knowledge, they should corrupt themselves with crime. There is crime in the mere act of deliberation, even if they do not decide on a criminal action. For this reason, since it is wicked merely to think about certain courses of action, they should simply have no place in your deliberations. Furthermore, no deliberation should ever be based on the expectation or assumption that you are going to conceal or cover up your actions. If we have made any progress at all in philosophy, we should be sufficiently convinced that, even if we could hide our actions from all mankind and from all the gods, we should never do anything greedy, unjust, lustful, or intemperate.

[38] To illustrate this truth Plato introduces the well-known Gyges.[27] Once when the ground had split apart after some violent rainstorms, Gyges climbed down into the cleft, as the story goes, and discovered a bronze horse. There were doors in the flanks of the horse, and when they were opened he saw the body of a dead human of unusual size. There was a gold ring on one of his fingers. Gyges removed the ring, put it on his own finger and then went back to the gathering of shepherds

---

[27] Plato, *Republic* II. 359D–360D tells the story of "the ancestor of Gyges the Lydian." It is also told by Herodotus, I. 8–12.

(he was one of the King's shepherds). There he discovered that, when he had turned the bezel of the ring toward his palm, he was invisible to everyone. But he was still able to see everything and became visible again when he had turned his ring back to its proper position. So, making use of the advantage offered by this ring, he seduced the queen, and with her as a helper brought about the death of his master, the King. He removed all those who he believed were standing in his way, and he was completely invisible as he performed these crimes. Thus, with the help of the ring he swiftly rose to be king of Lydia. The point is, if a wise man had this same ring, he would not think he was any freer to do wrong than if he did not have it. Good men seek right conduct, not conduct that has to remain concealed.

[39] At this point certain philosophers,[28] men who may have good intentions but who are not very clever, claim that Plato has propounded an invented and fabulous story as if he were really claiming that this either happened or could have happened. This is the point of the ring and of the fable: if no one were to know, if no one were even to suspect when you were about to commit a crime to gain wealth, power, ascendancy, or sexual satisfaction, if this act were to remain unknown for all time to the gods and to men, would you go ahead and do it? These philosophers say that those conditions could never occur. Of course they cannot possibly occur. But I am asking:

[28] Epicureans. The intent of this paragraph is difficult to grasp without some knowledge of the Epicurean position on wrongdoing. They taught that men are not deterred from crime by an innate law but rather by the fear of being detected. Even a perfect crime would be known to the man who committed it and he could never be absolutely certain that he would never be detected. Without such absolute certainty, his happiness would constantly be disturbed. Therefore crime, for the Epicurean, was not advisable. As for Plato's fable, the Epicureans object to it because the ring of Gyges magically assures that absolute certainty of escaping detection which they claim can *never* come about, and that claim is crucial to their analysis of wrongdoing. Cicero, however, claims that they fail to see that the story is a fable.

suppose the situation that these philosophers say can never arise actually did arise, what would they do? They insist on their objection with perfect stupidity. They keep saying it cannot arise and they persist in that assertion; they fail to see the force of the word "could." When I ask what they would do *if* they could conceal their actions, I am not asking *whether* they could conceal their actions. It is as if I were applying torture of some sort. If they replied that they would perform actions for their personal advantage if they had a guarantee of impunity, they would admit they were criminal types. If they said they would not, they would concede that all immoral acts must be avoided at all times. At this point let me return to my topic.

[40] Many situations commonly occur that confuse our thinking because they appear to be advantageous. These are not cases where one hesitates whether one should deviate from right conduct because of the size of the advantage, for that is criminal on the face of it. The situations occur when a man wonders whether what appears to be expedient can be achieved without a breach of morality. When Brutus denied command to his colleague Collatinus, he might have appeared to be acting unjustly; for Collatinus had been the companion and advisor of Brutus when they were expelling the kings. However, once the leaders had decided that the relatives of Superbus, the very name of the Tarquins and the memory of kingly rule must be removed (an advantageous action insofar as it benefited the country), Brutus' action was by the same token a right action and should have pleased even Collatinus himself.[29] Consequently, what was expedient won out because it was right conduct, and had it not been that it could not possibly have been expedient.

[29] L. Tarquinius Collatinus was a companion of Brutus in the expulsion of the last King of Rome, Tarquinius Superbus. But after that king was expelled, all those who bore the same name were suspect. Hence Cicero's anecdote. In Livy's version (*History of Rome* II.2), Collatinus resigns voluntarily from the consulship.

[41] The same thing was not true in the case of the king who founded Rome.[30] What motivated him was an apparent advantage. When he conceived the idea that it was more expedient to rule alone than with another man, he killed his brother. He ignored both decent respect and human feelings in order to gain what seemed advantageous to him but was really not. He even gave the excuse of the wall, a pretense of right action, neither credible nor completely adequate. [42] The point is, he committed a crime, which I trust he will allow me to assert, whether he is Quirinus the god or Romulus the man.

However, we must not relinquish our own personal advantages and surrender them to other people when we need them ourselves. Each man must protect his own advantage insofar as it can be realized without harm to another person. Chrysippus spoke intelligently on this point, as on many others: "A man running a race in a stadium ought to strive to win and compete as strongly as he can. But by no means should he trip up or push out of the track the runner with whom he is competing. In the same way, in life it is not wrong for each man to try to get for himself what might contribute to his advantage; but he has no right to take this away from another man by force."

[43] Friendships are especially liable to throw moral duties into confusion. It is a violation of your moral duty to fail to perform what you can properly do on behalf of a friend. But to do something unjust on his behalf is also a violation. The rule covering this whole area is short and easily grasped. You must never subordinate your friendships to ambitions that appear to you to be advantageous, election to office, for example, making money, sexual gratification, or other apparently advantageous

---

[30] Romulus is the mythical founder of Rome; Remus was his brother. The legend of the rivalry between the brothers and how Remus taunted Romulus by jumping over the wall he had just built around the newly founded city is retold by Livy and Plutarch. Romulus was later worshipped at Rome under the name Quirinus.

objectives. Yet a good man will never act against the state or against his oath and trust[31] for the sake of a friend, not even if he is actually the judge in a friend's trial. He puts aside the role of friend when he assumes that of judge. He will make concessions to his friendship insofar as he hopes that his friend's case is a good one, and he will arrange a convenient time to hear the case argued insofar as the law permits. [44] When as judge he has to pronounce the sentence under oath, however, he will remember that he is calling a god to witness. "God" means here, in my opinion, his own conscience, which the god himself bestowed on the man; and no human trait is more divine. In the same connection we inherited from our forefathers an excellent formula for petitioning judges, if only we were still using it. It asks him to do "what he can do without violating his oath." This petition has a bearing on those things that a judge can rightly concede to a friend, as I said a short while ago. If all the wishes of our friends had to be carried out, such relationships would not be considered friendships but conspiracies.

[45] I am, you understand, speaking about everyday friendships. No concessions of that sort are possible among wise and perfect men. They say that Damon and Phintias, the Pythagoreans, were devoted to each other in a remarkable way. When Dionysius the tyrant set the day of execution for one of them, the one condemned to death requested a few days delay to arrange for the maintenance of his relatives. The other friend went bail for his appearance in court; he had to die if his friend did not return. When the condemned man returned on the set day, the tyrant was amazed at their mutual trust and asked that they accept him as the third partner in their friendship. [46] Even in friendships, therefore, when you compare what seems advantageous with right action, the mere appearance of advantage should yield, and right action should prevail. Moreover, when

---

[31] The oath he took and the trust granted him when he took public office, such as the praetorship.

friends ask you to do things that are not right, the scruple of conscience and trustworthiness should take precedence over friendship. In this way we will select the correct duty, and it is a principle of selection that we are seeking.

In the government the securing of an apparent advantage very frequently causes wrongdoing, as the Romans did wrong in the sack of Corinth.[32] The Athenians acted even more harshly when they decreed that the people of Aegina, whose strength lay in their war fleet, should have their thumbs cut off.[33] This seemed to be advantageous. Because of its closeness, Aegina threatened the Piraeus. But nothing is advantageous that is barbarous; barbarity is extremely repugnant to the nature of human beings, and we ought to follow nature. [47] Also, those who prohibit foreigners[34] from making use of cities and who keep them beyond the city limits are not advocating a good action. Pennus did this in our fathers' time and Papius recently. It is right to forbid a noncitizen to pretend to be a citizen; a law to this effect was passed by the consuls Crassus and Scaevola, extremely wise men. But it is patently inhuman to deny completely the use of the city to foreigners.

There are some well-known examples of men rejecting what was apparently an advantage to the public in favor of right action. Our country's history is full of examples of this, but most remarkable was an event in the Second Punic War. After suffering defeat at Cannae, the country displayed finer morale than

---

[32] Cicero has already condemned the destruction of Corinth by the Romans; see I.35.

[33] Cutting off their thumbs would make them poor rowers, and rowing was important to the power of ancient warships. The date of the decree is not known.

[34] *Peregrini* ("foreigners") were citizens of any other place than Rome. Rome did not acknowledge double citizenship. At various times in Roman history attempts were made to detect noncitizens who were voting fraudulently. This was the intent of the law of 95 B.C., passed by Crassus and Scaevola. Pennus (126 B.C.) wanted actually to exclude *peregrini* from Rome and Papius (65 B.C.) attempted to revive Pennus' law.

it ever did when affairs were going well. There was no trace of fear, not a whisper about peace. The force of right action is so great that it puts the apparent advantage[35] in the shade.

[48] The Athenians had no way of resisting the invasion of the Persians and decided to abandon the city, to leave their wives and children at Troezen, to embark in their ships and defend the freedom of Greece with their fleet. At that time a certain Cyrsilus was urging them to stay in the city and to open their gates to Xerxes. They put him to death by stoning. He also seemed to be pursuing an advantage, but it was no advantage at all because right action was against it.

[49] After the Greek victory in this war with the Persians, Themistocles announced in the assembly that he had a plan that would insure the safety of the state but that there was no need for it to be widely publicized. He asked the people to send someone forward to whom he might reveal the plan. They sent forward Aristides. Themistocles told him that the Spartan fleet that had been beached at Gytheum could be set on fire secretly; that if this were done, the power of the Spartans would certainly be broken. When Aristides had heard this he returned to the assembly, which was in a mood of great curiosity. He said the plan that Themistocles had conveyed was extremely advantageous, but the opposite of right action. So, because it was not a right action, the Athenians considered it no advantage at all. At the urging of Aristides they voted down the entire plan, which they had not even heard. They acted better than we Romans: we tolerate pirates who pay no taxes and allies who are required to pay tribute money.[36] From the foregoing we may conclude that what is immoral is never advantageous, not even

[35] The apparent advantage to Rome after Cannae was to admit defeat and sue for peace.

[36] Cicero has in mind 1) pirates who were swept off the seas by Pompey and settled into communities that were granted tax privileges and 2) certain cities that were tax-exempt but took sides against Caesar and were later punished with reimposition of the taxes.

when you attain by immorality what you firmly believe to be advantageous. The mere act of mentally equating immorality and advantage is devastating to the character.

[50] As I said above, occasions often arise when expediency seems to conflict with right action. One must then examine carefully whether the conflict is absolute or whether expediency might be combined with right action. The following problems belong in this class: suppose, for example, an honest man imports to Rhodes a large cargo of grain from Alexandria. He imports it during a scarcity and famine among the Rhodians, when there is a very high market for grain supplies. Suppose that this particular man knows that a number of other merchants have set sail from Alexandria and that he saw on his voyage their ships, loaded with grain, making for Rhodes. Is he going to mention this fact to the Rhodians or is he going to keep quiet and sell his grain at the highest possible price? I am imagining an intelligent and honest man. I am asking about the inner debate and reasoning of a man who could not conceal the facts from the Rhodians if he decided that it is immoral; but he does wonder whether it is immoral or not.

[51] In cases of this type Diogenes the Babylonian, the great and impressive Stoic, thinks one thing, while Antipater, his disciple and a very clever man, thinks something else.[37] Antipater thinks everything should be revealed so that the buyer knows fully everything the seller knows. According to Diogenes, the seller has the obligation to point out flaws, insofar as the local law so requires, and to complete the transaction without fraud; but, since he is the seller, he should be eager to sell as profitably as possible. "I imported the goods, I put them on sale, I am

---

[37] Antipater succeeded Diogenes as head of the Stoic school in Athens. Diogenes came to Rome on an embassy in 156 B.C., in the company of two other prominent philosophers. Presumably Cicero is stating what he believes the two philosophers, representing two shades of Stoic opinion, would have said about these hypothetical problems in ethics. Cicero advances his own solutions in section 57 below.

selling my wares no higher than other people, perhaps even for less, when the supply is greater. Who is suffering injustice?"

[52] The reasoning of Antipater starts from another direction: "What are you saying? You ought to protect other men's interests and be of service to human society. You were born under the law, and you know two natural principles that you ought to obey and follow: that your own advantage should benefit the public as well and, in reverse, that the general advantage should be for your benefit. Are *you* going to conceal from other men the relief and supplies that are at hand?" Perhaps the reply of Diogenes would be in these terms: "To conceal is not the same as to keep silent. For instance, I am not now concealing something from you if I do not tell you what the nature of the gods is, what the highest moral good is. These things, were they known to you, would be more useful than knowing about the low price of wheat. But I am under no obligation to tell you everything that would be advantageous for you to hear." [53] [Antipater will say,] "On the contrary, you are under that obligation if you remember that there exists a brotherhood of men that is cemented by nature." "I do remember that," Diogenes will say, "but I wonder whether society is so constructed that nothing belongs to any private individual? If that is the case, men should never sell anything but should give everything away." You realize in this whole argument that no one says, "Although such-and-such is immoral, still I will do it because it is to my advantage." The arguments are that something is advantageous because it is not immoral; or, on the other hand, that something should not be done because it is in fact immoral.

[54] Suppose an honest man sells a house because of some defects that he is aware of but that others do not suspect. Suppose the house is unsanitary but is considered healthy; suppose no one knows that vermin can be seen in all the bedrooms, that the house is built of poor timber and quite dilapidated. No one except the owner knows these things. The question is, if the

seller does not tell these facts to a buyer and sells the house for much more than he thought he could get for it, did he act without justice and without honor?

Antipater says, "He certainly did. Not to give directions to a man who is lost is forbidden at Athens and punished by a public curse.[38] What is the difference between this and allowing a buyer to rush in and through his mistake become the victim of an enormous fraud? It is even worse than not giving directions; it means quite deliberately leading another man into deceit."

[55] Diogenes speaks in rebuttal: "Did the man force you to buy? No, he did not even encourage you. He put up for sale what he no longer wanted; you bought what you wanted. If people advertise a good, well-built house, no one thinks they have practiced deceit, even if the house is neither good nor built on the best plan; the imputation of deceit is a good deal less if they have not praised the house at all. What fraud can there be on the part of the seller when the final decision is up to the buyer? If men do not have to make good everything they mention, do you think that what is not mentioned has to be made good? Really, what is more absurd than having the seller name point by point the faults of what he is selling? What is so bizarre as having the auctioneer, on the orders of the owner, shout aloud, 'I am selling an infested house!'"

[56] In this way, in a number of doubtful cases, right action finds a defender on one side, while on the other side advantageousness finds someone to praise it in these terms: that not merely is it right action to do what seems to be advantageousness, but it is even immoral not to do it. Such is the notorious discrepancy that apparently arises time and again between advantageous actions and right actions. These cases must be decided. I did not expound them merely to raise questions but to

---

[38] Giving directions, along with giving fire, was cited in I.51 as an example of universally recognized duties. Ritual curses were pronounced at Athens by certain priests against those who failed to perform such acts.

resolve them completely. [57] It seems to me, then, that neither the Rhodian grain dealer nor the dealer in real estate should have practiced concealment on the buyers. The definition of "concealment" is not merely "keeping silent" about something: "concealment" is the desire to keep the interested parties in ignorance of what you know in order to contribute to your profit. Who does not understand what kind of concealment that is, what kind of men practice it? Surely those men are not frank, not straightforward, not innocent, not honest, not good men. On the contrary, they are cunning, deceitful, shifty, cheating, evil-minded, sharp operators, schemers, and liars. Is it to any person's advantage to be known by these vicious names and by various others?

[58] If those who keep silent ought to be criticized, what are we to think of people who deceive by using eloquence? Gaius Canius, a witty and rather well-educated Roman knight, once went to Syracuse, not for his vocation but for his vacation, as he used to put it himself.[39] He mentioned repeatedly how he wanted to purchase some small estate or other where he might invite his friends, where he might enjoy himself free from unwanted visitors. When this plan became widely known, a certain banker in Syracuse, Pythius by name, told him that he had a property which, although it was not for sale, Canius could use if he wished, as if it belonged to him. At the same time Pythius invited Canius to dinner in his gardens for the following day, and Canius promised to come.

Then Pythius, who was the friend of all classes of men because he was a banker, summoned the local fishermen and requested them to fish the next day in front of his estate, and outlined what else he wanted them to do. Canius came to dinner at the appointed time. There was a feast richly prepared by Pythius. There was a crowd of fishing boats before their eyes. Each fisherman brought forward the fish he had caught himself

---

[39] Canius makes a similar pun in Latin (*otium—negotium*); cf. I.156.

and spread them at the feet of Pythius. [59] At that point Canius said, "I am astonished at this, Pythius. So many fish? So many fishing boats?" Pythius answered, "What is so astonishing? Whatever fish there are in Syracuse are right here. Here they find fresh water. Those fishermen cannot do without this estate." Canius was aflame with greed and begged Pythius to sell. The latter answered reluctantly at first. Why go into details? Canius got his wish. The greedy, wealthy man purchased the estate at the price that Pythius named, and he bought it furnished. He visited his banker and closed the transaction.

On the next day Canius invited his friends; he himself came early, but he saw no boats, not even an oarlock. He asked the neighbor next door if there were some fishermen's holiday or other, because he did not see any crowd. "No holiday as far as I know," said the neighbor; "but then no one usually fishes here. In fact, I was wondering what was going on yesterday."

[60] Canius was enraged. But what could he do? My colleague and good friend Gaius Aquillius had not yet issued his regulations concerning criminal fraud.[40] When he was asked what criminal fraud was in connection with these regulations, he answered, "when what is represented differs from what is delivered." This definition is admirably succinct, as one would expect from an expert. Pythius and anyone else who delivers something that differs from what he represents is fraudulent, shameless, and malicious. Nothing whatsoever that he does can be advantageous since it carries the stigma of so much immorality.

[61] If Aquillius' definition is a true one, people must remove fraud and dissimulation from their whole life. Accordingly, an honest man will make no pretense about anything, will

---

[40] Aquillius was one of Cicero's colleagues in the praetorship in 66 B.C. The regulations referred to are *formulae;* the *formula* was a document issued by the praetor at a preliminary hearing that determined the charge under which the defendent was to be tried by the judge. Aquillius refined the *formulae* in cases concerning fraud.

not dissimulate anything in order to buy cheaper or sell higher. In fact, fraud of that sort had already been punished by law before the time of Aquillius; by the Twelve Tables, for example, in the case of guardianship. Fraud involving minors had been punished by the *Lex Plaetoria* and also by judgments not based on any specific law, in which was added the phrase "in good faith." In the remaining judgments concerning "good faith"[41] the following phrases are especially prominent: in the judgment about a wife's property, "better and more justly"; in the judgment about alienated returnable property, "honest action among honest men." What conclusions should we draw? Can there be any particle of fraud in what is done "better and more justly"? Or can any action be deceitful or malicious when the law mentions "honest action among honest men"? As Aquillius says, the essence of fraud is contained in "deceit." Consequently, in matters of contracts, falsehood of any kind must be avoided. The seller will not make use of a false bidder, the buyer will not employ someone to bid to his advantage.[42] Both parties,

[41] This sentence lists three laws antedating the *formulae* of Aquillius that dealt with fraud in specific areas. For Twelve Tables see *Glossary;* for *Lex Plaetoria* see *Index of Names.* The third item is not a single law, but refers to the other great source of Roman Law besides statute law, namely, the regulations put forward by magistrates, mainly the praetors, that supplemented statute law; see note to I.32. Where these regulations mentioned the phrase "in good faith," which is the opposite of fraud, they were, in effect, also regulations about fraud, and Cicero therefore adds them to his list. He then proceeds to cite two other parts of the regulations which also deal with offences that resemble fraud; he quotes relevant phrases from these regulations. The "wife's property" is her dowry, a common subject of litigation. "Alienated returnable property" refers to an agreement about transferred property in which the parties agree to an eventual return of the property to the original owner, this agreement depending on the good faith of the parties to the transaction. See further section 70 below.

[42] The seller would of course use a false bidder to inflate the price. How the buyer can use a false bidder is less clear; perhaps Cicero has in mind the use of a confederate to bid so low at the start of the sale that the apparent value of the object being sold is depreciated, or the use of a false bidder to conceal the identity of a well-known collector or agent.

when it comes to naming a price, will name their price once and once only.

[62] In fact Quintus Scaevola the son of Publius once asked that the seller name the price of a farm of which he was the prospective buyer. When the seller did so, Scaevola said that he thought it was worth more. He added 100,000 *sesterces* to the price. No one will deny this was an honest man's action. However, no one says it was the action of a wise man; they would have felt the same if Scaevola had sold a piece of property at a lower price than he could have obtained. This is that well-known plague, the distinction people make between good men and wise men. Ennius[43] makes a phrase out of this distinction: "The wise man is wise for no reason if he has no power to benefit himself." I could see the truth in this statement if Ennius and I could agree on what "to benefit" means.

[63] I see that Hecaton the Rhodian, a disciple of Panaetius, in the book on moral duties he wrote for Quintus Tubero, says "a wise man should maintain his private fortune but do nothing contrary to custom, the laws, and morals. We do not desire to be rich for ourselves alone but also for our children, neighbors, friends, and especially for our country. The resources and wealth of individuals are the wealth of the state." Hecaton would not be very pleased by the action of Scaevola that I mentioned just now. Hecaton implies that he will do anything for his own profit, as long as the action is not expressly forbidden. No great praise or gratitude should be wasted on that man.

[64] Be that as it may, whether fraud is misrepresentation as well as keeping silent or not, there are extremely few affairs that do not provide an opening for out-and-out fraud. Whether or not a good man is best defined as one who helps everyone and harms no one, it is certainly not easy for us to find a thoroughly good man. I conclude that it is never an advantage to

---

[43] Cicero paraphrases a line from Ennius' *Medea*, a tragedy no longer extant (fr. CV in Jocelyn; see note 20, p. 14).

break the law because it is always immoral; and because it is always the right action to be a good man, it is always advantageous.

[65] In the statutes concerning real estate Roman civil law provides that when a sale takes place, the seller should point out the faults that are known to him. According to the Twelve Tables it was enough to be responsible for those faults that were detailed orally, and the man who refused to do so paid a penalty of double the item's cost. In recent times the jurisconsults have instituted a penalty even for failure to mention faults. They decided that whatever fault existed in a property ought to be made good if the seller knew of it, unless it was specifically exempted. [66] For example, once when the augurs were going to conduct observations on the Capitol[44] and had ordered Tiberius Claudius Centumalus, who owned a house on the Caelian Hill, to demolish the high parts of it that interfered with the taking of the auspices, Claudius advertised the building for sale [and sold it]. Publius Calpurnius Lanarius purchased it. The augurs made precisely the same demand of the new owner. After Calpurnius had demolished the house, he happened to learn that Claudius had advertised the house after having been ordered by the augurs to demolish it. He brought Claudius before an arbitrator to discover "what he ought to pay or perform in good faith." Marcus Cato, the father of our present Cato, gave the opinion. (This man has to be named after his son just as others are after their fathers, because he fathered this great intelligence.) As judge, Cato decreed that "since when selling the property he knew this fact but did not declare it, he ought to recompense the buyer for the loss." [67] For this reason he decided that it is vital for good faith that a seller should make his knowledge available to the buyer if he knows about a flaw in the merchandise. If Cato's judgment was correct, it was not right for

[44] For augurs see *Glossary;* they used the Capitoline Hill as an observation post. The Caelian Hill is across the city in the southeasterly direction from the Capitol.

that grain seller to keep silent, nor was it right for the seller of the infested house.

Civil law cannot provide for all such cases involving failure to reveal a fault. Where it does take notice of them, however, the punishments are strict. Marcus Marius Gratidianus, a relative of mine, had sold back to Gaius Sergius Orata the same property that he had purchased from him a few years before. The property was under a servitude[45] [to Sergius], but Marius had not mentioned this in the instrument of purchase. The case was brought to court. Crassus defended Orata, Antonius defended Gratidianus. Crassus laid stress on the law: "the fault should be made good that the seller, in full knowledge, did not mention." Antonius stressed the equity of the case: "since this fault was known to Sergius, who had previously sold the house, there was no obligation to say anything, nor was the man deceived who knew the legal status of what he had bought." [68] I mention this case so that you can fully realize that men of sharp practice did not please our ancestors.

The law and the philosophers eliminate sharp practice in different ways. The law deals with the punishment of acts of criminal cleverness as far as it can; the philosophers try to deal with the understanding and explanation of sharp practice. It is only logical, they claim, never to do anything fraudulent, deceptive, or false. May not "deceit" be defined as "stretching the nets," even if you have no intention of scaring up or driving in game? The game often snares itself, with no one in pursuit. In an analogous way, when you advertise a house, you erect the signboard like a net [you are selling the house because of its faults], hoping someone might run into it without warning. [69] Since morality has begun to decline, I see that men do not normally consider this principle immoral and that neither the law nor civil statutes forbid it: and yet the law of nature forbids it.

---

[45] Some person other than the owner had a right to make some use of the property.

Although I have frequently said the following, I must still say it more frequently: society is in fact the most far-reaching community, involving all men with each other. The bounds are close among those who belong to the same race, even closer among those who belong to the same city. Accordingly, our ancestors understood that the law of nations and the law of states were separate. The law of a state should not necessarily be identified with the law of nations, but the law of nations should include the law of a state. We do not possess any rounded and finished portrait of the true law and its sister, justice: we use mere reflections and sketches. I wish we could obey even them! Those sketches are based on the best models in nature and truth.

[70] How important are those words, "that I not be defrauded or deceived because of you or my trust in you!" How precious are the words, "that there should be honest transactions between honest and openhearted men!" But it is a great question who are "honest" men and what are "honest actions." Quintus Scaevola, the *pontifex maximus,* used to say that all those decisions to which judges added the formula "in good faith" were of extreme importance. It was his opinion that the phrase "in good faith" had wide application, and that this concept was involved in cases of guardianship and corporations, of trusts and commissions, of property bought and sold, or in renting and hiring, transactions which are the very basis of human society. In these cases it requires an eminent judge to decide what services each person should perform, and to whom, especially since the bulk of these cases involves countersuits.

[71] For this reason we must do away with fraudulent dealings and with that malicious cleverness that, of all things, wants to be recognized as wisdom but is very far removed and distant from wisdom. It is the business of wisdom to choose between good and bad things; but malicious cleverness prefers bad things to good things, if bad things are defined as everything that is immoral. The civil law derived from nature condemns malice and deceit not only in the case of real-estate transactions, of

course. In the marketing of slaves, too, it forbids any fraud on the seller's part. The aediles have decreed in their edict that sellers who are aware of a poor state of health, of a tendency to escape, or a record of theft have to report these traits. (The case of heirs is not comparable.[46])

[72] Since nature is the source of law, the foregoing makes it clear that it is in accord with nature to avoid any action to enrich oneself because of another man's lack of knowledge. Life holds no greater curse than apparent intelligence that masks evil-mindedness. That is the source of those uncounted instances that make advantageousness appear to conflict with right action. Is it not rare to find a man who can resist doing an injustice if he has the freedom to do so and can escape completely from men's eyes?

[73] Let us attempt to find that man, if you like, by looking at precisely those cases where the majority of mankind would probably think no law has been broken. In this section there is no need to discuss assassins, poisoners, forgers of wills, extortionists, or embezzlers. Those people should be stamped out, not by talk and argument from philosophers, but by chains and imprisonment. Instead let us inspect the actions of men whom people usually consider honest.

Certain individuals once brought back to Rome from Greece the forged will of Lucius Minucius Basilus, a very wealthy person. In order to make its probate less difficult, they wrote down as cobeneficiaries with themselves Marcus Crassus and Quintus Hortensius, men who were extremely powerful in that era.[47] Although Crassus and Hortensius suspected the will

---

[46] A purchases slaves from B, who shortly afterwards dies and leaves his property to C. A may not then claim damages from C for faults in the slaves that were not revealed at the time of sale.

[47] The forgers hoped by including such powerful men among the heirs to discourage close examination of the document. Crassus and Hortensius would not feel themselves directly guilty of fraud and would receive a small part of the estate.

to be false, still they were not guilty of any collusion and did not reject the slight benefit derived from someone else's crime. The result? Was it not sufficient that they did not *appear* to break a law? I for one do not think so, although I was very fond of Hortensius while he lived and abandoned my hatred for Crassus when he died.[48] [74] But there was no justice, because Basilus had wished Marcus Satrius, his nephew, to bear his own name and had made him his heir.[49] (I am speaking about the Basilus who was *patronus* of Picenum and Sabinum, a shameful brandmark on this age [that name]!) Two of the chief men of the state got the property,[50] Satrius inherited nothing except the name.

Now I argued in the first book[51] that the man who does not ward off or repulse an injustice from his dependents when he can, is acting without justice. But what should we think of the man who not only fails to repulse an injustice, but actually encourages it? Even genuine inheritances do not seem to me examples of right conduct if they have been sought after with evil-intentioned flatteries, by the falsification of moral duty and not by its truth. Yet from time to time advantageousness and right conduct in such affairs appear to be separate courses of action. [75] But not in truth, for the same measuring stick applies to advantageousness that applies to right conduct. No fraud, no

[48] Relations between Cicero and Crassus were strained because Cicero accused him of participating in the Catilinarian conspiracy. They were reconciled shortly before Crassus' death in 53 B.C.

[49] Cicero knew that Basilus' actual will provided that Marcus Satrius should inherit all his property and take his name. For *patronus* in the next sentence see *Glossary*. Cicero is indignant both because Satrius was an adherent of Antony and because the Italian towns he mentions, which enjoyed all the rights of Roman citizenship, should nevertheless need the protection of a *patronus* at Rome.

[50] Cicero may mean "part of the property," since presumably the forgers (whom he does not name) made themselves chief beneficiaries of the forged will.

[51] See I.23.

crime will keep its distance from the man who does not perceive this clearly. "Of course that is right conduct, but this is to my advantage," he may argue. Thinking such thoughts, the man will have the insolence to force apart through his ignorance what nature joined together. That is the origin of deceits, misdeeds, and crimes of all sorts.

If an honest man had such power that, if he snapped his fingers, his name could sneak into the wills of wealthy men, he would not make use of this power, not even if he were perfectly assured that no one at all would even suspect the fact. Suppose, however, that you granted Marcus Crassus the power to have his name written into a will as an heir by the snapping of his fingers when he was in fact not an heir: he would dance in the Forum.[52] A just man, however, and the man whom we acknowledge to be an honest man, would take nothing from anyone to transfer to himself. Whoever doubts this admits that he does not know what an honest man is.

[76] If anyone really wished to unwrap the ideal stored in his own mind, he would soon teach himself that a good man is one who helps anyone he can, who harms no one unless he is wounded by injustice. And then? Does the man not do harm who, by some magic spell or other, arranges to displace the legal heirs and moves himself into their place? Someone will say, "You mean, then, that he is not to do what is advantageous, what is profitable?" No, and let him recognize that nothing is advantageous, nothing is profitable that is unjust. The man who has not learned this cannot be a good man.

[77] When I was a boy I used to hear from my father how Gaius Fimbria, the ex-consul, was the judge in the case of Marcus Lutatius Pinthia, an undoubtedly honest Roman knight. Lutatius had made a bond forfeitable unless he proved he was a good man. Under these circumstances Fimbria told him that he would never pass judgment on this case. He did not want to

---

[52] See I.145, with note, and section 93 below.

deprive a worthy man of his reputation if he judged against him, or appear to have decreed that any man is a good man, when that condition is defined by duties and praises that are beyond enumeration. To that kind of a good man nothing whatsoever can appear to be advantageous that is not also right action. Fimbria—and not only Socrates![53]—recognized that a good man will not dare to perform anything that he would not dare to announce openly. He would not even conceive of such a thing.

Is it not shameful that philosophers debate matters over which even countrypeople do not hesitate? There is a proverb, already worn thin with long use, that had its origin among them. When men praise someone's trustworthiness and honesty they say, "he is a man with whom one can play morra[54] in the dark." The essence of the proverb is this: nothing is advantageous that is not proper, even if you can obtain it and no man can prove anything against you. [78] Do you not see that according to this proverb, no pardon can be granted to our Gyges,[55] nor to the man I was imagining a short while ago, who by snapping his fingers could pile up in one heap everyone's inheritances? Just as you see that immorality, even though it may be hidden, can never become right action, in the same way a wrong action can never be turned into something advantageous, since nature rejects this and fights against it.

[79] Someone might object that, when the rewards are exceptionally great, there is an excuse for breaking the law. At one point Gaius Marius had lived in obscurity for more than six years following his praetorship.[56] He had long been deprived of any hope of becoming consul. It seemed that he was never even going to seek the office. But after he had been sent to Rome by his commander, Quintus Metellus, an outstanding citizen whom he served as lieutenant, he accused Metellus before

[53] See section 11 above and II.43.
[54] See Glossary.
[55] See section 38 above and following.
[56] The normal course of office would allow a two-year interval.

the Roman people in these terms: Metellus was prolonging the war; if they made Marius consul, he would make short work of delivering Jugurtha, dead or alive, into the power of the Roman people. So they made Marius consul;[57] but he turned his back on trustworthiness and justice. By a false accusation he brought hatred down upon a very good and well-respected citizen, whose lieutenant he was and whose mission he was carrying out.

[80] Nor did my relative Gratidianus carry out the duty of a good man. The case occurred when he was praetor, and the tribunes of the people had convened the college of praetors so that financial matters could, by common agreement, be put on a firm footing. In those days the coinage was so unstable that no one was able to find out what he owned. Together they drafted an edict on coinage that included penalties and legal procedures in case of infringement. Both the praetors and tribunes agreed that they would all ascend the *rostra* at the same time after midday. All the other men went their separate ways, but Gratidianus went directly from the *subsellia*[58] to the *rostra* and announced by himself what they had drafted together in joint agreement. That action, as I believe you know, was considered to have done him a great honor. He had statues in every ward, with candles and incense at their feet. Why go into details? No one was ever more beloved by the crowd.

[81] These are the kinds of cases that commonly disturb us when we think about them, when the substance of the violation of fairness does not seem great, and the advantage gained from that violation seems to be very great. For example, it did not seem very immoral to Gratidianus to steal from his colleagues and the tribunes of the people their popularity with the crowd; it seemed to him extremely advantageous to become consul as a result of that theft, and that is what he had planned for himself. But there is one rule for all cases, and I want you to

[57] Marius held the consulship in 107 B.C.; he celebrated his triumph over Jugurtha in 104.
[58] For *rostra* and *subsellia* see *Glossary*.

know it as well as possible: either the action that seems advantageous should not be immoral, or, if it is immoral, it should not appear to be advantageous. What then? Can we decide that either Marius or Gratidianus is a good man? Unroll your thoughts and shake out your mind. See what idea, [outline], or notion of a good man it contains. Does it then suit the notion of a 'good man' to tell lies for his own profit, to accuse others, to forestall, and to cheat? Nothing could be more contrary.

[82] Is there anything of such great value or any advantage so much worth winning that you are willing to lose the glory and reputation of being a 'good man?' What can your so-called advantageousness bring you of value equal to what it can remove if it whisks away your reputation as an 'honest man' and takes away your trustworthiness and justice? What is the difference between a man changed into a real beast and a man who acts like a beast beneath his human appearance?

What about other cases? Some men reject whatever is right and honest as long as they attain power. They are acting just like the man who did not even hesitate to marry a certain man's daughter, since he planned to use his father-in-law's ruthlessness to attain power.[59] It seemed advantageous to him to grasp at more power while leaving the unpopularity to someone else. He did not see how unjust toward the country and how immoral this was. Moreover, the father-in-law himself always used to have on his lips Greek verses from the *Phoenissae*.[60] I will translate them as best I can, not elegantly perhaps, but still so that you can understand the idea:

If there must a breaking of the law, let it be broken
So that you can rule; in other things cultivate respect.

[59] Pompey the Great, who married Caesar's daughter, Julia.

[60] Lines 524–525 of Euripides' *Phoenician Women*. Eteocles, who was supposed to share the rule of Thebes with his brother, justifies his refusal to do so by making an exception of ruling and by saying that it is permissible to break the law to preserve oneself in power. See *Index* under Epigoni.

The speaker, Eteocles, or rather Euripides, should be put to death. He made an exception of the one thing that was criminal beyond all else!

[83] Why are we listing these trivial items, forged wills, fraudulent buying and selling? Look at the man who lusted to be king of the Roman people and master of the whole world—and attained that desire! Whoever says that that is a respectable ambition is out of his mind. He thereby approves the death of law and liberty; he believes that the foul and shocking suppression of the law is something splendid. Someone might assert that, while it is not respectable to reign as king[61] in a city that was free and that ought to be free, still it is advantageous to the man who can do it. What argument, or rather what reproach should I use to try to rescue him from such a gross error? By the immortal gods! Can parricide against the fatherland, the most sordid and repulsive of acts, be an advantageous event for anyone, even though the browbeaten citizens name the man who committed it their father?[62] I conclude that advantage should be guided by right action and in such a way that although the two words clash in meaning, they seem to harmonize in action.

[84] I cannot imagine what advantage is greater in the common man's opinion than that of being king. On the other hand, when I begin to call the argument back to the standard of truth, I find nothing more disadvantageous to the man who attained this position unjustly. Is it possible that there is advantage to

[61] Julius Caesar never took the title *rex*, or "king," which was so hated by the Romans, but his enemies associated the word with him, as did some flattering or ambitious friends.

[62] In this sentence Cicero alludes to the honorary phrase *Pater Patriae*, "Father of the country." Cicero won the right to use the phrase in 63 B.C. after his suppression of the Catilinarian conspiracy; Caesar won it after the battle of Munda in 45 B.C. Since Cicero regarded Caesar as the destroyer of the Republic, the "Father of the country," in his case, was also its parricide.

any man in worries, anxieties, fears by day and night, a life filled with traps and dangers? Accius[63] says,

Many are hostile and treacherous toward my throne,
Few [are] men of good will.

And of what kingdom does he speak? One that was held legally, one handed down from Tantalus to Pelops. How many more anxieties do you think beset the king who oppressed the Roman people themselves with a Roman army, who forced a city to obey him, a city that was not only free but even ruled other people overseas? [85] What wounds and corruptions do you think this man had in his conscience? What man's life can be of any advantage to himself when it is a condition of this life that the man who assassinates him will earn the greatest possible gratitude and glory?[64] If the things that seem most advantageous are not so because they are full of shame and immorality, it should be sufficiently clear that nothing is advantageous that is not right action.

[86] Indeed, this point has often been demonstrated in various situations. A remarkable case happened in the war with Pyrrhus, when a difficult decision was made by Gaius Fabricius, second time consul, and by the Roman Senate. King Pyrrhus had waged an aggressive war against the Roman people, and the struggle with this noble and strong king concerned the power to rule. A deserter came from him into the camp of Fabricius and promised Fabricius that, if he would guarantee him a reward, he would go back to the camp of Pyrrhus just as secretly as he had left it and would assassinate him by poisoning. Fabricius saw to it that this deserter was escorted back to Pyrrhus, and the Senate praised his action. Now, if we are looking for the mere appearance, the common notion, of advantageousness, that deserter acting alone could have done away with that long war and an important enemy of Roman

---

[63] Lines from a play of Accius about the descendants of Pelops. The "king" who oppressed the Roman people with their own army was Caesar.

[64] On the morality of assassinating tyrants, see II.23 and III.19.

rule. But it would have been a great shame and disgrace to overcome an enemy by a crime and not by courage: the struggle with Pyrrhus involved Rome's reputation.[65]

[87] Is it more advantageous to fight an enemy with weapons or with poison? Is there more advantage to Fabricius, who was the equivalent in Rome of Aristides at Athens, or to the Roman Senate, which never distinguished between advantageousness and its self-respect? If men are trying to rule because of the glory involved, they must not entangle themselves in crime: there can be no glory in crime. If the object is to seize power for its own sake by any means available, power cannot be an advantage if it is bound up with shame. A proposal once made by Lucius Philippus, the son of Quintus, was not an advantage. Lucius Sulla, after accepting a payment of money, had granted tax exemptions to certain cities by a decree of the Senate. Philippus urged that they pay taxes again and that we should not return the money they had paid for their exemption. The Senate agreed with him. This was a blot on our government. There is more good faith among pirates than there was in the Senate. The senators might say, in support of their opinion, "But the tax receipts went up, and so it was advantageous." How long will people have the insolence to say that anything is advantageous that is not right action?

[88] Can dislike and hatred be of advantage to any government that should be founded on glory and good will toward its allies? I have often disagreed with my friend Cato. I used to think that he supervised the treasury and tax system too strictly. He usually rejected petitions for adjustments from our allies and never granted the *publicani* a single adjustment of their contracts.[66] We should actually be of good will toward the

---

[65] For Cicero's distinction between wars of domination and wars involving reputation see I.38.

[66] Cicero criticizes the inflexibility of Cato by citing two separate incidents. The *publicani*, who contracted with the Senate to gather taxes, found in 61 B.C. that their contract was very disadvantageous to them. Accordingly they peti-

allies and behave toward the *publicani* just as we usually do with our tenants. An even more compelling reason for this is that the cooperation of the orders is connected with the safety of the state. When Curio was arguing that the case of the Transpadanes was just, it was poor policy to keep on saying, in addition, "Let profit prevail!" He was actually demonstrating that their cause was not just because it would not be profitable to the state.[67] Should he say that it was not advantageous, he would then be asserting that it was just.

[89] The sixth book of Hecaton's work on man's obligations is full of problems like the following:

—"Is it the sign of a good man not to feed his slaves when there is an extreme shortage of grain?" He argues the question on both sides, but finally guides duty by advantage as he conceived of it, rather than by humanity.[68]

—"If something has to be thrown overboard, should a valuable stallion be jettisoned or some decrepit little slave?" In this case feeling for one's property pulls in one direction, feeling for humanity in the other.

—"If a stupid man snatches a plank from a shipwreck, is a wise man going to wrench it away from him if he can?" Hecaton says not, "because there would be violation of rights."

—"What about the master of the ship? Is he going to seize his own property?" "Of course not, no more than on the high seas he would throw a passenger off the ship because it be-

---

tioned the Senate for an adjustment in the contract, but Cato, "supervising the treasury," refused. Cicero goes on to say that this refusal increased animosity between the Senators and the Knights, which upset the cooperation of those two orders of Roman society. The second example of Cato's obstinacy ("to the allies") alludes to his harsh treatment of the Ptolemaic ruler of Cyprus in 58 B.C.

[67] Curio was arguing that residents north of the river Po, who had been granted some limited rights, should be awarded fuller rights, as they desired. Cicero says that he vitiated his argument by pointing out that the new grants were not only just but would also be profitable.

[68] Hecaton's rule is quoted in section 63 above. In this case he apparently would advise that the slaves go hungry.

longs to him. When arrangements have proceeded to the point where the ship is hired, the ship is not the master's but the passengers'."

[90] —"What about this? If there is one plank, two survivors and both of them wise men, should neither one seize it for himself, or should one give way to the other?" "In fact, one should give way; the plank should go to the man whose life is more important either to himself or to his country."

—"What about this? Suppose these considerations are equally valid for both men?" "There will not be a struggle, but one man will yield to the other as if defeated in a lottery of some kind, or by playing *morra*."

—"What about this? If a father were robbing a temple, digging a secret tunnel into the treasury room, for example, should the son point this out to the magistrate?" "That, of course, is absolutely forbidden. In fact he should even defend his father if he were accused." "You mean the fatherland does not take precedence over all other obligations?" "It does by all means, but it is in the fatherland's interest to have citizens who respect their parents."

—"What about this? Suppose a father attempts to become tyrant or to betray the fatherland, will the son keep silent?" "No. On the contrary, he will beseech his father not to do it. If he accomplishes nothing that way, he will argue with his father, even threaten him and finally, if the matter will obviously involve the ruin of the fatherland, he will rank the country's safety higher than the safety of his father."

[91] Hecaton also puts this problem:

—"If a wise man accepts counterfeit money in place of genuine money without noticing it, should he spend it in place of genuine money when he realizes it is counterfeit, if he owes something to someone?" Diogenes says yes, Antipater says no, and I rather agree with Antipater.[69]

---

[69] Diogenes and Antipater appeared as controversialists above in section 51 and following. They reappear here without warning; up to now in this

—"Should a man who knows that the wine he is selling will turn bad mention this or not?" "Not necessary," is Diogenes' opinion. "A good man would," is the thought of Antipater. These situations are comparable to the "controversial laws" of the Stoics.[70]

—"In the sale of slaves, should their faults be announced? Not the ones that, under civil law, cause the slave to revert to the seller if he does not declare these faults, but ones like the slave's tendency to lie, gamble, steal, or drink?" One man thinks they should be declared, the other thinks not.[71]

[92] —"If some man thinks he is selling *orichalcum*, but he is really selling gold, will a good man point out to him that it is gold, or should he buy for one *denarius* what has the value of a thousand *denarii?*"[72] By now it is quite clear what kinds of controversies arise between the philosophers I have named and what my opinion is.

It is a question whether or not men should always keep agreements and promises "not entered upon by constraint or by deceit," as the praetors always say. Suppose someone has given a medicine for dropsy to someone else and has stipulated that, if he is cured by it, he should never afterward use the same medicine. Suppose that the medicine did cure the patient, and some years later he falls victim to the same disease. But this time the man with whom he made the agreement refuses him permission to use the medicine. What should be done? Since the man who refuses the medicine is acting inhumanly and since he suffers no personal injury if the medicine is used, the man who is ill must act to preserve his own life and health.

---

passage the solutions of the hypothetical problems have been based on Hecaton's rule.

[70] Stoic logicians distinguished between absolute laws and laws subject to discussion.

[71] The laws governing the sale of slaves were also mentioned in section 71 above.

[72] For *orichalcum* and *denarius* see *Glossary*.

[93] What about this? Suppose someone proposed to make a wise man his heir and to leave him in his will one hundred million *sesterces*. But suppose the wise man were required to dance publicly in the Forum[73] by daylight before he could receive his inheritance, and suppose he promised he would do this because otherwise the wealthy man would not put him in his will as heir. Should he carry out the promise or not? I would want him not to make the promise, and I consider this in accord with respectability; but since he promised, it would be more correct to break the promise than to carry it out if he considers it degrading to dance in the Forum. It would be more correct for him to receive nothing from the inheritance than to take something, unless perhaps he applied the cash so derived to help in some great crisis or other in the state; in that case even dancing would not be immoral, since he would be doing it in the interest of the fatherland.

[94] The particular promises that you should not keep are the ones that are not advantageous to those to whom you made the promise. To return to examples from mythology, Sol told his son Phaëthon that he would do whatever his son wished. Phaëthon requested to be allowed to drive his father's chariot. He was carried through the sky but went up in smoke after being struck by a thunderbolt before he could return to earth.[74] How much better it would have been in this story if the father had not kept his promise!

What about the promise that Theseus forced Neptune to carry out?[75] After Neptune had granted him three wishes, he wished for the death of his son Hippolytus because he had

[73] See I.145, with note.

[74] The best-known version of this story is in Ovid's *Metamorphoses* I.750 ff. The young Phaëthon lost control of the sun-chariot and did much damage to the world until Zeus destroyed him.

[75] The myth of Theseus and Hippolytus was also used in I.32 as an example of disadvantage in honoring promises. The myth forms the basis of Euripides' *Hippolytus*.

aroused his father's suspicions with his step-mother. When Theseus got what he wished, he was stricken with profound grief.

[95] What about this? After Agamemnon had dedicated to Diana as a sacrifice the most beautiful creature born in his kingdom in that year, he had to immolate Iphigenia; nothing more beautiful than she, of course, had been born that year. Agamemnon should have avoided carrying out his promise rather than permit such a horrible crime. I conclude that sometimes you should not fulfill promises and that objects left on deposit with you should not always be returned. If someone has deposited a sword with you when he was of sound mind, but asks it back when he is insane, it would be a transgression to give it back; it is your duty not to return it.

What about this? If a man who deposited money with you should wage war against the fatherland, should you return what he left with you or not? No, I believe not, for you would be acting against the state, and the state should be dear to you beyond everything else.

By these arguments, many actions that naturally appear to be right actions turn into wrong actions in certain circumstances. To fulfill promises, to abide by agreements, to return things entrusted to you: these turn into wrong actions if the advantage you hoped to secure has disappeared. I think I have said enough about actions that, contrary to justice and under the guise of wisdom, assume the appearance of being advantageous.

[96] In the first book I derived responsibilities from the four sources of right action.[76] Let us follow that plan and retain the same headings as I show you how great the contrast is between apparent (but false) advantageous actions and right actions. The argument about wisdom, which malicious cleverness attempts

---

[76] Cicero returns to the four cardinal virtues: wisdom, justice, courage, and temperance. He points out that the first two have been covered by the discussion that extends from section 7 to section 95 of this book.

to imitate, is complete. I have also dealt with justice, which is always advantageous. Two divisions of right action remain. The first of these is displayed in the heroism and courage of a noble spirit; the other is displayed in the formation and regulation of the spirit by temperance and self-control.

[97] One of his tricks seemed advantageous to Ulysses, at least as some tragic poets tell the tale. (Homer, our best authority, never mentions that Ulysses used this particular deceit.) The tragedians, however, accuse him of attempting to evade military service by pretending to be mad. This plan was not right action. Someone might attempt to claim that it was an advantage to Ulysses to be king and to live quietly at Ithaca with his parents and his wife and son. "Do you think," they might say, "that any distinction won in daily toil and in dangers can compare with tranquillity like that?" I believe that such tranquillity must be rejected and discarded, because I do not think that anything is advantageous that is not also right action. [98] What do you think men would have said about Ulysses if he had persisted in that pretense? Even after he had performed unsurpassed feats in the war, Ajax still spoke about him in these terms:

> He alone set aside his oath, as everyone here knows,
> The very man who was the leader in pledging it.
> He decided to pretend to be mad, so that he did not have to
>   go along.
> If the clear-sighted wisdom of Palamedes
> Had not spied out the evil-minded cunning of that man,
> He would have evaded the fulfillment of his sworn oath for
>   all time.[77]

[99] For Ulysses it was really better to fight it out with the enemy and even with the waves, which is what he did, than to desert

[77] In this quotation from a play of Pacuvius, Ajax describes Odysseus' (= Ulysses') attempt to evade military service in the Greek expedition against Troy. The "oath" was the promise of the leading Greeks to support Menelaus in seeking revenge for the rape of Helen. Palamedes devised a trick that revealed that Odysseus' apparently insane actions were in fact simulated.

the Greeks when they agreed to wage war against the barbarians.

Let me pass over mythologies and foreign tales. Let me come to a real action, and a Roman one. Marcus Atilius Regulus, then consul for the second time, had been captured by a trick in Africa. His captor was the commander Xanthippus from Sparta, under the generalship of Hamilcar, the father of Hannibal. They sent Regulus to the Roman Senate under oath, the condition being that Regulus himself should return to Carthage unless the Romans agreed to return certain captive nobles to the Carthaginians. When he came to Rome, he saw how attractive his personal advantage would be, but he decided this advantage was false, as the result makes clear. The attraction was this: to remain in his fatherland, to live in his own home with his wife and his children, and to retain his rank of consular authority, adopting the opinion that the defeat he had sustained was nothing extraordinary in the fortunes of war. Who do you suppose denied that these things are advantageous? Regulus, with his nobility and courage, said they were not advantageous.

[100] Do you require any more reliable authorities? It is the essence of nobility and courage not to fear anything, to hold in contempt anything merely mortal, and to assume that it is possible to endure anything that can happen to a man.

What did Regulus do? He came into the Senate and explained his commission, he refused to pronounce his opinion and said that, as long as he was bound by the oath given to the enemy, he was not a senator. He even said (someone or other will say, "What a foolish man! How he fights against his own advantage!") that it was not a good idea to return the Carthaginian prisoners. He explained that they were young men and good leaders, while he was already worn out by old age. His prestige prevailed, the prisoners were not released, Regulus himself went back to Carthage, and neither his affection for his fatherland nor for his own family held him back. Of course, at that point he knew very well that he was returning to an extremely cruel enemy and refined tortures, but he maintained his belief that he must respect his oath. The Carthaginians murdered him by forced lack of sleep. Yet, I maintain that even so the reasoning for his decision was more valid than if he had stayed in Rome, an old man, a man who had once surrendered to the enemy, a man of consular rank who had broken his oath.

[101] "But he acted foolishly," someone might reply. "Not only did he argue against sending back the prisoners, but he even dissuaded others who wanted to return them!" In what way did he act foolishly? Did he act foolishly even though he was helping the government? In fact, is it possible that an action that harms the state can be of advantage to an individual citizen?

Men distort truths that are the very basis of nature when they force a separation between advantageousness and right action. Granted, each one of us is seeking his own advantage. We are pulled along toward that end, and in no way can we act differently. Who would run away from advantages, or rather, who does not pursue them with the greatest eagerness? But I cannot discover any advantage anywhere except in honor, in glory, and in right action. Therefore I consider these goals to be primary and supreme over all others. Advantage should not be thought of as something separate and glorious in itself, but as something bound up with these higher goals.

[102] Someone might say, "But what is there in an oath, anyway? Are we afraid of the anger of Jupiter? There is no reason for that fear. Let me cite an opinion common to all philosophers, both those who believe that a god himself has no worries and does not interfere with mortals and also those[78] who think a god is always active and always working in the world: they both assert that God never grows angry and does not do any harm. What greater harm could an angry Jupiter have done than the harm Regulus willingly caused himself? There was no power in religion that could have upset the advantage Regulus could have enjoyed, had he remained in Rome."

Someone else might say, "Was he afraid of acting immorally?

[78] The two schools of philosophy are the Epicureans and Stoics respectively.

As the saying goes, his problem was to choose the lesser of two evils. After all, was the immorality really as full of evil as his torture? And then there is also that quotation from Accius:[79]

—Did you break your oath?
—I did not give it, and I do not give it
To anyone at all who is without trustworthiness.

Although an impious king said this, still it is brilliantly said."

[103] Just as I might say that some things appear to be advantageous that really are not, these critics also say that some things appear to be right actions that really are not. "For example, the very act of returning to face torture in order to keep an oath seems to be a right action. But it should not have been considered right. He should not have honored an oath that he made because the enemy applied force." They also assert that almost anything that is extremely advantageous might turn out to be right action, even if it did not seem so previously.

These are pretty much the points they raise against the conduct of Regulus. Let us examine the initial objections.

[104] "There was no need to fear that Jupiter in his anger would do harm; he neither gets angry nor does harm." This argument has no more force against the oath of Regulus than against any oath in the world. Where an oath is involved, our attention should not be focused on fear of possible punishment but on the essence of taking the oath itself. An oath is a sacred and binding undertaking; and what you promise as an obligation, with God as witness, as it were, you must honor. At that point it does not involve the wrath of the gods, which does not exist, but it involves justice and trust. Ennius, you remember, wrote a famous line:

A nourishing Trust, fitted with wings, and the oath of Jupiter![80]
The man who violates an oath violates Trust, which our ances-

---

[79] From the *Atreus* of Accius. The implication of the verses is that an oath given to a faithless enemy should not be considered binding. The quotation is referred to again in section 106.

[80] This line, identifying Trust with the word of Jupiter, comes from a tragedy of Ennius, possibly his *Thyestes* (fr. CLXXXIV in Jocelyn; see note 20 on p. 14).

tors understood to be "the neighbor of Jupiter Optimus Maximus on the Capitoline," as a speech of Cato puts it.

[105] "But still, even Jupiter in his wrath would not have done more harm to Regulus than he did to himself." Of course, if it were true that nothing is evil except suffering. However, philosophers with the strongest authority contend that suffering is by no means the worst evil, but in fact is not an evil at all. Please, I entreat you, do not slander the testimony of those philosophers, which is not slight, nor that of Regulus himself, who, I suspect, is the most impressive witness of all. Indeed, what more authoritative witness can we want than a leader of the Roman people who willingly underwent torture to remain true to his duty?

As for their third contention that "the lesser of two evils" should be chosen, that is, that one should act immorally rather than undergo destruction: is there any evil greater than immorality? If there is something not very agreeable in a deformity of the body, how great must seem the distortion and ugliness of a demoralized soul! [106] That is why men who judge these matters very strictly go so far as to say that the *only* evil is immorality; and even those[81] whose judgment is less strict do not hesitate to call that the greatest evil. As for the quotation about an oath cited above,

I did not give it, and I do not give it
To anyone at all who is without trustworthiness,

the poet was justified in writing it because he was dealing with Atreus and had to be consistent with the character. If anyone assumes that an oath sworn to an untrustworthy person is void, he should beware, because he might thereby be creating a loophole for perjury.

[107] [There is also the law of war. Your fidelity to an oath often has to be maintained with an enemy.] An oath given in such a way that the mind intends to keep the oath must be observed. If the oath is not so sworn and is then not kept, there is no perjury. For example, if you do not give to some pirates

---

[81] The Stoics were "very strict" on this point, the Peripatetics "less strict."

the ransom you agreed upon for your life, there is no deceit, not even if you agreed under oath to pay a ransom. By definition a pirate is not on the list of fair enemies but rather is everyone's common enemy. No one should enter into an agreement or take an oath with him. [108] Swearing to something false is not perjury by itself. Rather, perjury is failure to perform an action which you have sworn to do "upon your conscience," as the traditional phrase expresses it. Euripides wrote cleverly,

I swear in words, my mind remains unsworn.[82]

In fact, Regulus had no right to perjure himself and renounce the conditions and agreements of war between enemies to which he consented. The Romans were conducting hostilities with a legally and properly declared enemy, to whom the Fetial law applied and many treaty regulations.

If the Romans had not observed this code of laws, the Senate would never have put a number of famous men in chains and surrendered them to the enemy.

[109] When Titus Veturius and Spurius Postumius were consuls for the second time, a disastrous battle took place near Caudium, and Roman legions were sent under the yoke. But the consuls were surrendered to the Samnites because they had made peace with them and had done so without the consent of the people and the Senate.[83]

In the same era, Tiberius Numicius and Quintus Maelius, who were then tribunes of the people, were surrendered to the Samnites in order to repudiate their peace with them. The peace had been concluded only on their authority. In fact, the same Postumius who had been previously surrendered at the time of Caudium was among those who advocated and urged this surrender.

Many years later Gaius Mancinus met the same fate. He spoke in the Senate in favor of the motion to surrender himself to the

---

[82] Line 612 of Euripides' *Hyppolytus.*

[83] After the Roman defeat at Caudium in 321 B.C., the Senate refused to ratify the battlefield agreement entered into by the consuls.

Numantini,[84] because he had concluded a treaty with them without authority from the Senate. Lucius Furius and Sextus Atilius introduced a *senatus consultum* to this effect, and when it passed, he was turned over to the enemy. Mancinus acted more correctly than Quintus Pompeius, who, in the same situation,[85] refused to consent, and the law did not pass. Here, what seemed advantageous had more power than right action. In the previous cases, however, the false appearance of advantageousness was overcome by the authority of right action.

[110] The critics of Regulus argue, "But an action performed under duress should not have been binding."[86] As if duress could really be applied to a brave man!

"Then why did he set out for the Roman Senate, especially since he intended to dissuade it from returning the captives?" These people are criticizing the most impressive aspect of the case. Regulus did not act on his own decision, but he undertook the mission so that there could be a decision by the Senate. The Romans would certainly have returned the captives to the Carthaginians, except that Regulus himself advocated the opposite decision in the Senate. Had the captives been returned, Regulus would have remained safe in his fatherland; but he did not think their return was advantageous to his fatherland, and so he believed it was right action for himself both to declare that opinion and to suffer.

As to their assertion that an extremely advantageous action may prove to be right action, they should rather say that it is truly right, not that it may prove to be right. There is nothing advantageous that is not also right action. Nothing is right action because it is advantageous; but because something is morally right, it is advantageous. Because of this, one will not find

---

[84] Mancinus negotiated a peace with the Spanish defenders of Numantia in 137 B.C.

[85] That is, had also made a peace settlement in Spain that was not acceptable to the Senate at Rome, and he was also present at the debate.

[86] The argument returns to the case of Regulus.

it easy to select from among the many splendid stories in Roman history one more praiseworthy or more outstanding than that of Regulus.

[111] Amidst all this praise of Regulus one fact remains most worthy of admiration: that Regulus himself advised that the captives should not be released. Nowadays it seems to us an amazing thing that he went back, but in those days he could not act differently. To praise that action, therefore, is not praise of Regulus, but of his age; for our ancestors believed that the binding force that would keep trust most securely in place must be a man's given word. The laws of the Twelve Tables show this, as well as the "sacred" laws, and the treaties by which faithfulness is enforced, even with the enemy. The investigations and penalties imposed by the censors also show this: their judgments were stricter about oaths than about anything else.

[112] For example, when Lucius Manlius the son of Aulus was dictator, Marcus Pomponius, a tribune of the people, served notice of an indictment on him because of his own accord he had added on a few days to the term of his dictatorship. Pomponius also accused Manlius because he had banished his son from human company and had ordered him to take up residence in the country. (This was the son who was later given the name Torquatus.) But when the young man heard that this trouble was being caused for his father, he is said to have hastened to Rome and arrived at dawn at Pomponius' house. When his arrival was announced to Pomponius, he thought that the young man was angry and was going to report some evidence against his father. Pomponius got up from bed, sent all witnesses away and ordered the young man to approach him. When the young man entered, he immediately drew out his sword and swore that he would kill Pomponius on the spot unless he swore that he would drop the charges against his father. Fear forced Pomponius to swear this oath. He later reported the incident to the people. He told them why it was necessary for him to withdraw from the case, and he

dropped the charges against Manlius.[87] That shows how strong an oath was in those days. [And this Titus Manlius is the one who earned his *cognomen*[88] at the Anio by tearing off the collar of a Gaul whom he had killed after being challenged by him. It was in his third consulate that the Latins were dispersed and put to flight near the Veseris. He was among the foremost great men, and the same person who was so thoughtful toward his father was later severely strict toward his own son.]

[113] Just as it is proper to praise Regulus for keeping his sworn oath, it is proper, by the same token, to blame those ten Roman prisoners whom Hannibal sent under oath to the Senate after the battle of Cannae, if it is a fact that they did not return.[89] The Carthaginians had captured some Roman camps, and the ten Romans swore that they would return there unless they obtained terms for ransoming prisoners. Not all writers describe their behavior in the same way: Polybius, among the most reliable authorities, says that of the ten high noblemen who were sent on that occasion nine went back, since the Senate did not grant the terms demanded. One of the ten remained in Rome: he *had* gone back a short time after he had left the camp, on the pretext of having forgotten something. He argued that by *that* return to the camp he had freed himself from his sworn

---

[87] Another version of the story of the cruel dictator Manlius is told by Livy in his *History of Rome* VII.3–5. In Livy's account Manlius incurs the hostility of the people because, although he was named dictator specifically in order to carry out an ancient apotropaic ritual, he used his term in office to recruit armies by ruthless methods and wage a war against the Hernici. Livy says that Manlius banished his son because the young man was slow in speech. But Livy, like Cicero, emphasizes the loyalty of the son to the father who treated him cruelly.

[88] The *cognomen* of T. Manlius was Torquatus; tradition connected this name with *torquis*, a collar or neck-chain worn by the Gaul whom Manlius defeated in single combat.

[89] The same episode is referred to in I.40. Cicero expresses uncertainty because the historians he remembers or has consulted are in conflict. The case is closely parallel to that of Regulus.

oath. The argument was wrong, for fraud aggravates perjury, it does not lessen it. Therefore this was foolish cleverness that mocked and mimicked wisdom. The Senate decreed that the deceiver, clever as he was, should be led in chains back to Hannibal.

[114] But the following is the most impressive example: Hannibal held eight thousand men captive, not captives from the battlefield or deserters who were afraid of death, but soldiers who had been abandoned in camp by the consuls Paullus and Varro. The Senate did not think those men should be ransomed, although it could have done so at small expense. The Senate ruled that Roman soldiers were trained either to win or to die. Polybius[90] writes that the optimism of Hannibal was checked when he learned of the decision, because the Senate and the Roman people had maintained such a heroic spirit when things were in a state of disaster. Thus it is that actions that seem advantageous are put in the shade when they are compared to right action.

[115] [However, Gaius Acilius, who wrote his Roman history in Greek, says that there were more men who returned to the camp by the same trick, hoping to be released from their sworn oath; he says they were listed by the censors with all the marks of disgrace.] Let this end the discussion. It is quite clear that actions performed in a shrinking, timid, cast-down, and broken spirit are not advantageous because they are shameful, dishonorable, and immoral. Such would have been the conduct of Regulus if he had given advice about the captives that seemed beneficial to him instead of beneficial to the state, or if he had wished to stay at home.

[116] There remains the fourth category of virtue that is defined by propriety, moderation, modesty, restraint, and tem-

[90] Polybius, VI.58. Severity toward their own men who had been taken prisoner was traditional among the early Romans, although there were some examples of ransom being paid. This episode followed the battle of Cannae, 216 B.C., which was a disastrous defeat for the Romans.

perance. Can anything be advantageous that is opposed to such a multitude of virtues? But there are those Cyrenaics, followers of Aristippus, and the followers of Anniceris, so-called philosophers, who defined the *summum bonum* as pleasure.[91] They thought that virtue should be praised because it created pleasure. When those men were no longer in vogue, Epicurus appeared, an advocate and promoter of practically the same teaching. If our purpose is to defend and maintain right action, then we must fight these men with "troops and horseflesh," as the saying goes.

[117] Suppose that an entirely happy life (and not merely an advantage) is defined as a strong physical constitution accompanied by the assurance that the constitution will remain healthy. Metrodorus puts forward this claim. This supposed advantage, this *summum bonum,* which is what they call it, will certainly come into conflict with right action. First of all, will there be a place for wisdom? Will its function be to seek out titillations from every direction? But how wretched it is to use a virtue as a slave to pleasure! What is the function of wisdom? To choose intelligently among pleasures? Granted that nothing may be more attractive than that, yet what can conceivably be more immoral? As for courage, which is contempt for pains and hard work, what place does a man assign to it who concludes that pain is the greatest evil? It may be that Epicurus often speaks rather bravely about pain, as he says. Yet one should pay attention, not to what he actually says, but what might be the logical thing to say for a thinker who defines good as pleasure, evil as pain.

---

[91] From this point to the end of section 119 Cicero deals briefly with the attitude of the hedonist schools toward virtue. He mentions four different schools of hedonism: the Cyrenaics, the followers of Anniceris, Epicurus, and Metrodorus. He has not taken any pains to distinguish their doctrines, but lumps them together as philosophies that encourage the pursuit of pleasure. He then tries to imagine what place the four cardinal virtues will have in a life devoted to that pursuit.

If I were to listen to him on the subject of self-control and temperance—well, he says, of course, many things in various passages. "But the water won't run," as they say. Who can praise self-control when he seeks the *summum bonum* in pleasure? Everyone knows that moderation is the enemy of sensuality, while sensuality is the close ally of pleasure.

[118] In discussing wisdom, courage, and moderation, these philosophers twist and turn however they can and not without cleverness. They bring wisdom into their system under the guise of knowledge that provides pleasure but drives out pain. They also work courage in somehow or other when they draw up a plan for ignoring death and for enduring pain. They even bring in moderation. They of all people can not do this very easily, but they find the means somehow, for they assert that the degree of pleasure is determined by the removal of pain. Justice, for them, shuffles along, or rather lies there useless, along with all those good qualities that are revealed in human association and in the cooperative structure of human society. There can be no goodness, no generosity, no courtesy, no more than there can be friendship, if these qualities are not sought out for their own sake, but are considered to be relative to pleasure or to advantageousness.

Let us summarize. [119] Just as I have demonstrated that there is no advantage that conflicts with right action, in the same way I assert that all pleasure is opposed to right action. For this reason I conclude that Calliphon and Dinomachus should be reprimanded more severely: they thought they would solve the dilemma if they yoked pleasure with right action—like mating human beings with cattle. Right action does not accept that relationship, it despises and rejects it. Nor in truth can the supreme good, which ought to be simple, be a mixture and patchwork of conflicting elements.

[120] But I have written more on this subject in another book,[92] for it is a great topic. Now to the point. Enough, I think,

---

[92] Cicero discussed the relationship of virtue and pleasure in Book Two of his *De Finibus Bonorum et Malorum*.

has been said above about how the problem is to be solved if an apparently advantageous action conflicts with a right action. However, even if we admit that pleasure has a semblance of advantageousness, no connection between this and right action is possible. We may want to assign some value to pleasure; perhaps we can say that there is something decorative about it, but assuredly nothing of real usefulness.

[121] Marcus, my son: you now have a present from your father that is valuable, at least in his own opinion. But it will be as valuable to you as you make it. Of course, you have to make room for these three books as house guests among your notes on Cratippus' lectures. If I had come to Athens myself, I believe you would occasionally have been my student, too. I would certainly have made the voyage, except that my fatherland raised its clear voice and called me back from my journey. You might have heard me speak in my own voice, but now it has reached you in these books. Devote as much time to them as you are able, which means as much time as you wish. When I hear at last that you delight in this kind of knowledge, then I hope we shall be pursuing it with each other. In the meantime, I shall have to address you across the distance that separates us. So farewell, my Cicero. Please believe that you are dear to me beyond all others, but I will cherish you even more if you take pleasure in teachings and lessons like these.

GLOSSARY

aedile. These were annually elected officials who had charge of temples, archives, public buildings, markets, and games in Rome. They were also in charge of grain supply and other details of life in the city. As commissioners in charge of producing games and festivals, aediles had the opportunity to capture popular favor by spending large sums of their own money, an abuse that Cicero condemns (II.57) while recognizing its importance to political advancement. The minimum age for election was thirty-six.

apophthegmata. Greek: "wise saying; a terse, witty proverb or maxim;" English: "apothegm." Various Romans made collections of them (I.104; III.1).

as. The smallest Roman coin, made of copper.

augurs. This group of sixteen official diviners preserved the knowledge and practices by which the will of the gods might be determined. The decisions of the augurs were the auspices, which could be favorable or unfavorable. If not favorable, public business or the project contemplated was temporarily suspended or abandoned. The readings of omens in the sky (see III.66), in the behavior of animals, as well as the interpretation of extraordinary natural manifestations were the means by which the augurs reached their decisions. Since public events, such as elections, could be stalled or even declared invalid because of unfavorable auspices, the augurate was a position of political importance.

auspices. *See* augurs.

censor. Every five years two censors were elected at Rome for an eighteen-month term. Their task was to supervise the census, to maintain the lists of senators, and to investigate and punish irregularities in personal conduct. The exclusion of citizens from the voting lists was one way of applying penalties (see also III.115).

cognomen. This was the third of the three traditional personal names of the Romans. It was either the family name or frequently referred to some personal characteristic of appearance or distinction. Cicero alludes to how Manlius Torquatus acquired his *cognomen* (III.112) and to the *cognomen* of Crassus, *Dives*, "Rich" (II.57).

consul. Every year two consuls were elected at Rome; they were the chief magistrates, presided over the Senate, and held the chief military authority; their term was usually extended one year to allow them to serve as proconsul outside of Rome, where they governed a province or held a military command. The candidate for consul had to be forty-two years old and ordinarily would already have served as quaestor, aedile, and praetor, though, as Cicero notes, the aedileship might be omitted (II.58). Roman years were expressed by naming the consuls, e.g., "when M. Tullius Cicero and L. Antonius were consuls" = 63 B.C.

curule office. Certain magistracies at Rome (consuls, praetors, censors, and curule aediles) entitled their holders to use a special ivory chair on public occasions. This was the *sella curulis* and hence these magistracies were collectively called curule offices.

deme. A topographic division of Athens; all Athenian citizens were registered in one of the demes, which served as administrative units of local government.

denarius. A small silver coin equal to one-fourth of a sesterce.

dictator. A magistrate who could be appointed for a term of six months to exercise absolute authority during an emergency. He could raise, command, and discharge armies, could punish at will, and all other magistracies except tribune of the people were suspended during his term. The office was abused by Sulla and Caesar and was abolished soon after the latter's assassination.

ephors. One of five magistrates of Sparta who formed a board of advisors to the kings of Sparta and kept surveillance on their activities.

eukairia. Greek: "the right moment." Cicero contrasts this term with *eutaxia*, "the right order or arrangement," in his discussion of correct order and timing in actions (I.142).

eutaxia. *See* eukairia.

Fetial law. The *Fetiales* were a board of twenty priests who administered the technicalities of formal relations between Rome and other states. The important duty of these priests was to apply the Fetial law that governed the making of treaties and the rituals of declaring war.

guest-friend. Receiving a man as a guest in your home obligated him to show you the same courtesy. This courtesy extended to an informal, but frequently important relationship between leading citizens of different countries (II.64; 82).

hormai. Greek: "impulses, eager desires."

hostis. Cicero discusses this word (I.37) to show that the older Romans used it to mean merely a "stranger or foreigner," even though the man was in reality a formal enemy, or *perduellis*. In Cicero's own time the word *hostis* meant "enemy." Cicero claims that the increasing harshness in the meaning of the word illustrates the loss of diplomatic nicety in relations with formal enemies of the state.

jurisconsults. Lawyers; experts in legal knowledge.

kathekon. Greek: "fitting, proper," a Stoic technical term.

katorthoma. Greek: "a virtuous, upright action," a Stoic technical term.

knights. A class of citizens at Rome who engaged especially in banking and contracting; membership in the class was determined by a property qualification (400,000 *sesterces*), and the class wielded considerable power because of its wealth and cohesion.

mina. A sum of money in the Greek monetary system, equal to one hundred drachmas; a fairly large amount.

modius. A Roman dry measure approximately equivalent to one peck.

morra. A game in which each player suddenly displays a number of fingers while the other player tries to guess and match the number. Since seeing the partner's fingers is crucial, to play the game in the dark implies unlimited trust in the partner's honesty.

orichalcum. Some alloy of copper, or a yellow ore; perhaps brass.

pathe. Greek: "emotions, passions."

patronus. A man who represented and protected by his position, influence, and legal knowledge another man, or group, or perhaps whole towns and provinces, who were his *clientelae*. Slave owners would become *patroni* of their freed slaves, and generals became *patroni* of peoples they had conquered.

perduellis. *See* hostis.

phronesis. *See* sophia.

pontifex. The numerous temples and cults of Rome were in the charge of groups of priests who also performed various duties in the state, such as keeping records of notable events and supervising the calendar. The chief official in religious matters was the *pontifex maximus*, who had an official residence, supervised the Vestal Virgins, and published the decisions of the boards of priests.

praetor. One of the eight officials of Rome elected annually to administer legal matters between Roman citizens, and between Roman citizens of foreigners. Praetors and propraetors were also administrators of provinces. The age for election was thirty-nine.

prepon. Greek: "what is proper, fitting."

proconsul. *See* consul.

propraetor. *See* praetor.

publicani. This name was given to those men who contracted to collect taxes and duties for the government or to construct public works. They were drawn from the class of knights.

quaestor. The quaestors were elected annually and served as finance officers in Rome (*quaestor urbanus*) and the provinces. The minimum age for election was thirty.

rostra. The *rostra* was a platform in the Forum that served as a place from which orators would address large crowds. Its front was decorated with the rams of captured ships. Below and in front of the *rostra* were benches (*subsellia*) reserved for the use of tribunes of the people.

Senate. The Senate was the governing body of Rome; it prepared legislation, and a resolution of the Senate (*senatus consultum*) had great power if not strictly the force of law. The Senate appointed special courts, administered finances, dealt with foreign relations, appointed governors of provinces, and controlled religious matters. It was a large body composed mainly of men who had held magistracies.

senatus consultum. *See* Senate.

sesterces. The *sesterce* was a small coin equivalent to four *denarii*. Large amounts of money were commonly expressed in thousands of *sesterces*.

sophia. Greek: "wisdom, knowledge." Cicero repeats a distinction between *sophia*, "contemplative, philosophical wisdom," and *phronesis*, "practical wisdom, prudence." The equivalent Latin words are *sapientia* and *prudentia* (I.153).

subsellia. *See* rostra.

summum bonum. The phrase means the "highest good" and refers to the ideal goal of a philosophy, e.g., for the Stoics to live in harmony with nature; for the Epicureans to live a life of pleasure (i.e., a life without pain).

tibia. This is the Roman name of the Greek *aulos*, a reed pipe.

tithe-offerings. An offering of one-tenth of property or spoils made to Hercules usually before or after an important venture. The offering was spent on an expensive sacrifice from which the people would benefit by feasting on the sacrificial animals afterwards. Cicero cites the case of Orestes (II.58), who offered such a sacrifice merely to capture popularity.

tribune (military). An officer in the Roman army; six military tribunes shared the command of each legion.

tribune (of the people). One of the ten annually elected officials who represented the interests of the lower classes. Their chief power was the right to block the action of any other magistrate and the right to hold assemblies of the people to advance legislation. Cicero frequently views their activities as disruptive, demagogic, and radical.

triumph. When the Senate so authorized, a Roman general could celebrate an important military victory with a procession inside the city of Rome. The parade would include the civil magistrates of the year, captives, spoils of war, and such exhibits as the model of captured Marseilles mentioned in II.28. The triumph terminated on the Capitol, where a sacrifice was offered.

triumvir. The triumvirate was an unofficial alliance of Pompey, Caesar, and Crassus, formed to reconcile their spheres of interest in 60 B.C.

Twelve Tables. A codification of Roman law that a special board published in 450 B.C. It formed the basis of later Roman law, but by Cicero's time it had been much modified, although it was still studied. Cicero quotes it as a reflexion of ancestral standards of conduct. The Twelve Tables do not survive complete but only in numerous fragments.

INDEX OF NAMES

(The *Index of Names* serves to identify the proper names that occur in *On Duties* and to supply pertinent information about them. The references are to book and section, e.g., I.109 means book I, section 109. The initial letters in Roman names stand for the following: A. = Aulus; C. = Gaius; Cn. = Gnaeus; D. = Decimus; L. = Lucius; M. = Marius; M'. = Manius; P. = Publius; Q. = Quintus; Ser. = Servius; Sex. = Sextus; Sp. = Spurius; T. = Titus; Ti. = Tiberius.)

"Academics." Cicero's philosophical dialogue of this name dealt with theories of knowledge; it was issued in two separate editions, the first in two books, of which one survives, the second in four books, of which fragments survive; both versions were written in 45 B.C. II.8.

Academics. Followers of Platonism; the name was derived from the Academy in Athens where Plato taught; the Academic philosophy that Cicero studied as a youth was a form of scepticism not directly corresponding to Plato's original doctrines. I.6; III.20.

Accius (170—ca. 86 B.C.). Roman writer of tragedy and other literary works; Cicero knew him and was fond of quoting from his plays, especially the *Atreus,* some of whose phrases became nearly proverbial. III.84, 102.

Acilius. Roman historian active in the mid-second century B.C. whose narrative, written in Greek, dealt with Rome's history from the beginnings to his own day. III.115.

Aeacus. In myth the son of Zeus and the nymph Aegina; a hero remarkable for his piety; Pyrrhus, the Greek general, claimed to be descended from him. I.38, 97.

Aegina. An important island in the Saronic Gulf whose naval power rivaled that of Athens for many years until the Athenians subjected the population in 456 B.C. III.46.

Q. Aelius Tubero. Legal expert and historian; a strict Stoic to whom several philosophers dedicated books. III.63.

Aemilius Lepidus Mamercus. Consul in 77 B.C. with D. Junius Brutus. II.58.

L. Aemilius Paullus. Hero of Rome's war against Macedonia, which he ended with a victory at Pydna in 168 B.C.; twice consul; the father of P. Scipio Aemilianus. I.116, 121; II.76.

L. Aemilius Paullus. Consul for the second time with C. Terentius Varro in 216 B.C., when Hannibal defeated and slaughtered a large Roman army at Cannae, a disaster in which Aemilius perished. III.114.

M. Aemilius Scaurus. Consul in 115 B.C.; an extremely energetic politician, admired by Cicero for his long public career and great oratorical ability. I.76, 108.

M. Aemilius Scaurus. Son of the preceding; aedile in 58 B.C. when he spent lavishly; accused of bribery in 54, he was successfully defended by Cicero; attempted to gain consulship in the same year, was accused of electioneering intrigue and went into exile. I.138; II.57.

Aequi. Primitive people of central Italy; resisted Roman domination until they were finally subjected and nearly exterminated in 304 B.C. I.35.

Aesopus. A famous Roman tragic actor of the first century B.C.; he once gave Cicero lessons in elocution. I.114.

Africa. A portion of the Mediterranean coast of Africa, conquered and taken from the Carthaginians; under Roman domination from 146 B.C.; it was enlarged and reorganized by Julius Caesar in 46 B.C. I.112; III.99.

Africanus. See Cornelius.

Agamemnon. In Greek mythology the commander-in-chief of the Greeks in the Trojan War; when the fleet transporting the expedition could not sail because of adverse winds, Agamemnon, in order to appease the angry goddess Artemis (= Diana) who was causing the delay, vowed to sacrifice to her the most beautiful creature born in his kingdom that year, which turned out to be his own daughter Iphigenia. III.95.

Agesilaus. King of Sparta who reigned for nearly forty years (died 360 B.C.); he enjoyed success and, much later, fame as a military commander. II.16.

Agis. Agis IV, king of Sparta (reigned 244–241 B.C.), who attempted to introduce economic and political reforms; his partial success generated reaction, and he lost his life to his opponents; his reforms may have been inspired by Stoicism; his career itself inspired later reformers. II.80.

Agrigentum. City founded by Greeks on the south-west coast of Sicily. II.26.

Ajax. A hero in Homer's *Iliad* and subject of a play by Sophocles; Cicero cites him as an obstinate, surly, and quarrelsome character. I.113–114; III.98.

T. Albucius. Propraetor in Sardina in 104 B.C.; convicted of extortion in the following year, he retired to Athens and there pursued his cultivation of Epicureanism. II.50.

Alexander the Great. Macedonian king and general (ruled 336–323 B.C.), founder of a great empire in the Greek world, the Near East, and Egypt; his achievements and character were studied as models; Cicero judges that he was undoubtedly great as a general but that his character was faulty. I.90; II.16, 48, 53.

Alexander of Pherae. Tyrant (ruled 369–358 B.C.) of Pherae in Thessaly; married Thebe, his niece; notorious for his cruelty and suspicion; eventually he was murdered in a plot led by his wife; Cicero says her motive was jealousy, other writers say it was hatred of Alexander's cruelty. II.25–26.

Alexandria. City in Egypt, founded by Alexander the Great in 332 B.C.; capital of Egypt under the Ptolemies; an important cultural center and seaport. II.82; III.50.

Anio. River of central Italy, a tributary of the Tiber; it formed the boundary between Latium and Sabine territory. III.112.

Anniceris. Hedonist philosopher of the Cyrenaic school of the latter half of the fourth century B.C.; modified pure hedonism to acknowledge duties toward parents, friends, and homeland. III.116.

T. Annius Milo. Tribune in 57 B.C.; the lengthy enmity between Milo and Clodius expressed itself in repeated violence between their rival street gangs; Milo secured the murder of Clodius in 52 B.C., and Cicero was willing to defend Milo because Clodius had worked for the exile of Cicero in 58 B.C., while Milo had worked for his recall in 57. II.58.

Antigonus (ca. 382–301 B.C.). General of Alexander the Great; an important military and political figure in the Greek world following Alexander's death. II.48.

Antiope. Title character of a play by Euripides imitated by the Roman Pacuvius (220–130 B.C.); in mythology she gives birth to two sons fathered by Zeus; is loved by King Lycus; suffers the persecution of Lycus' jealous wife Dirce; is finally saved by her sons. I.114.

Antipater. *See* Cassander.

Antipater of Tarsus. Stoic philosopher, leader of the school about 140 B.C.; teacher of Panaetius; a few fragments of numerous writings survive; Cicero represents him upholding social morality against the strict legalism of Diogenes of Babylon. III.51, 54, 91.

Antipater of Tyre. Stoic philosopher of first century B.C.; friend of Cato the younger; Cicero mentions his criticism of Panaetius. II.86.

M. Antonius. Consul in 99 B.C.; grandfather of Marc Antony the triumvir; admired and idealized by Cicero as one of the best Roman orators. II.49; III.67.

Apelles. *See* Coan Venus.

Apollo. Greek god; his temple at Delphi in Greece, where his epithet was "Pythian," housed a prophetess who was the most famous of many ancient oracles; her responses to questions about the future were thought to come from Apollo himself. II.77.

Appius. *See* C. Claudius Pulcher.

C. Aquillius Gallus. A contemporary of Cicero; praetor in 66 B.C.; retired from public life to devote himself to legal studies. III.60–61.

M'. Aquillius. Consul in 101 B.C.; accused of extortion following his proconsulship in Sicily; prosecuted by L. Fufius; defended with success by M. Antonius. II.50.

Aratus (271–213 B.C.). General of the Achaean League from Sicyon who liberated his native city from tyranny in 251 B.C.; allied himself with the rulers of Macedonia but lost trust in them when they became aggressive toward Greece. II.81–82.

Areopagus. Name of a council in Athens charged with overseeing legal matters; its importance was upheld in Solon's constitutional reforms. I.75.

Arginusae. Small islands near Lesbos, the scene of a sea battle between Athens and Sparta in 406 B.C. I.84.

Argos. City of the Peloponnesus in Greece. II.81.

Aristides. Athenian statesman and general during the Persian Wars and the years following; general at the battles of Marathon and Salamis; a rival of Themistocles; called "The Just" because of his reputation for integrity and tenacity. III.16, 49, 87.

Aristippus. Philosopher from Cyrene, a companion of Socrates in Athens; he (or possibly his grandson of the same name) was the founder of the Cyrenaic school (see Anniceris) whose ethics were based on the idea that pleasure should be the chief goal of human action. I.148; III.116.

Ariston. Stoic philosopher from Chios, flourished about 250 B.C.; pupil of Zeno, the founder of Stoicism. I.6.

Aristotle (384–322 B.C.). Pupil of Plato; founder of the Peripatetic school; Cicero contrasts Aristotle the philosopher with Isocrates the rhetorician. I.4; II.56; III.35.

Arpinum. Town in central Italy; birthplace of Cicero. I.21.

Athens. I.1, 75, 84, 86, 104; II.64, 86; III.6, 46, 48, 49, 54, 87, 121.

M. Atilius Regulus. Consul in 267, again in 256 B.C.; victorious over Carthage's fleet, and on land in Africa; but suffered defeat and capture in 255; sent back to Rome to arrange an exchange of prisoners (Cicero's version) or possibly to negotiate peace, probably in 249; he urged the Senate not to deal with Carthage, returned there as he had promised the enemy and died in prison; his heroic conduct throughout this embassy and his subsequent torture were the subjects of much moralizing elaboration. I.39; III.99, 102–105, 108, 110–115.

Sex. Atilius. Consul in 136 B.C. III.109.

Atreus. Example of cruelty from Graeco-Roman tragedy; he murdered his brother's children and his step-brother. I.97; III.106.

Cn. Aufidius Orestes. Consul in 71 B.C. II.58.

C. Aurelius Cotta. Consul in 75 B.C. II.59.

Bardulis. A king of Illyria, defeated in 358 B.C. by Philip II of Macedonia. II.40.

Basilus. See Minucius.

Brutus. See Junius.

Q. Caecilius Metellus Macedonicus. Consul in 143 B.C., a rival in politics of the younger Scipio Africanus. I.87.

Q. Caecilius Metellus Numidicus. Victor over Jugurtha; consul in 109 B.C. III.79.

Chrysippus (280–207 B.C.). Succeeded Cleanthes as head of the Stoic school in 232 B.C.; regarded in antiquity as the embodiment of orthodox Stoicism; a voluminous writer and famous logician. III.42.

Cicero. *See* Tullius.

Cimbri. Celtic tribe that migrated from Germany to northern Italy, was finally defeated by the Romans in 101 B.C. I.38.

Cimon. Athenian general and statesman; died in 449 B.C.; mentioned by Cicero as an example of generosity. II.64.

Circe. An island nymph of witch-like powers in Homer's *Odyssey* who detained Ulysses (= Odysseus) for a year on his voyage home. I.113.

T. Claudius Centumalus. Unknown apart from Cicero's reference. III.66.

M. Claudius Marcellus. Roman military hero, five times consul; conqueror of Syracuse (211 B.C.), winner of battlefield honors including honorable burial by his great enemy Hannibal. I.61.

C. Claudius Pulcher. Son of Appius Claudius Pulcher; aedile in 99 B.C.; consul in 92. II.57.

Cleombrotus. Commanded Spartans at battle of Leuctra in 371 B.C.; he fought the battle contrary to good military judgment because he feared criticism for friendliness to his Theban enemies. I.84.

P. Clodius. Enemy of Cicero who secured Cicero's exile, attempted to force his own election to praetorship by violence, was opposed by Milo whose hirelings killed him in a brawl in 52 B.C. II.58.

Clytemnestra. In mythology the wife of Agamemnon; she slew him upon his victorious return from Troy; subject of tragedies by Aeschylus and Accius. I.114.

Coan Venus. A painting of the goddess Venus by Apelles (fourth century B.C.), known as the greatest painter of antiquity; the painting was probably executed on the island of Cos and was later brought to Rome by Augustus. III.10.

Cocles. Horatius Cocles, a legendary exemplar of early Roman virtue; he held back an Etruscan army that was attacking Rome by single-handedly defending the Sublician bridge over the Tiber. I.61.

Collatinus. *See* Tarquinius.

Conon. Athenian admiral defeated by Lysander at Aegispotami (405 B.C.), defeated the Spartans in 394 B.C. I.116.

Corinth. Important and wealthy city in Greece, ruthlessly destroyed by the Romans under Mummius in 146 B.C. I.35; II.76; III.46.

P. Cornelius Lentulus. Consul in 57 B.C.; Cicero mentions his great expenditures as aedile (63 B.C.), which were famous. II.57.

Cn. and P. Cornelius Scipio. Brothers, heroes of the second Punic War; both died in Spain in 212 B.C. after many military successes. I.61; III.16.

P. Cornelius Scipio. Adoptive father of Scipio Africanus the Younger. I.121.

P. Cornelius Scipio (Africanus Major) (236–ca. 183 B.C.). Greatest Roman general of his time, active in Spain and Africa. II.80; III.1–2, 4.

P. Cornelius Scipio (Africanus Minor) (185–129 B.C.). Renowned military and cultural leader; conquered Carthage in 146 B.C., Numantia in 133; in literature the leader of the Scipionic Circle, a group of writers and philosophers that included Panaetius and Polybius. I.76, 87, 90, 108, 116; II.76.

P. Cornelius Scipio Nasica. Consul with D. Junius Brutus in 138 B.C.; leader of opposition to Ti. Gracchus. I.76, 109.

L. Cornelius Sulla (ca. 138–78 B.C.). Already an acknowledged military leader when he became consul in 88; throughout his early life a rival of Marius; he marched Roman armies that were loyal to him personally against Rome in 88 in a violent attempt to crush his opponents; escaping trial, he moved East, sacked Athens, campaigned against Mithridates, then returned as a rebel to invade Italy; elected dictator in 81, he purged his opponents ruthlessly and attempted to reform the government by increasing the Senate's power; died in 78 B.C. I.43, 109; II.27, 51; III.87.

P. Cornelius Sulla. Relative of the preceding; Cicero notes that he helped with the public auction of property that was confiscated in the purges carried out by Sulla the dictator in 81 B.C. and then by Caesar in 46, undoubtedly becoming wealthy on both occasions. II.29.

Cotta. *See* Aurelius.

Crassus. *See* Licinius.

Cratippus. Peripatetic philosopher from Mitylene, teaching in Athens from about 50 B.C.; teacher of Cicero's son. I.1; II.8; III.5–6, 33, 121.

Curio. *See* Scribonius.

Cynics. Philosophical school whose most famous teacher was Diogenes of Sinope; his teachings included the virtue of poverty and contempt for social conventions; Cicero mentions the school only to condemn it. I.128, 148.

Cyrenaics. *See* Aristippus.

Cyrsilus. An Athenian who was stoned to death because he advised surrender to the Persians; an example of cowardice. III.48.

Cyrus (ruled 559–529 B.C.). Founder of the Persian Empire; cited by Cicero as a wise and successful ruler. II.16.

Damon. A Sicilian Pythagorean; known as the friend of Phintias; their friendship, grounded on Pythagorean philosophical principles, was put to the test by Dionysius II the Younger, ruler of Syracuse, as in the story retold by Cicero. III.45.

Decii. Father and son both named P. Decius Mus, who sacrificed their own lives on the battlefield in 360 and 295 B.C. respectively; the act, called *devotio,* was religiously inspired, intended to secure victory (as it did in both cases), and made traditional heroes of the Decii. I.61; III.16.

Demetrius of Phaleron (ca. 354–ca. 283 B.C.). Greek statesman and student of philosophy; pupil of Theophrastus, orator and writer. I.3; II.60.

Demetrius Poliorcetes. King of Macedonia from 294 to 287 B.C.; the enemy of most other rulers in Greece and the East during his reign; a coalition finally drove him to defeat and off the throne. II.26.

Demosthenes (384–322 B.C.). The greatest Greek orator; Cicero mentions that his career began at an early age and contrasts it with that of Plato. I.4; II.47.

Diana (Roman name of Greek goddess Artemis). *See* Agamemnon.

Dicaearchus. Peripatetic philosopher from Sicily, student of Aristotle, contemporary of Theophrastus; none of his numerous writings on history, philosophy, and geography survives. II.16.

Dinomachus. A Greek philosopher (dates uncertain), mentioned by Cicero in conjunction with Calliphon as men who attempted to reconcile pleasure and morality. III.119.

Diogenes of Babylon. Stoic philosopher, student and successor of Chrysippus; on embassy to Rome in 156 B.C.; teacher of Panaetius. III.51–52, 55, 91.

Dion (409–354 B.C.). Sicilian ruler, relative of the tyrant Dionysius I; admirer and student of Plato. I.155.

Dionysius the Elder (430–367 B.C.). Tyrant of Syracuse; became the stock example of a cruel ruler living in continuous fear and suspicion. II.25.

Dionysius. *See also* Damon.

Drusus. *See* Livius.

Q. Ennius (239–169 B.C.). Earliest Roman literary figure of importance; composed an epic, tragedies on Greek models, as well as comedies and works in other forms. I.26, 51–52, 84; II.23, 62; III.62, 104.

Epaminondas. Greek general from Thebes; student of Pythagoreanism; the victor at Leuctra, leading Theban forces against Spartans; died at the battle of Mantinea, 362 B.C. I.84, 155.

Epicurus (342–270 B.C.). Founder of Epicurean philosophy; Cicero distorts Epicurus' account of happiness; it is less hedonism than asceticism; Epicureanism was more logical and austere than most Romans believed. III.116–117.

Epigoni. Figures in a tragedy of Accius after Greek models; in a quarrel over who should rule Thebes, the city was attacked by an army with seven commanders who were defeated and all but one killed; ten years later the survivor led the sons (Epigoni) of the commanders in a return attack, which was more successful. I.114.

Eteocles. King of Thebes in mythology, son of Oedipus; he and his brother Polyneices killed each other in a struggle over rule of the city. III.82.

Euripides (480–406 B.C.). Athenian tragic poet; Cicero quotes his *Phoenissae* and *Hippolytus*. III.82, 108.

Q. Fabius Labeo. Consul in 183 B.C. I.33.

Q. Fabius Maximus. Consul five times, twice dictator; remembered as the general who opposed Hannibal in Italy by a campaign of delay and harassment; died in 203 B.C. Cicero contrasts Fabius' patience with Cleombrotus' haste. I.84, 108.

C. Fabricius. Consul in 282 and 278 B.C.; example of old Roman severity and uprightness; refused to yield to Pyrrhus' temptations when on an embassy; refused to deal with a traitor from Pyrrhus' camp or to take unmilitary advantage of an enemy; the Roman counterpart of Aristides the Just in Athens. I.40; III.16, 86–87.

Fimbria. *See* Flavius.

C. Flavius Fimbria. Roman orator and lawyer; consul in 104 B.C. III.77.

L. Fufius. Roman orator about 100 B.C.; remembered for his prosecution of M'. Aquillius. II.50.

L. Furius. Consul in 136 B.C. III.109.

Gracchus. *See* Sempronius.

Gratidianus. *See* Marius.

Greece and Greeks. I.1, 3, 8, 51, 108, 111, 142, 153; II.18, 60, 80, 83, 87; III.48, 73, 82, 99.

Gyges. King of Lydia in the seventh century B.C.; according to the famous story retold by Cicero, he was a shepherd who became king with the aid of a magic ring. III.38, 78.

Gytheum. Main seaport of Sparta; on the Laconian Gulf. III.49.

Hamilcar. Father of Hannibal; commander of Carthaginian armies in Sicily and Spain. III.99.

Hannibal (247–183 B.C.). Carthaginian general in Punic Wars; defeated Romans in Italy at Trasimene (217) and Cannae (216); defeated by Romans at Zama (202); the Romans thought him ruthless and cruel. I.38, 40, 108; III.99, 113–114.

Hecaton. Stoic philosopher from Rhodes; pupil of Panaetius, author of a book on duty dedicated to Tubero. III.63, 89.

Hercules. In mythology the son of Zeus and Alcmene; semi-divine hero, carried out the twelve labors; later regarded by philosophers as a model of humanity striving toward virtue; hence the famous story of the choice at the cross-roads between virtue and pleasure. I.118; III.25.

Herillus. Stoic philosopher, pupil of Zeno; claimed that knowledge is the supreme good and everything else indifferent in value. I.6.

Hernici. People of Latium, sometimes allies, sometimes enemies of Rome; finally subdued in 306 B.C. I.35.

Herodotus. Greek historian of fifth century B.C.; the story of the just man chosen king of the Medes is told of Deioces in I.96–101 of his *Histories*. II.41.

Hesiod. Greek poet of about 700 B.C.; his *Works and Days* contains, among much else, proverbial wisdom of the kind cited by Cicero. I.48.

Hippolytus. Son of Theseus, step-son of Phaedra, Theseus' second wife; the latter falsely accused Hippolytus of adultery when he rejected her love, and he died when Neptune (= Poseidon), the sea-god, carried out a wish of Theseus that Hippolytus be killed. I.32; III.94.

Homer. Traditional Greek author of the *Iliad* and *Odyssey;* Cicero quotes the story of how Ulysses (= Odysseus) attempted to evade military service; the story fell outside the limits of Homer's narrative but was the subject of later dramas. III.97.

Q. Hortensius. Aedile in 75 B.C.; consul in 69; a renowned orator and important political figure of Cicero's times. II.57; III.73.

C. Hostilius Mancinus. Consul in 137 B.C.; general in Spain against Numantians; arranged battlefield treaty after a defeat, but it was not ratified by the Roman Senate; he was delivered over to the enemy with his own consent, but later regained favor at Rome. III.109.

Illyria. See Bardulis.

Iphigenia. See Agamemnon.

Isocrates (436–338 B.C.). Greek orator; rival of Demosthenes. I.4.

Italy. II.75–76.

Ithaca. Ulysses' home, an island near the west coast of Greece. III.97.

Janus. Roman god, probably originally of stream-crossings, whose name was apparently given to a district or street of Rome near the Forum, in which he had an arch. II.87.

Jason of Pherae. Thessalian ruler and general; tyrant of Pherae from ca. 380 to 370 B.C. I.108.

Jugurtha. King of Numidia; at first an ally of Rome, then an enemy (112–106 B.C.); eventually captured and executed at Rome. III.79.

C. Julius Caesar (100–44 B.C.). Many of Cicero's references to Caesar in *On Duties* are oblique; he regards Caesar as a man of great abilities who perverted them because of ambition; cited are Caesar's confiscations, his acquiescence in Catiline's conspiracy, his cruel treatment of Marseilles, his delight in breaking the law. I.26, 43, 112; II.2, 23–28, 83–84; III.19, 32, 82, 85.

C. Julius Caesar Strabo. Writer and orator; aedile in 90 B.C.; fond of wit and humor; killed in the purges of Marius the Great in 87 B.C. I.108, 133; II.50.

L. Junius Brutus. Led the revolt against the Tarquins; first consul of Rome (509 B.C.) with Collatinus; the latter was suspected of favoring the expelled Tarquins and forced to resign his office. III.40.

M. Junius Brutus. Father and son of the same name; the father was one of the three founders of the study of civil law at Rome; the son was a vigorous and aggressive prosecutor, so much so that Cicero blames him for having acquired the *cognomen* "Accusator," "The Prosecutor." II.50.

M. Junius Pennus. When tribune in 126 B.C. sponsored a law expelling noncitizens from Rome. III.47.

D. Junius Silanus. Mentioned by Cicero for his expenditures on games as aedile; consul in 62 B.C. II.57.

Jupiter. In mythology the king of the gods. I.118; III.102, 104–105.

Lacedaemonians. See Spartans.

Laciadae. Citizens of the deme Lacia in Athens, the deme of Cimon. II.64.

"Laelius." Alternative title of Cicero's essay *On Friendship.* II.31.

C. Laelius Sapiens. Consul in 140 B.C.; intimate of Scipio the Younger; in philosophy a Stoic; pupil of Diogenes of Babylon and Panaetius; in public life distinguished himself under Scipio against Viriatus in Spain. I.90, 108; II.40; III.16.

Latin (language). Cicero urges his son to combine Greek and Latin in his studies. I.1–2, 133; II.87.

Latins (tribe). People of Latium; dwelled in earliest territory acquired by Rome; defeated at battle of Veseris (Trifanum). I.38; III.112.

Lentulus. See Cornelius.

Leuctra. Town in Boeotia in Greece where Epaminondas, leading the Thebans, defeated the Spartans in 371 B.C. I.61; II.26.

Lex Plaetoria. A law passed in 192 B.C.; established distinction between minors (under 25 years of age) and adults; provided penalties for fraud against minors. III.61.

L. Licinius Crassus. Consul in 95 B.C.; the greatest Roman orator before Cicero; splendid aedileship (? 98 B.C.); prosecutor of Carbo, the supporter of the Gracchi; expelled illegally enrolled citizens from Rome. I.108, 133; II.47, 49, 57, 63; III.47, 67.

M. Licinius Crassus. Consul in 70 and 55 B.C.; triumvir with Caesar and Pompey; remembered for his wealth and fatal expedition into Parthia. I.25, 109; III.73, 75.

P. Licinius Crassus. Consul in 98 B.C.; father of the triumvir; mentioned because of expenditures during aedileship. II.57.

L. Licinius Lucullus and **M. Licinius Lucullus.** Brothers associated in the aedileship in 79 B.C.; Lucius was consul in 74 B.C.; successfully campaigned against Mithridates; was a man of wealth. I.140; II.50, 57.

M. Livius Drusus. Tribune of the people in 91 B.C. who attempted a revival of Gracchan policies; a distinguished orator. I.108.

Lucullus. See Licinius.

Lusitania. See Viriatus.

Q. Lutatius Catulus. Father and son; the father consul in 102 B.C. with Marius; both distinguished in public life. I.76, 109, 133.

M. Lutatius Pinthia. A Roman knight of whom nothing seems to be known aside from this reference. III.77.

Lycurgus. Legendary lawgiver of Sparta; by tradition the man who formed Sparta's militaristic constitution. I.76.

Lydia. See Gyges.

Lysander. Spartan military leader; defeated Athens at the battle of Aegispotami (405 B.C.). I.76, 109.

Lysander the Ephor. An associate of Agis; ephor in 243 B.C. II.80.

Lysis. Pythagorean philosopher of Tarentum; fifth century B.C.; a teacher of Epaminondas. I.155.

Macedonia. Area in northern Greece, homeland of Philip and Alexander the Great. I.37, 90; II.26, 53, 76.

Q. Maelius. Probably tribune-elect in 321 B.C. III.109.

Mamercus. See Aemilius.

Mancia. A doubtful name. Some Roman aristocrat is referred to, but the name is otherwise unknown and does not appear to be authentic. I.109.

Mancinus. See Hostilius.

L. Manlius Capitolinus (father) and **T. Manlius Torquatus (son).** The father was dictator in 363 B.C.; the son was renowned for having killed his own son for disobedience at the battle of Veseris. III.112.

Marathon. The seacoast northeast of Athens where Miltiades defeated Darius the Persian in 490 B.C. I.61.

Marcellus. See Claudius.

L. Marcius Philippus. Son of Q. Marcius Philippus; orator of high rank in Cicero's estimation; consul in 91 B.C. I.108; II.59, 73; III.87.

C. Marius. Military leader against tribes from the north; conqueror of Jugurtha (105 B.C.); consul seven times; a reforming leader, violent and cruel; died in 86 B.C. I.76; III.79.

Numantia. Capital of Spanish people of Celtiberia; destroyed following prolonged siege by Scipio the Younger. I.35, 76; III.109.

Ti. Numicius. Tribune of the people, colleague of Maelius in 321 B.C. III.109.

Cn. Octavius. Commanded Roman fleet in victory against Perseus, 168 B.C.; consul in 165 B.C. I.138.

M. Octavius. As tribune sponsored a revision of the grain regulations of C. Gracchus; not otherwise known. II.72.

"Oeconomicus." *See* Xenophon.

Orestes. *See* Aufidius.

Palamedes. In mythology exposed the simulated madness of Ulysses; *see* Ulysses. III.98.

Palatine. The most important of Rome's seven hills; a wealthy residential district in Cicero's time. I.138.

Panaetius. *See* Introduction. I.7, 9, 90, 152, 161; II.16, 35, 51, 60, 86; III.7–12, 18, 33–34, 63.

C. Papius. Tribune of the people in 65 B.C.; sponsored a revival of M. Junius Pennus' law expelling noncitizens from Rome. III.47.

Paullus. *See* Aemilius.

Pausanias. King of Sparta; commanded Greek forces at Plataea against Persians in 479 B.C. I.76.

Peloponnesian War. The prolonged struggle between Athens and Sparta, 431–404 B.C.; subject of Thucydides' *History.* I.84.

Pelops. In mythology ruler at Pisa, site of the Olympic games; son of Tantalus, father of Atreus and Thyestes. III.84.

Pennus. *See* Junius.

Pericles. Athenian general, orator, statesman; died in the plague of 429 B.C. I.108, 144; II.16, 60.

Peripatetics. The followers of the philosopher Aristotle. I.2, 6, 89; II.16; III.11, 20.

Persians. The Persian empire of Asia Minor invaded Greece twice, under Darius in 490 B.C., under Xerxes in 480; was defeated both times. I.37; III.48–49.

Phaëthon. *See* Sol.

Phalaris. Tyrant of Agrigentum in Sicily in sixth century B.C.; a stock example of a cruel ruler. II.26; III.29, 32.

Phaleron. One of Athens' harbors; *see* Demetrius.

Philip. Son of Antigonus, of whom little is known. II.48.

Philip. King of Macedonia, father of Alexander the Great; ruled in Macedonia until 336 B.C.; Cicero quotes fictional letters from Philip to Alexander in which the father advises the son on conduct. I.90; II.48, 53.

Philippus. *See* Marcius.

Phintias. *See* Damon.

"Phoenissae" (*The Phoenician Women*). A tragedy of Euripides. III.82.

Picene Lands. A district in north-east Italy that, with Sabine territories, had M. Satrius as its *patronus*. III.74.

Piraeus. The main harbor of Athens. III.46.

Piso. *See* Calpurnius.

Plataea. Town in Boeotia where the Greeks won their great land victory over the Persians in 479 B.C. I.61.

Plato. I.2, 4, 15, 22, 28, 63–64, 85, 87, 155; III.38–39.

Plautus. Roman playwright, twenty-one of whose comedies are preserved; died 184 B.C. I.104.

Polybius (ca. 200–ca. 118 B.C.). Greek historian of Rome; resided in Rome and was a member of the Scipionic Circle. III.113.

Cn. Pompey (106–48 B.C.). The triumvir; distinguished in military campaigns; married Caesar's daughter Julia; was lavish in aedileship and in providing public buildings; fought Caesar and was defeated at Pharsalus in 48 B.C. I.76, 78; II.45, 57, 60; III.82.

Q. Pompey. Consul in 141 B.C.; a commander in the war against Numantia. III.109.

Sex. Pompey. A person whose legal, mathematical, and philosophical learning Cicero found worthy of praise. I.19.

M. Pomponius. Tribune in 363 B.C.; brought an action against L. Manlius for attempting to prolong his dictatorship beyond the legal term of office. III.112.

C. Pontius Herennius. Samnite general victorious over the Romans at the Caudine Forks (321 B.C.). II.75.

M. Popillius Laenas. Consul in 172 B.C. I.36.

M. Porcius Cato (234–149 B.C.). Orator, statesman, soldier; "The Censor"; advocate of Carthage's destruction; a traditional model of stern old Roman morality, anti-Greek and against luxury. I.36, 37, 79, 104; II.89; III.1, 16, 104.

M. Porcius Cato Uticensis (95–46 B.C.). Great-grandson of the Censor;

Stoic, orator, soldier; after defeat at Thapsus in Africa he committed suicide. I.112; III.66, 88.

Posidonius (ca. 135–ca. 51 B.C.). Pupil of Panaetius; teacher of Cicero at Rhodes; guest of Cicero at Rome. I.159; III.8, 10, 109.

Prodicus. Philosopher of fifth century B.C.; originator of the story of Hercules' choice. I.118.

Propylaea. The ramp, stairway, and gates leading up the Acropolis in Athens that were part of Pericles' building program. II.60.

Ptolemy II Philadelphus (309–247 B.C.). King of Egypt; wealthy patron of culture. II.82.

Punic Wars. Series of wars between Rome and Carthage. I.39–40, 79; III.47.

Pyrrho. Greek philosopher of fourth century B.C.; founder of Scepticism; rejected possibility of certainty of knowledge. I.6.

Pyrrhus (318–272 B.C.). Descendant of Aeacus; king of Epirus; adventurous soldier, invaded and campaigned in Italy. I.38, 40; II.26; III.86.

Pythagoras. Greek philosopher of sixth century B.C.; mathematician, teacher of a semi-religious discipline; his followers organized into closed societies. I.56, 108, 155; III.45.

Pythian. See Apollo.

Pythius. A banker in Syracuse, known only from this reference. III. 58–60.

Quirinus. Alternate name of deified Romulus. III.41.

Regulus. See Atilius.

Rhodes. Large island south of Asia Minor. III.50, 57, 63.

Romulus. Mythical founder of the city of Rome; see Quirinus.

Sex. Roscius Amerinus. Accused by an agent of Sulla of having murdered his own father; successfully defended by the young Cicero. II.51.

Rupilius. An actor known only from this reference. I.114.

P. Rutilius Rufus. Consul in 105 B.C.; student of Panaetius; abandoned public career in 92 B.C. to devote himself to philosophy. II.47; III.10.

Sabines. People of central Italy; adversaries of Rome until federated in 290 B.C. I.35, 38; III.74.

Sabine Lands. See Picene Lands.

Salamis. Island and straits near Athens where the Greeks defeated Persia's fleet in 480 B.C. I.61, 75.

Salmacis. A legendary spring whose waters made strong men weak. I.61.

Samnites. People of south-central Italy who opposed Rome successfully for many years before accepting Roman rule and citizenship. I.38; II.75; III.109.

Sardinians. Inhabitants of Sardinia, the large island west of Italy, a Roman province from 227 B.C. II.50.

M. Satrius. Adopted and made heir by L. Minucius Basilus. III.74.

Scaevola. See Mucius.

Scaurus. See Aemilius.

Scipio. See Cornelius.

C. Scribonius Curio. Consul in 76 B.C.; an opponent of Cicero. II.59; III.88.

M. Seius. Wealthy Roman knight; aedile in 74 B.C. II.58.

C. Sempronius Gracchus. Brother of Tiberius Gracchus; tribune in 123 and 122 B.C. II.43, 72, 80.

P. Sempronius Gracchus. Grandfather of the tribunes. II.43.

Ti. Sempronius Gracchus. Father of the tribunes; soldier and twice consul. II.43, 80.

Ti. Sempronius Gracchus. Tribune in 133 B.C.; popular orator; advocate of reforms in favor of lower classes; regarded by Cicero as a disruptive revolutionary. I.76, 109; II.43, 80.

C. Sergius Orata. Praetor in 97 B.C. III.67.

Sicilians. II.50.

Sicyon. Greek city near Corinth. II.81–82.

Silanus. See Junius.

Socrates (469–399 B.C.). Greek philosopher; several Greek philosophical sects regarded him as their founder or forerunner; Cicero mentions the Academics and Peripatetics, the Cynics and Cyrenaics. I.2, 90, 104, 108, 134, 148; II.43, 87; III.11, 77.

Sol. Roman god of the sun, father of Phaëthon; in the legend Sol rashly lent Phaëthon his sun-chariot to drive through the sky, and the boy was killed. III.94.

Solon (638–558 B.C.). Traditional lawgiver of Athens; reformed the Areopagus; is said to have pretended to be mad in order to urge the Athenians to conquer Salamis, when to advocate such a policy was forbidden. I.75, 108.

Sophocles (495–406 B.C.). Athenian tragic poet; general in Athens' campaign against Samos (440 B.C.). I.144.

Tubero. *See* Aelius.

M. Tullius Cicero (son). *See* Introduction. I.1, 3, 15, 78; II.1, 8, 44; III.1, 4–5, 33, 121.

Tusculum. Italian town near Rome, site of one of Cicero's country villas. I.21, 35.

Ulysses. Roman form of Odysseus' name. I.113; III.97–98.

Varro. *See* Terentius.

Venus. *See* Coan Venus.

Veseris. A stream or town near Mt. Vesuvius, scene of a battle at which P. Decius Mus sacrificed his own life for victory. III.112.

T. Veturius. Consul in 321 B.C. III.109.

Viriatus. Native leader in Spain who successfully defied the Romans (148–146 B.C.). II.40.

Volscians. People of central Italy made citizens of Rome in 188 B.C. I.35.

Xanthippus. Greek mercenary soldier from Sparta working for the Carthaginians in Africa. III.99.

Xenocrates (396–314 B.C.). Student and successor of Plato. I.109.

Xenophon (ca. 430–ca. 354 B.C.). Greek writer and soldier; student of Socrates; author of *Oeconomicus*, an essay translated by Cicero, and other historical and biographical works, including Socratic dialogues. I.118; II.87.

Xerxes. King of Persia; invaded Greece, defeated in 480 B.C. by the Greeks at Salamis. III.48.

Zeno. Founder of Stoicism in the fourth century B.C. III.35.

The Library of Liberal Arts

SCHILLER, J., Wilhelm Tell

SCHLEGEL, J., On Imitation and Other Essays

SCHNEIDER, H., Sources of Contemporary Philosophical Realism in America

SCHOPENHAUER, A., On the Basis of Morality
Freedom of the Will

SELBY-BIGGE, L., British Moralists

SENECA, Medea
Oedipus
Thyestes

SHAFTESBURY, A., Characteristics

SHELLEY, P., A Defence of Poetry

SMITH, A., The Wealth of Nations (Selections)

Song of Roland, Terry, trans.

SOPHOCLES, Electra

SPIEGELBERG, H., The Socratic Enigma

SPINOZA, B., Earlier Philosophical Writings
On the Improvement of the Understanding

TERENCE, The Brothers
The Eunuch
The Mother-in-Law
Phormio
The Self-Tormentor
The Woman of Andros

Three Greek Romances, Hadas, trans.

TOLSTOY, L., What is Art?

VERGIL, Aeneid

VICO, G. B., On the Study Methods Our Time

VOLTAIRE, Philosophical Letters

WHITEHEAD, A., Interpretation of Science

WOLFF, C., Preliminary Discourse on Philosophy in General

XENOPHON, Recollections of Socrates and Socrates' Defense Before the Jury